Jane Eyre's Sisters

Jane Eyre's Sisters

HOW WOMEN LIVE AND WRITE THE HEROINE'S STORY

JODY GENTIAN BOWER

*This publication has been generously supported by
The Kern Foundation*

QUEST

BOOKS

THEOSOPHICAL PUBLISHING HOUSE
WHEATON, ILLINOIS • CHENNAI, INDIA

Theosophical Publishing House
PO Box 270
Wheaton, IL 60187-0270

www.questbooks.net

Cover image: *Girl Beside a Stream*, by Arthur Rackham
Cover and type design and typesetting by Drew Stevens

Library of Congress Cataloging-in-Publication Data

Bower, Jody G.
Jane Erye's sisters, how women live and write the heroine's story
/ Jody Gentian Bower.
     pages   cm
Includes bibliographical references and index.
ISBN 978-0-8356-0934-0
1. Fiction—Women authors—History and criticism. 2.
Fiction—Authorship. 3. Women in literature. 4. Heroines in
literature. 5. Women—Mythology. I. Title.
PN3352.W66B69 2015
809'.89287—dc23   2014031325

5 4 3 2 1 • 15 16 17 18 19 20
Printed in the United States of America

For Margot and Maya

Contents

Foreword

IT IS ALWAYS a joy to hold in one's hands a book by a former student and to see how she has transformed her discovery of her own voice and her central themes into a gift for others—which is what Jody Bower has done in this book now in your hands.

As I began reading, I could not help but think of how only a few months ago I was asked to pick out one sentence from all my books that might best communicate the heart of everything I've written about. Surprisingly, that turned out be easy; the words come from my first book, *The Goddess,* and go like this: "We need images and stories to help us see who we are and who we might become." This, I believe, is precisely what Jody provides in her book—figures and stories that might help us see more clearly, not only who we are and where we have been but, perhaps even more importantly, who we might be.

Like me, Jody is lifelong reader (and re-reader)—someone who is inhabited by stories, hungry for them, nourished by them, and particularly drawn to stories by women about the female journey through life. She writes eloquently about how male stories about women's lives and male depictions of the human journey (as described, for example, in Joseph Campbell's *Hero with a Thousand Faces)* and even some female attempts to distinguish the heroine's journey from that of the hero just don't feel right. They don't fit her own experience—and don't really correspond with the plots of the great, female-authored nineteenth-century

novels about women or with the plots of the contemporary fiction Jody most values.

Her fascination with how women have written about women's
lives has led her to discover a particular pattern, one that she came
to recognize as her own, one that has not only enabled her to see
more clearly where she has been but has also encouraged her to
imagine forward. She wrote this book in the hope that a careful
delineation of the stages of this plot might help others to do the
same (though she, of course, acknowledges that this is not the
only female story). Thus, in her book she retells and analyzes the
plots not only of classical novels by Jane Austen, the Brontës, and
George Eliot that serious readers of women's fiction are likely to
know but also of more recent works. (Less of a snob than I, Jody
also discusses current genre fiction, especially science fiction, and
movies and television shows out of a conviction that these often
reveal the contemporary *zeitgeist* most clearly.)

To distinguish the pattern she wants to focus on from the
ones more often put forward, Jody decided to write about the
Aletis rather than the heroine. The Aletis, she tells us, is a female
who from early on knows herself to be essentially on her own,
unseen, unprotected, but who somehow finds the courage to
leave an untenable situation, perhaps characterized by abusive or
absent parents or a too-early and all-wrong marriage. Thus she
finds much more focus in these accounts on the life-situation
that propels the protagonists out into the world than is true of
most hero-narratives. The Aletis knows she has to go forth; she
becomes a wanderer. Not in that clear-cut, goal-directed way
that Campbell describes, not in order to return with a boon, with
a great discovery that will benefit the hero's community. There
is nothing circular about her path. The Aletis is compelled to

leave—without knowing clearly where she might be going, only that it is *away,* toward something altogether *new*—not toward the conventional female path of marriage and motherhood nor of the masculine path of great achievement. (One of my favorite lines in the book communicates this so well: "The war between the sexes takes place primarily in our own psyches.")

The Aletis becomes a wanderer in search of herself. Jody clearly describes the resolve and imagination this brave stepping-forth requires. She writes beautifully about the joyous fulfillment these fictional characters experience in finally being able to say: "*This* is who I am."

Yet, having said all this, I also need to admit that the contemporary fiction that most moves Jody Bower, the plot she finds so empowering, is *not* the one to which I'm most drawn. She is pulled to what I call the happy ending, not the *old* happy ending ("They lived happily after") but a happy ending that focuses on the achievement of a kind of in-one's-self-ness. It focuses on an inner wholeness achieved only by moving out of constraining relationships to a point where one can then be open to the possibility of genuinely mutual relationships or of doing without. At the same time, it is very important to Jody to emphasize that even this is not really an *end.* She cares about the *after,* believing that the Aletis is too essentially a wanderer not to be *still on the way*—albeit now in satisfying, creative ways. My own pull, as she knows, is to darker novels, ones that focus on all that makes such outcomes unlikely, on never fully resolved dissatisfactions, on unfulfilled hopes, failures, losses, disappointments. Nonetheless, though it's hard to do, I have to admit that in many, many ways what for Jody is *the* story is in truth *my* story, at least in its second half. One does not need the inauspicious beginning to be propelled forward. I believe that just about any woman will experience an inner connection to the story-line that *Jane Eyre's Sisters* makes so visible.

At the very end of her marvelous book, Jody writes about how the goal of the female plot she has described so well is to move beyond the search for one's own wholeness and integrity by finding how to use what we have learned along the way in the service of communal healing and transformation. It seems to me that, in writing this book and sending it out into the world, Jody Bower has done just that!

—Christine Downing
September, 2014

Acknowledgments

FIRST AND FOREMOST, I must thank Richard Smoley of Quest Books, whose encouragement set me, in 2006, on the path that led to this book. Sharron Dorr at Quest, my editor, not only loved the book but understood what I was trying to say so well that her suggestions for changes were always an improvement, and I'm grateful.

I owe immeasurable thanks to Christine Downing, teacher and mentor extraordinaire, for her encouragement, her unfailing willingness to talk through ideas with me, and her ruthless eye for irrelevancies, unfounded generalizations, and mistaken ideas.

I found great inspiration in the works of James Hillman, not just because of his ability to "see through" to the essential, but his *way* of working with ideas, which I have tried to emulate in this book. Many others who shaped my thinking are also cited in the text.

Words cannot convey the depth of my gratitude for my sweet sister-friend Kathy Merwin, my "beta" reader whose editorial eye not only caught errors but also saw when I was veering into polemic or an irrelevant tangent and brought me safely back again. On more than one occasion, her enthusiasm for this book gave me the push I needed to keep going.

I am fortunate to come from a long line of strong New England women. I've been inspired in particular by my mother, Sarah Smith Skinner; my sister, Elizabeth Skinner; my aunt, Constance

Smith Whitman; my great-aunt, Inez Haynes Irwin; and all the "Smith girl" cousins who traversed unknown terrain and ventured into foreign lands to create the lives they wanted to live.

My father, Alfred Skinner, was the first to teach me critical thinking skills. I also want to acknowledge Stephens Burtchaell, Sharon Chapman, Pete Dieckerhoff, Sue Dieckerhoff, True Heart, Elizabeth Skinner, Molly Skinner-Day, Shannon Sloan-Spice, Emma Tresemer, and the "Spring Flingettes"—Cheryl Ellsworth, Gay Burton, Jackie Odell, Kate Clark, and Martha Rhodes—for many great conversations and the wonderful meals that usually accompanied them, as well as for their unwavering faith in me.

And finally, to all the great writers whose works have not only given me pleasure but also have helped me to understand my own journey, my gratitude.

Introduction

UNTIL MIDLIFE, the course of my life resembled the path a ball takes through a pinball machine. I bounced from one place to another, one career to a totally dissimilar one. Only later could I look back and see how all my experiences connected and contributed to the sense of purpose that descended on me quite suddenly in my fifties.

I came to the ideas this book expresses in much the same way. I never intended to be a scholar of stories about women. I just loved to read. In the early 1980s, I joined a women's book club. Our reading choices varied from fantasy to nonfiction, but we primarily read novels by women authors of the mid-twentieth century. I found these books tiresome after a while, because they all seemed to have the same plot: the heroine is unhappy in her childhood or adolescence and marries to get away from home; her husband turns out to be too controlling, or has affairs, or bores her; they divorce; she undergoes a time of poverty before finding her true calling; in the end she is alone but finally knows who she truly is. We read so many novels with this plot that I came to call it "the standard feminist novel."

Once I saw this pattern, I began to notice similarities to it in the great classic novels by women of the nineteenth century such as Jane Austen's *Pride and Prejudice,* Charlotte Brontë's *Jane Eyre,* Anne Brontë's *The Tenant of Wildfell Hall,* Elizabeth Gaskell's *North and South,* and George Eliot's *Middlemarch.* Then I found that the same pattern often held true in the biographies and auto-biographies of famous women. Ultimately, I realized that my life was also following this pattern.

Intrigued, I started looking for books that addressed what I was seeing. I was shocked to find that while scholars have ana-lyzed stories of the quest of the hero in depth and some have explored the "heroine's journey" (as Maureen Murdock called it), almost none address how *women* tell this story. Instead, psycholo-gists like Murdock describe the psychological pattern of women's development throughout their lives, based on what they observe in clients, while mythologists and folklorists selectively choose particular myths and folk tales that speak to their own models (often based on the masculine heroic quest model) of the hero-ine's journey. There is a lot of overlap; the authors who focus on folktales and myths often interpret those stories in psychological terms, while the therapists back up their observations with exam-ples from stories.

I have problems with both of these approaches. The writers who focus on myths and folk tales rely, for the most part, on sto-ries that were probably written (or written down and changed) by men. Unfortunately, such stories often reflect unconscious biases about women, a problem I discuss in chapter 2. Many of these writers also assume that Joseph Campbell's model of the heroic quest, described in *The Hero with a Thousand Faces*, can be made to fit women's lives with just a little adjusting here and there. This approach requires such writers to ignore all the motifs in women's stories that don't fit the model.

Psychologists, on the other hand, tend to focus on the first and second acts in a woman's life: the difficult stage of childhood and adolescence in a society that tells girls they must conform solely to a pastel palette of possibilities, and the crisis-ridden period of midlife where women often seek out therapeutic advice as they struggle to break free of that mindset and live a life in rich colors saturated with experience and joy. It makes sense to me that women probably do not talk to counselors about the parts of their lives that *aren't* a problem. Happy and fulfilled women might not seek out counselors at all, so books of this type may not reflect the totality of a woman's life. Novelists, however, tend to include all the details—the highs, the lows, and the ordinary.

A few writers have seen many of the things I see in women's tales, but they tend to limit their analyses to a few specific motifs. For instance, quite a few authors have written books about women's search for the goddess as a way of reclaiming the feminine in their own lives. While this idea sounds lovely, I personally do not relate to it. Such books all talk about a necessary "descent" to find the dark feminine, the aspects of women that society represses or will not allow, as a huge and usually one-time event in a woman's life. But my opinion is that many women know the Underworld very well, stepping in and out of it frequently (perhaps, even, monthly). I myself made the descent for the first time when I was eleven, after the sudden death of a beloved brother in an accident. This incident predisposed me to bouts of depression, and, for many years, I was more familiar with the Underworld than the bright light of the upper world. I didn't need to read about it.

Also, I dislike the concept often expressed in these books that there are three stages in a woman's life: those of the nubile Maiden, the fecund Mother, and the wise Crone. For one thing, *these roles are defined by a woman's relationship to others.* The Maiden is the desirable mate a man seeks; the Mother lives for her children;

and the Crone dispenses advice to those who need it. But what about women who do not desire men? What about women who never become mothers? What about women who refuse to let age define them in any way? In short, what about women who forge their own paths through life as unique individuals?

I found some answers in biographies of famous women. The artist Beatrix Potter, for example, struggled for years to express her true self while limited by the prejudices and conventions of Victorian society. Her early success with her books was overshadowed by a domineering mother and the loss of her first love. But she eventually got away from her mother and found lasting love and happiness at midlife. Her life only became richer and more interesting as she aged. Her lasting legacy includes not just her many delightful books, but the conservation of thousands of acres of England's beautiful Lake District and the preservation of the area's indigenous species of sheep. Potter's biographer Linda Lear wrote, "Her life was not without tragedy, but she was one of those rare individuals who is given a real third act. Beatrix Potter made the most of this gift, and it is this coda that I have found the most revealing of her essential nature."[1]

The idea of a "real third act" struck me to the core. It explains my problem with so many of the novels I've read: they lack a third act. They do not take the heroine forward from the point at which she realizes and steps into her unique being and finally starts to live life as she wills. And that was what I most wanted to know: what happens next? I wanted a third act for myself; I wanted a guide for how to make that happen.

The biographies gave me some answers. I found more in speculative fiction (also known as science fiction and fantasy), where authors are free to imagine cultures and worlds with different rules from our own—including different rules for how women are expected to behave. I also found that scriptwriters for television and movies love to imagine women who break the rules and forge their own paths. Many of these writers understand that a woman's life can have "a real third act," and it is in that third act that we see who a woman really is.

Eventually, I realized that if I wanted to read a book that talked about all these issues I would have to write it myself. So I went to graduate school to study the stories in depth. I identified the motifs and characters that recurred over and over in these stories and wrote my doctoral dissertation on "Recurrent Motifs in Women's Narratives." That work led to this book.

A chance conversation during my student days helped me to see that I had come to my ideas through an approach called *ground truthing,* a term taken from mapmakers. Mapmakers may rely these days on data from satellites and aerial photographs, but these data only give the big picture. To understand the distinct details of the terrain, one must go out and walk it, observing all the details that can neither be measured nor seen from a distance. This process uses the body as much as the mind. We experience the thing we want to know about through our senses as well as the intellect. Archetypal psychologist and philosopher James Hillman, whose work has had a major impact on my own thinking, taught that such an approach allows us truly to *see* what is there in front of us, instead of staying stuck on a **reductionist** idea (see box) that "explains" it.

We can practice ground truthing as we read by focusing on our *experience* of the images in the story. When we stop trying to explain an image in terms of an abstract theory, stop trying to hang a label on it and be done, and instead become aware of the

REDUCTIONISM

Reductionism is the idea that everything can ultimately be reduced to the simplest possible terms and made to fit one over-arching theory. A scientific reductionist believes that everything has a physical, scientific explanation and that all other explanations are false. Love, for example, can be explained as a purely biological phenomenon.

In the Dogon language of West Africa, the word *explain* is translated as "to make flat." An answer that explains something flattens out all the parts that may trip us up: the mystery of the thing. Once a thing is made flat, we don't have to look at it again or think about it anymore; instead, we may walk right over it. Reductionism is a two-dimensional response to a three-dimensional world.

Archetypal psychologist James Hillman argues that a reductionist view—trying to make everything fit under a "single explanatory principle"—blinds us to different ideas and thus to the full range of possibilities in what we see.[2] It is like putting on glasses that only allow vision through a narrow slot. What we see may be accurate, but it is not the whole picture.

physical and emotional *sensations* evoked by an image every time we look at it, the ground truth of the image will reveal itself to us. This experience-based approach may bring us closer to understanding certain aspects of the world around us than the logical, conceptual kind of thinking that has dominated Western thinking for centuries.

Just as a landscape changes under the influence of weather and time, the meaning of an image in a dream or a book is fluid and changeable. The truth that an image or pattern reveals to one person may not be what others see. In current Internet lingo, "your mileage may vary." Nor will the meaning necessarily remain the same if a person looks at the same image later on. As an inveterate re-reader of books, I have found that the best books give me something new every time—even a book I have read dozens of times. I believe that we must not become too enamored of any of our ideas about a book, or an image, or a person—including ourselves! We need to look anew each time to see if the book, the image, the person, or our own unconscious has something new to say to us.

I attempt to keep this "beginner's mind" attitude throughout this book. I name all the different characters and motifs that have revealed themselves to me in my readings of women's stories and do my best to include the ideas that others have had about these characters and motifs as well. But I do not claim to have captured all the possible interpretations of these stories. In the end, it is up to a story's readers to decide what a particular image or motif means to them at any given moment.

One more thing must be said: My original intent with this book was to describe what I have come to call the story of the *Aletis* or wandering heroine, *Aletis* being the Greek word for "wanderer" according to classicist Deborah Lyons (see chapter 1). But inevitably, I had to address issues of the female voice in literature: how women have had to struggle against accepted cultural norms to be published in the first place and then to have their work accepted as legitimate—a struggle that continues to this day. This struggle is a reality of Western history and must be acknowledged. However, I have no desire to engage in blaming, which does nothing to solve a problem. The process by which human beings came to see the world as consisting of polar opposites (male/female, good/evil, black/white, etc.) and then chose one side of each pair as "better" and "masculine" and the other side as "worse" and "feminine" is a long and complicated one with many tangled roots—and has been addressed by others far better qualified than I. The consequences are as problematical for men as they are for women, for the first and most immediate arena of that battle lies within each of us, in our own psyche, our own sense of self. I address some of the ways that this battle plays out for men, but as this is a book about women's stories, my emphasis is necessarily on how this polarized thinking influences a woman's journey to individuality and freedom.

IDYLL

Jane Eyre's Journey

JANE EYRE'S MOTHER married a man of lower social status and was cut off from her family as a result. When Jane is orphaned early in life, she is taken in by her mother's favorite brother, the only one who is willing to overlook her mother's social lapse. His family, however, is not. After this uncle dies, his wife and children make Jane's life miserable through both physical and emotional abuse.

Jane rebels against this treatment and is sent away to Lowood School. Life is no better there; the girls are under-fed and poorly clothed, and Jane is unfairly punished by the headmaster. After an epidemic of typhus kills many of the girls, including Jane's friend Helen, the school comes under new management and conditions improve for the students. Jane does better after that and eventually becomes a teacher at Lowood herself.

Yet Jane longs for a greater life. She leaves Lowood to become a governess at Thornfield Hall, where she falls in love with the mysterious Mr. Rochester and he with her. They plan to marry, but at the altar it is revealed that Rochester has a living wife, the insane Bertha Mason who has been locked away in the attic of Thornfield. Shocked and despairing, Jane runs away and becomes lost on the moors. She is close to death when she is found and taken in by the Rivers family. After Jane regains her health, St.

John Rivers arranges for her to run her own day school for the village girls. Jane strives to be content with her life and forget Rochester. But then St. John Rivers begins to press her to marry him—not because he loves her, but because he thinks plain, hardworking Jane is an ideal wife for a missionary.

Once again Jane flees. She finds out that Bertha burned down Thornfield Hall and died in the fire, and that Rochester was maimed while trying to save her. Jane seeks out Rochester and they renew their love. They marry and live out their lives together.

CHAPTER 1

The Wandering Heroine

[She was] a being who had been cast upon herself; a female
Robinson Crusoe, as unaided and unprotected, though in
the midst of the world, as that imaginary hero in his unin-
habited island . . . to be rescued from famine and death by
such resources as she could find, independently, in herself.

—Fanny Burney, *The Wanderer*

THE STORY OF A WOMAN who must travel from place to place searching for love or freedom or answers has been told for centuries. Fanny Burney, an English novelist who wrote in the late eighteenth and early nineteenth centuries, named one of her novels *The Wanderer* in honor of her heroine Juliet Granville, who flees from France by herself and learns how to survive on her own in England. Burney's description of her heroine applies equally well to Jane Eyre and many other famous fictional women.

Psyche of Roman myth travels alone across the wilderness and descends to Hades to win back her husband, Cupid. Vasilisa the Beautiful, a central figure in Russian fairy tales (who is also called "the Virgin Traveler"), goes alone into the forest to win aid from the fearsome witch Baba Yaga. Sethe of Toni Morrison's *Beloved* walks away from slavery; a century later, Celie of Alice Walker's *The Color Purple* walks away from bondage of a different kind. These are just a few of the myriad of stories about a wandering heroine who must rely primarily upon herself. Clearly, she is a figure of archetypal status.

Archetypes

In today's parlance, an *archetype* often means a trope, a stock character such as the Hero, the Innocent Child, the Prostitute with the Heart of Gold, the Wise Old Teacher, and so on. Pioneering depth psychologist Carl Gustav Jung had a different take, however. He believed that archetypes originate from our instinctive reactions to life.[1] James Hillman, the founder of archetypal psychology, saw archetypes as representing the deepest patterns of psychological function—even, perhaps, the "roots of the soul."[2] For him, archetypes represent *styles* of being, ways we live out or express a particular instinctive energy in the world.

Much as we might like to think differently, we are not rational or objective in our initial reactions to things. Instead, we react much like an animal would, out of a basic feeling such as anger or fear, hunger or sexual desire, or an urge to protect. These feelings tell us whether we should run away or fight, whether we should protect something or try to have sex with it—or eat it— or whether we can safely ignore it. But because we humans also have a thinking forebrain, when we feel these instincts we come up with an idea or image to explain them. These images are what Jung called "archetypal images." They are our attempts to express that instinctive energy to ourselves and others.

Also, because we are all unique individuals, we are capable of creating an endless multiplicity of images to express an archetype. Each image only captures part of the energy. Thus, a literary

COMPLEXES

We all know what it's like to accidentally "push someone's buttons." Those "buttons" are what depth psychologists call complexes. According to Freud, complexes are "perversions" of sexual instincts that are "innate in everyone": we are born with them and can't change them.[3] But post-Jungian psychologists think of a complex as a tangle of emotions that has gotten attached to a specific memory. Every time the memory surfaces, all those feelings come up again. And vice versa: every time a person experiences those feelings, he may remember the original incident that triggered them and even act as if the original incident is happening again.

A complex exists outside of time. In the grip of a complex, we stop reacting to how things really are in the present. One sign that someone is in the grip of a complex is when they say that someone or something is "always" or "never" a certain way, even if there is plenty of evidence to the contrary.

or cinematic trope is *not* the same thing as an archetype, for the archetype is always going to be much greater than the image.

But as individuals, we often do restrict our ideas about an archetypal energy to just one image. Our instinctive reactions are colored by our prior experiences, biases, and personal blind spots. We tend to connect experiences that *feel* similar. When we see a person we have met before, for example, or perhaps even someone who looks or acts much the same, we remember our earlier experiences with the first person as well as feelings and ideas we hold about him or her. But those old ideas may have nothing at all to do with how the second, "similar" person is behaving in the moment; and, in fact, the one who reminds us of someone else may have a very different character altogether. Clinging too tightly to just one idea of, for instance, the archetypal energy we associate with "Mother" or motherhood can limit our ability to see different *styles* of maternal behavior and perhaps even lead us to ignore or condemn those different styles. Thus, another way to define *archetype* might be "a complex that many people have in common." A **complex** (see box) can be so powerful that it can override our ability to think clearly in a certain situation. Instead, we only perceive what we expect to see and hear.

For example, most people have strong emotions about death, and their particular cultures have images and stories and rituals around the idea of death that reinforce those emotions. Images of the devil speak to a shared belief in and fear of punishment in the afterlife. But those who do not believe in an afterlife or in hell will have no emotional reaction to such images.

Jung believed that all humans have the ability to tap into a shared source of memories and experiences that may have nothing to do with our own personal lives. He called this source the *collective unconscious*—*collective* because it is shared by everyone and *unconscious* because people access this source without consciously thinking, as in when they are dreaming or when inspiration strikes from out of the blue. Jung first got the idea of the collective unconscious by listening to the dreams of his patients. Many of them would describe or draw images similar to those of other cultures, despite the fact that the dreamers knew nothing about those cultures. To Jung, the only explanation was that the dreamers, while asleep, had access to a deeper source of knowledge not available to their conscious minds (hence "depth" psychology).

The explanation for why such images occur in different societies may be simpler than Jung thought, however. Humans have different cultures, but biologically we are all pretty much the same. Since our instinctive feelings are similar, in even disparate cultures similar images can emerge—such as a skeletal figure to represent death.

Also, although all humans have similar instinctive reactions, the images people use to represent experiences often depend on context. For example, if someone wakes up at night because of a strange noise, her instinctive reaction will likely be a sense of danger. The image or concept that the forebrain attaches to this feeling of danger might be *intruder* if the person is inside her home, or *bear* if she is camping in the woods (or, if she lives in Africa, *lion*).

Thus *intruder*, *bear*, and *lion* are all archetypal images, symbols that the forebrain creates in response to the instinctive reaction of danger. Once again, archetypal images are not the same as the archetype itself. Images are the way we try to express the *feeling* of the archetype. The archetype itself cannot be contained in a single image, because the same instinctive feeling can give rise to many different expressions of it.

I believe that our endless capacity to express the same ideas in different images explains why people tell the same stories over and over, changing them a little each time, or make movies of the same popular story every few years with a different cast, or paint the same scene again and again. Archetypal images *always* fall short of what we want to express; they never quite capture the totality of the archetypal energy. People retell old stories with new archetypal images in the ongoing attempt to convey important ideas and feelings to each other.

The Archetype of the *Aletis*

What is a heroine? Some have criticized the word *heroine* itself for being a diminutive form of *hero,* the diminutive implying that a heroine is not the equal of a hero but a smaller, less impressive character. It's true that female protagonists of most women's stories are usually not heroic in the same sense that a hero is. They don't tend to accomplish some big, nearly impossible, death-defying deed. Their bravery is of a different kind. But that doesn't mean it is any less impressive.

Some writers have tried to come up with a better name for the heroine, but many of them are still based on hero, like *she-ro*, *female hero*, and *hera*. Fortunately, there is a better choice. Classics scholar Deborah Lyons found that ancient Dionysian rituals used *Aletis*, the Greek word for "wanderer," to mean a heroine.[4] Not surprisingly, this word has already found its way into popular culture (popular culture is always ahead of the scholars when it comes to recognizing and portraying new archetypal characters). Fantasy author Jo Clayton wrote her *Diadem from the Stars* series about a woman named Aleytys who wanders from planet to planet having adventures; one of the mutant heroines of Marvel Comics' X-Men franchise is also named Aleytys.

Still, *heroine* does mean a female protagonist of a story, and it's the word most of us are used to when talking about such a character. Also, the phrase "the heroine's journey" has become a popular way to refer to these stories. Therefore, in this book I use both *heroine* and *Aletis* to describe the protagonist of stories about women who must wander in search of themselves and their true place in the world.

Men also write the Aletis story. In his second-century work *Metamorphoses*, Lucius Apuleius wrote about Psyche, who must wander the earth and even descend to Hades in her quest to become, eventually, a goddess. In *Twelfth Night*, Shakespeare gave us Viola, a woman who disguises herself as a man to survive in a hostile land. Daniel Defoe took Moll Flanders through many adventures to the New World. Charles Dickens put aside his usual submissive, sticky-sweet heroines in his last completed novel, *Our Mutual Friend*, to give us Lizzie Hexam, a woman with the moral strength to run away from an attractive, would-be seducer and the physical strength to rescue him from drowning. Today, Alexander McCall Smith writes about believable women struggling with real-life issues as the heroines of his *Ladies No. 1 Detective Agency* and *Isabel Dalhousie* series.

Male fantasy and science fiction writers love spunky heroines. J. R. R. Tolkien created the prototype for today's warrior princesses when he created Éowyn of *The Lord of the Rings*. Tolkien's fellow British fantasy writer Terry Pratchett writes many wonderful heroines, including the fearless twelve-year-old nascent witch, Tiffany Aching, who defeats her first demon in *The Wee Free Men* by the practical expedient of bopping it on the head with her mother's frying pan. Another daring twelve-year-old is Lyra Belaqua, heroine of Phillip Pullman's *His Dark Materials* series, whose fearless nature leads her across a magical bridge to other worlds and eventually down into the land of the dead, where she changes the very nature of reality.

Pratchett's *Wyrd Sisters* series also features a pair of elderly witches, Granny Weatherwax and Nanny Ogg, who are equal to any challenge thrown at them, whether it be vampires, scheming kings, or snotty adolescents. Pratchett's heroines are rarely beautiful; some are built on a larger scale, others are flat-chested and awkward; one is a werewolf-turned-cop; but all of them possess an inner strength that eventually wins the day (and, often, the heart of a decent man).

All these examples lead me to believe that the Aletis represents a feminine archetype every bit as important as the masculine archetype of the hero. This is why people keep writing her story, trying to put down in words something felt and understood unconsciously, something important about women.

CHAPTER 2

The Power of Story and the Imagination

We are all of us imaginative in one form or other.

—George Eliot

SOME CRITICS CONDEMN fiction, especially **genre fiction** (see box) such as romance and fantasy, as being escapist if it does not reflect life as we actually experience it. But the "escape" that fiction offers can also mean distancing ourselves to the point where we can be more objective about our own circumstances. Psychotherapists often encourage their clients to use methods such as journals, letters, or poems as a way of detaching from or gaining objectivity about distressing events. Turning real experiences into a story may enable a person to reexperience those events in a safe way and so see things more clearly.

Such a story can also help others who've had a similar experience. For example, a soldier who served in Afghanistan found that reading *The Lord of the Rings* helped him heal from his war traumas. In an interview, the soldier stated that the story "has elements in it that I was dealing with at the same time: hope and dread, adversity, perseverance and an overwhelming enemy."[1] Reading a fantasy story about a war that never really happened

GENRE FICTION

For science fiction and most fantasy works, I prefer the term "speculative fiction." These genres allow an author to explore what human beings might be like in another setting, under a different set of rules, or even as a different form of humanity.

Writers of speculative fiction hypothesize about the future. They imagine what humans would be like if the parameters of life changed in some way. For example, Ursula Le Guin's *The Left Hand of Darkness* explores how society might be structured if people were hermaphroditic, capable of being both female and male by turns. Then the author can make a statement about the essence of being human—about what remains true for us in all circumstances.

allowed the soldier a buffer—a safe way to think about his own experience and gain some perspective.

Children who are being bullied understand what J. K. Rowling's boy wizard Harry Potter experiences at the hands of his hulking cousin Dudley. They also understand what happens when Harry finally stands up to Dudley. Through Harry's example, they may find the courage to do the same with their own bullies, even though they don't have magical powers or a wand. Like the traumatized soldier who read *The Lord of the Rings*, children who read the *Harry Potter* books may experience a kind of wizardry that can help them in life.

For such magic to happen, the story—even a fantasy—must be similar enough to the reader's own experience to provide a useful mirror of that experience. The story must be plausible: the reader must be able to identify with the views and social realities put forth in the text. Only then can the story provoke thoughts and feelings that grant a new clarity and meaning to past, actual events. Tolkien was a foot soldier in the Battle of the Somme in

World War I. Even though his story's war is fought by imaginary beings such as hobbits and elves and orcs, he *knew* what being in battle felt like, and his story could strike a chord with a veteran of modern guerrilla warfare in Afghanistan.

Many romance novels mirror a woman's actual experience by featuring a heroine who finds herself adrift, lost, or forced to run away from home to escape a fate she does not want. Although there may be a rugged hero who "rescues" her at the right moment, most of the time she has to rely on her own wits and ingenuity to keep herself safe and find what she's looking for. Women may read these novels to drool over the bulging chest muscles and piercing eyes of the hero, but they also like the message about an independent heroine who in the end manages to get what she really wants through her own efforts.

The great novels by women of the nineteenth century, such as *Jane Eyre* and *Pride and Prejudice,* continue to be popular today because they raise issues that women still deeply care about: how to be free to follow one's heart and think for oneself when everyone around seems determined to prevent that; when and how to say "no" to the demands of others; what a partnership of true equals looks like; and how to get in touch with one's creativity. Jane Eyre would fit right in with women talking about their lives at the playground or over lunch today, and she and her sisters-in-fiction provide role models for how women can live the fullest life possible.

How Stories Change Reality

Stories do not just allow us to escape from an unsatisfying life. They can also allow us to imagine a new reality for ourselves, a reality we can then strive toward. In the earliest texts available to us—such as *The Iliad* or the great Indian work, *The Mahabharata*, both of which were written nearly three thousand years ago—we can see how our ancestors thought of themselves: as people with no wills of their own, as pawns of the gods. The great Greek tragedies of 2,500 years ago took this idea further and gave us characters like Oedipus, who, although powerless to change his fate, questioned why things had to be the way they were. The same theme can be seen in the poetry of Sappho (circa 600 BCE). But then from the Golden Age of Greece (roughly 500 to 300 BCE) forward, the idea that perhaps a man might be the prime mover of his own life gained ground. (As we will see, it took a while for most people to be able to imagine the same thing for women.)

Literary theorist Nancy Armstrong argues that the art form of the novel that came into its present form in the eighteenth century in Europe was also a medium for dealing with contemporary ideas about what it means to be an individual.[2] Writers of that era—and every subsequent era—imagined a new kind of person and then wrote that person into being. That is what artists do. Art history is the history of how artists keep finding new ways to look at the world and then portray what they are seeing so that others can see it, too. Literature, like art, is constantly presenting us with new ideas about ourselves and our world. Once we learn to see the world through these artists' eyes, we are forever changed.

Whether we are aware of it or not, we live our lives as stories. The popularity of social network sites attests to our desire to describe the stories we're living, bewail plot reversals we didn't see coming, and celebrate our little victories. We cast certain people in our lives as villains and others in the roles of friends and mentors. Most of us can't rest, it seems, until we've found someone to play our True Love.

Opposing lawyers tell the story of a case from different perspectives when they write their briefs. Doctors encourage patients to talk about their histories to gain a better picture of a problem than the lab results alone can provide. In the television series *Castle*, a New York City homicide detective relies on the insights of a crime novelist who has a knack for seeing what story the clues are trying to tell.

The best stories, the ones we tell over and over again, take on lives of their own and grow in surprising ways. The King Arthur story, for instance, has roots in ancient British legends, Welsh myths, romantic prose epics from France and Germany, and possibly even legends out of ancient Persia brought back to France and England by Queen Eleanor of Aquitaine. Different writers compiled these stories over the centuries. Each changed the stories slightly and added their own touches.

For example, the earliest German stories tell of a stone or stone platter called the *Gral* that was an unending source of food and drink. As the Arthurian stories became increasingly Christianized, the *Gral* evolved into the Holy Grail, the Cup of Christ, which only the purest knight could find.

And the process of reworking the story is still ongoing. From the beginning of the legends to as recently as the 1960 musical *Camelot*, Queen Guinevere was what Jung would call an "anima woman," a beautiful woman who provokes men to love or lust after her, to abduct her and fight over her, while she takes no action herself. But in the 2004 film *King Arthur*, Guinevere is a warrior who fights alongside Arthur and Lancelot. And in the TV series *Merlin*, which ran from 2008 to 2012, Merlin is not in his traditional character of the old wise man who advises the young King Arthur but is rather an even younger boy struggling to come

A SMEAR JOB

In the earliest Arthur myths from Wales, Gawain was not only noble and silver-tongued but also the champion of the goddess and of all women. Gawain punished rapists and any other man who offered violence toward women. But he was supplanted in later stories, first by the French Lancelot and the German Parsifal, and finally by the English Galahad.

John Matthews argues in his book *Gawain, Knight of the Goddess: Restoring an Archetype* that Gawain got demoted because he was too strongly linked to myths of the goddess of the land. As the Christian influence on the stories strengthened, this goddess devolved into a witch—the evil Morgan le Fay, architect of Arthur's fall.[3]

As the goddess lost her stature, so did her faithful knight. In Tennyson's *Idylls of the King*, written in the nineteenth century, Gawain has become a liar and a rapist himself—a sad fate for the original First Knight.

to terms with his power (rather like Harry Potter). Writers keep reimagining these characters to be the people we can relate to *now*.

How Writers Change Reality

When writers write the Aletis story, they imagine a new woman, a woman who up until that moment may not have even existed. Once she is created, she immediately becomes a role model for other women. Doris Lessing says that her masterpiece, *The Golden Notebook*, "was written as if the attitudes that have been created by the Women's Liberation Movement already existed."[4] But when she wrote the book, such attitudes were still to come. Lessing had to invent characters that could serve as role models to other women without having any such model herself. She used her imagination to create a new future for women; and, when women read her book, they could imagine it, too. *The Golden Notebook* was only one of many books that gave women of the 1960s ideas about a future they actually wanted and so helped spur the Women's Liberation Movement. For as soon as women had a vision of a possible future, they could work to create that future in real life.

This act of imagining and creating the future is a spiral process. Each time women have gained more freedom, authors have promptly imagined a new future with even more freedom for women. Each advance in the imagination changes reality as women live up to that new vision and then wonder what could happen *next*.

No act of imagination happens in a vacuum, of course; nor is it a simple matter of one thing causing another. Fiction writing has always occurred within the context of a myriad of incessant discoveries and shifts in every field of human endeavor, most of which are interconnected in ways so complex and subtle that we can never hope to understand them fully. It is not a question of whether the chicken came first, or the egg; chickens and eggs are inextricably bound together. One cannot exist without the other.

The culture we dwell within is likewise a dynamic web. We are not separate from but integral parts of it, affecting the web at the same time that it affects us, in an ever-changing, unceasing dance. We *cannot* ask a question until the culture has reached a point that makes it possible for us to ask it. Once that point is reached, the question inevitably *will* be raised. Over and over in the history of science, the same discovery is made by different people almost simultaneously, even when they are unaware of each other's work—a phenomenon known as "multiple independent discovery." The state of knowledge has advanced to where the discovery not just can happen but *has* to happen, and it may happen in many places at the same time.

Once the new breakthrough is made, the matrix changes again, and the dance goes on. Just as with scientific discoveries, as soon as the culture changes, the new woman is not just possible but inevitable—and she will change the culture for her daughters, whose daughters will have lives today's new woman cannot yet imagine.

Overcoming Tradition

This process of change is not, however, an easy one. As soon as a shift—in any area of human life—becomes the norm, almost immediately cultural ideas about that norm become calcified and difficult to overcome. Each generation feels that they are the first to fight against the weight of centuries of tradition, not realizing that the prior generation felt exactly the same way.

For example, most of the folk and fairy stories we love best were changed by those who wrote them down. It is evident from comparison with older versions of the same stories collected by others that the Grimm Brothers often edited folk stories to fit Christian sensibilities and make the stories more palatable to children (or, perhaps, to their parents; children can be remarkably bloodthirsty).

Moreover, they often made the stories up! The belief that the Grimm Brothers collected all their stories directly from old wives in villages has been discounted by folklore scholars such as Elizabeth Wanning Harries, Jack Zipes, and Maria Tatar.[5] Harries tells us that the literary genre of fairy tales was essentially invented in

France around the year 1690, primarily by educated women of the court known as *conteuses* (storytellers).[6] The term "fairy tale" (*conte du fées*) itself only came into use later, in the middle of the eighteenth century. Many of the Grimms' stories are now thought to have been written by their friends and relatives. (One major contributor was Henriette Wild, who later married Wilhelm Grimm.)

The conteuses took the credit for their stories. But some male writers, notably Charles Perrault and the Grimms, deliberately encouraged the idea that their stories were old tales handed down in peasant villages. Perrault's *Mere Loye* (Mother Goose) is depicted in the frontispiece of one of his books as a peasant woman telling stories as she spins yarn. To maintain this fiction, Perrault adopted a simple style for his stories that contrasted sharply with the sophisticated and witty style of the conteuses.[7]

Literary critics of the time praised Perrault's stories for being authentic while dismissing the stories by the conteuses as frivolous—ignoring the evidence that Perrault stole his plots for many of his stories directly from them. In other words, the critics determined that the norm for fairy tales should be based on how *men* wrote those stories.[8] This norm remained the standard for centuries. The stories "collected" by the Grimm Brothers and Perrault are still read as authentic fairy tales, while the stories written by conteuses such as Marie-Catherine d'Aulnoy, Catherine Bernard, Henriette-Julie de Castelnau, and Perrault's niece Marie-Jeanne Lhéritier are largely unknown. (Today, the conteuses are often arranged with the magical realists like Isabel Allende and Gabriel García Márquez in the adult-fiction part of the library, while Perrault and the Grimms are relegated to the children's section.)

Heroines written by women authors often go against what the critics will accept, because the critics' idea of a heroine is based on conventional social norms. But women's heroines tend to violate societal ideas of what women ought to be like, think, and feel. Instead, these heroines do what they are not supposed to do and refuse to do what they are expected to do. It is understandable, however, why many critics might find such heroines unbelievable: fiction has been all too often the only arena in which women could behave like this. Before the mid-twentieth century, real women rarely got the chance.

What such critics still do not—in some cases—realize is that many women characters in male-authored stories are not believable to *women* readers, for they are **anima figures** (see box). Such characters are depicted primarily as lovers, wives, mothers, and daughters *of men*. They do not have any kind of life apart from their relationship to a male character or any thoughts of their own, and so they often bear little resemblance to real women.

THE ANIMA

Jung uses the word *anima*, a Latin word for "soul," to mean the inner feminine aspects of a man's psyche that he is unaware of or tries to repress.

When people repress a trait in themselves, they often see it in other people instead. Jung calls this process projection. For example, men who believe that people should not show emotion may judge women as overly emotional. They may also blame women when they themselves become emotional—like the abuser who says a woman "makes" him angry.

When a male writer invents a female character that embodies such internal ideas about women, she may be what Jung calls an anima figure. Yet the anima can also serve as a guide for men, someone who helps them find their creative, intuitive selves.

This contrast can be seen when we compare most of the heroines of Charles Dickens to those of his contemporaries, the Brontë sisters. Almost all of Dickens's books feature a female character who puts aside all thoughts of herself to serve a father, brother, or husband, no matter how unreasonable or even abusive he might be toward her. She is the ideal Victorian heroine. But Charlotte's Jane Eyre, Anne's Helen Graham, and Emily's Cathy Earnshaw refuse to bow their heads and accept such lives. They protest—and when protest is futile, they run away. Many critics at the time found these stories improbable, as they could not imagine a woman venturing alone into the world.

Cultural ideas about what women should be like have dictated not just how female characters should be written but what good writing itself entails. One example is given above: once the critics decreed that a folk or fairy tale ought to sound like a peasant talking to children, the sophisticated stories of the conteuses were dismissed as inauthentic and, therefore, poorly written. It didn't matter that the men were making the stories up, too (or stealing their ideas from women); what mattered was *how* the stories were written. By the same token, a female character that critics found unbelievable was taken as proof that the author was a bad writer.

The idea that the *way* women write is wrong came into play as soon as Western women started to get their fiction published. Lady Mary Wroth's *The Countesse of Mountgomeries Urania*, written in the early 1600s, is perhaps the earliest known full-length prose romance by an English woman to make it into print. One of the main characters, Pamphilia, is a woman who writes songs and refuses to be silent, chaste, or obedient; for these sins she is rewarded, not punished, and becomes the queen of a fictional country. Although the noted writer Ben Jonson praised Wroth's work, the overwhelming response was so negative (some critics called her "a monster") that she never published the second half of the book and kept a low profile for the rest of her life.

A generation later, Aphra Behn, one of the first Englishwomen to earn her living as a writer, was criticized by Alexander Pope for her references to female sexuality in her novels. The leading critic of the early 1800s, William Hazlitt, castigated Fanny Burney's *The Wanderer* for its emphasis on "Female Difficulties," which he said were trivial and uninteresting: "difficulties created out of nothing."[9] Charlotte Brontë's writing was characterized as coarse by both male and female reviewers because of the scenes where Rochester tells Jane that his wife had affairs and that he himself has had mistresses. Such honesty about sexual matters between a man and a woman other than his wife was not acceptable to these critics.

Women writers remain a problem for some critics even today. In *Archetypal Patterns in Women's Fiction,* Annis Pratt gives several examples of twentieth-century critics who have condemned authors like Doris Lessing and Erica Jong for "hysterical" and "nymphomaniac" characters.[10] In her introduction to a later edition of *The Golden Notebook,* Lessing remarks that "apparently what many women were thinking, feeling, experiencing, came as a great surprise" to these critics.[11]

As recently as 2011, a study showed that reviews of works by men outnumbered reviews of works by women by 250 percent in the *Times Literary Supplement.* Sir Peter Stothard, editor of the magazine, responded by saying that "while women are heavy readers, we know they are heavy readers of the kind of fiction that is not likely to be reviewed in the pages of the *TLS.*" He then said that "the *TLS* is only interested in getting the best reviews of the most important books."[12] In other words, what half the population writes or likes to read is not important.

Reimagining Women's Lives

That women are, of course, fully capable of reading—and writing—great literature does not preclude a preference for books about the issues which concern them most nearly. And as noted in the above section, they are often concerned with gaining more freedom. In the earliest published works by European women, such as Christine de Pizan's fifteenth-century *The Book of the City of Ladies*, authors imagined a world in which women are, in fact, *allowed* to read—something few women of the medieval era could do. In women's stories from the fifteenth to the seventeenth centuries, an era when women were not regarded as individuals and an unprotected woman was fair game, female writers often envisioned a world in which a woman could say "no" to a man and have her word respected.

In the eighteenth century, visionary authors such as Burney explored the possibility of a woman's marrying for love instead of socially approved considerations of rank and money. Often their plots involve a woman marrying "up" in society against opposition. The hero of these stories is a man who is rich, often has a noble title, and displays good sense and correct morals. He marries the heroine because he recognizes that she is worthy in the same way. (She is also usually quite beautiful, as he is handsome.)

It might be easy to dismiss such a plot as romantic wish-fulfillment, but the idea of a lower-class woman marrying into nobility was radical for the time. As the woman's children would take over the family and inherit the property, these romantic novels promoted a gentle kind of revolt against the existing class structure as well as for women.

The heroines Jane Austen created in the early 1800s demand not just love but an equal partnership of mind. They generally don't care if the man they love is rich or not; they only want to marry men who suit them. When Elizabeth Bennet of *Pride and Prejudice* first realizes that she loves Mr. Darcy, it is not because he is handsome and wealthy but because they are right for each other:

> She began now to comprehend that he was exactly the man who, in disposition and talents, would most suit her. His understanding and temper, though unlike her own, would have answered all her wishes. It was a union that must have been to the advantage of both; by her ease and liveliness, his mind might have been softened, his manners improved; and from his judgment, information, and knowledge of the world, she must have received benefit of greater importance.

As is so often the case in life, Elizabeth only comes to this realization when she thinks Mr. Darcy is lost to her forever. Fortunately, Darcy is equally convinced of their compatibility and not about to give up.

Moreover, although Austen's protagonists are usually good-looking, she does dare to suggest that some of her characters are not conventionally handsome or beautiful, except in the eyes of those who love them. Darcy first dismisses Elizabeth as having no beauty, but by the end of the book finds her to be "one of the handsomest women" he has ever seen. A generation later, Charlotte Brontë went a step further in *Jane Eyre* and imagined soul mates who were "plain" on the woman's part and "not handsome" on the man's. Looks, Brontë implied, are as unimportant as wealth and standing to a good marriage.

As the nineteenth century went on and the Industrial Revolution upset the old class structure even more, women often created characters who chafed at and tried to circumvent the restrictions placed on them. For example, both George Eliot and Elizabeth Gaskell invented women characters who long to correct social injustices. Because society will not allow them to do so directly, they marry men who will act as they would like to act.

This way of escaping societal restrictions often necessitated a switch in roles to a heroine who is both richer and from a higher class than the hero—a change from the popular novels of Austen and others where a rich and upper-class hero condescends to marry "beneath" himself. When Dorothea of Eliot's *Middlemarch* marries the penniless dilettante Will Ladislaw, she inspires him to go into law and work on behalf of others. Wealthy heiress Margaret Hale of Gaskell's *North and South* chooses to marry a mill owner who is far beneath her socially, happy to give her money to a man who treats his employees well.

Toward the end of the nineteenth century, many women writers imagined female characters escaping from the confines of marriage altogether. The heroine of Kate Chopin's 1899 novel, *The Awakening*, for instance, leaves her wealthy husband and her children to dwell alone in a small house, inspired by a woman she has met who seems perfectly happy not to be married. Edna revels in her freedom for a while, but in the end drowns herself when she realizes how limited her options really are. She cannot go forward and refuses to go back, so she takes the only way out she can think of. The narrator of Sarah Orne Jewett's 1896 collection of linked stories, *The Country of Pointed Firs*, is a woman writer who has come to a fictional town on the Maine coast to work. The author makes no hint that she has or ever did have a husband or children, treating such considerations as irrelevant.

This new idea—that marriage and family did not have to be the central issue of a woman's life—quickly gained ground. Women novelists in the twentieth century gave equal weight to issues of career or life purpose for women. Anna and Molly of *The Golden Notebook* not only wrestle with questions about relationships and their careers but are also deeply concerned about politics and racism. In Great Britain, Margaret Drabble and her sister A. S. Byatt wrote about the challenges faced by women who pursue academic careers in books like *The Radiant Way* and *Possession: A Romance*. In the United States, Mary McCarthy followed the lives of eight Vassar graduates in *The Group* as they try to balance careers and relationships.

Now, in the twenty-first century, the heroines of science fiction and fantasy are pushing aside the heroines of "literary" fiction in the popular mind. Sookie Stackhouse of the books by Charlaine Harris and the *True Blood* television series; Arya Stark and Daenerys Targaryn of G. R. R. Martin's *Game of Thrones* TV series; Katniss Everdeen, heroine of Suzanne Collins's *Hunger Games* novels; and Tris of Veronica Roth's *Divergent* book series are just a few examples of current popular heroines. These heroines face challenges of mythical proportions where all the odds are stacked against them, yet they manage—by standing up for themselves while at the same time building strong relationships with others—to win out and transform the world.

These characters may be fictional, but the actors who play them are real people who often embody the same traits. Many actors who portray action heroines are devotees of martial arts and perform most of the stunts in their movies themselves. And several are also working to transform the culture. One example is Jennifer Lawrence, who plays Katniss in the movies based on the *Hunger Games* books. Lawrence uses her status as an "A-list" actor to speak out for the right to have a normal body instead of starving herself to comply with Hollywood's standards of female beauty.

Yet despite these changes from the early 1600s to the early 2000s, the essential pattern of the Aletis story remains remarkably the same. I also found the same basic plot and characters in biographies and autobiographies of famous women who were groundbreakers in their fields. This similarity confirmed for me that the Aletis is not just a fictional character. She is a true archetype, and, as such, can provide a role model for how women can live their lives.

The Goddess's Underworld Journey

*IN GREEK MYTHOLOGY, Persephone is the daugh-
ter of Demeter (whom the Romans called Ceres), goddess
of the grain. When Hades, god of the Underworld, steals
Persephone from the daylight world to be his queen, Demeter is so filled with grief that she lets all the crops die. This
threatens the life of everyone on earth. At first Zeus tells
Demeter there is nothing he can do, but eventually he
becomes desperate—for what is a god without people to
worship him?—and insists that Hades return Persephone
to her mother.*

*But Hades has already convinced Persephone to eat six
pomegranate seeds. In myth and folklore, eating anything
that a god or fairy or other supernatural being offers you
represents a binding contract. Thus, Hades has a claim on
Persephone for six months of each year.*

*Every year when Persephone returns to her, Demeter
celebrates with spring; each year when Persephone goes
back to the Underworld, Demeter mourns and the plants
die.*

*The descent story of the Sumerian deity Inanna also
involves two goddesses: this time, sisters. Inanna, queen of*

heaven, descends to see her sister, Ereshkigal, queen of the Underworld, who has just lost her husband. Jealous Ereshkigal first humiliates Inanna by stripping her naked, then kills her and hangs her body on a hook in the cave to rot.

Ereshkigal is placated when androgynous beings empathize with her suffering in childbirth. After three days, Ereshkigal agrees to let Inanna return above ground if Inanna's husband, Dumuzi, will spend six months of each year as Ereshkigal's consort. Inanna has no trouble agreeing to this because Dumuzi did not mourn for her when she was gone. But each year when he leaves her, she misses him. Dumuzi is the god of fertility, and, when he is underground, nothing grows.

The Metamorphoses *by Lucius Apuleius, a Roman novel dating from the second century CE, tells the story of Psyche and Cupid. Psyche is a human woman, but so beautiful that people liken her to Venus (Aphrodite, to the Greeks), the goddess of love and beauty. Jealous Venus sends her son Cupid (Eros) to prick Psyche with one of his arrows so that Psyche will fall in love with a horrible monster. But Cupid falls in love with Psyche instead, causes her to be brought to a secret villa in the woods, and makes love to her. He keeps his identity secret; he only visits her in the night and will not allow her to see him.*

Psyche is happy with her mysterious husband but misses her family. Cupid arranges for her sisters to be brought to her. But when her sisters (jealous of Psyche's beautiful home and her descriptions of her wonderful lover) spur Psyche to light a candle so that she can see Cupid, he disappears—as does the villa.

Alone in the wilderness, pregnant Psyche wanders in search of her lover. Eventually Venus finds her and insists that Psyche serve her. Three times, Venus sets impossible tasks before Psyche, but each time magical helpers come to Psyche's aid and allow her to finish the task.

Finally, Venus tells Psyche that she must descend into Hades and ask for a gift for Venus from Proserpina (Persephone), queen of the Underworld. Venus gives Psyche a box and tells her not to return unless she brings back some of Proserpina's secret beauty remedy. Psyche, again with magical help, overcomes all the terrors of the descent and succeeds in her quest. However, on the way back, she can't resist peeking inside the box and is overcome with a death-like sleep.

Cupid, meanwhile, has regretted his flight and is now searching for Psyche. He finds her, wakes her, and takes her to Olympus so that she can give the gift to Venus, fulfilling her quest. Jupiter (Zeus) gives Psyche ambrosia to drink—turning her into a goddess—warns Venus to stop persecuting her, and solemnizes the marriage.

CHAPTER 3

Heroic Quests and Heroine Journeys

*I used to think, I could be dressed up as a warrior, with
a lance and plume and sword and all, but it wouldn't fit,
would it? What would I do with the sword? Would it make
me a hero? I'd be myself in clothes that didn't fit, is all,
hardly able to walk.*

— "Tenar" in *Tehanu,* by Ursula K. Le Guin

THE STORY OF THE HERO'S QUEST has been a part of
human culture for thousands of years. Joseph Campbell identified its elements in *The Hero with a Thousand Faces.* Campbell
found that no matter what culture or religion he studied, he could
find the same story, which he called the Monomyth, "the one,
shape-shifting yet marvelously constant story."[1] It is the story of
Odysseus and Beowulf, of King Arthur and Percival, of Moses
and Prince Arjuna, of Luke Skywalker, Frodo the Hobbit, and
Harry Potter. People tell each other this story over and over again,
creating variation upon variation yet never straying far from the
same basic plot, the same set of characters.

Doing is the theme of the hero's quest. There is something he
must accomplish to prove himself a hero: find the Holy Grail,
destroy the One Ring, or pull the Sword from the Stone. Fantasy
author Sheri Tepper calls this "the single wondrous thing" in her
novel *Raising the Stones.* Accomplishing the single wondrous thing
usually solves all problems both for the hero and for his realm.

The young hero is different from other boys. He may be an orphan; he may be the third or the seventh son; he may just be a little odd. Somehow he is set apart, separate from the rest of his community. Often his uniqueness is more apparent to those around him than to himself.

The first stage of Campbell's heroic quest is the Call to Adventure. This call comes from outside: Caesar sends a messenger calling the general-turned-farmer back to Rome, a wizard named Gandalf or a giant named Hagrid knocks at the hero's door, or R2D2 the robot shows the hero a hologram of a mysterious woman. The hero may resist or refuse to answer the call at first, but sooner or later he has to go.

The hero often has companions on the quest. They may be friends who volunteer to come along, like the hobbits who travel with Frodo, or they may join him along the way, as Luke Skywalker is joined by Han Solo, Chewbacca, and Leia. The hero is also guided by a strange man of supernatural powers who appears and disappears suddenly. Arjuna rides in the chariot steered by Krishna, Frodo is guided by Gandalf, Luke Skywalker is taught the ways of the Force by Obi-Wan Kenobi. This wise guide disappears at some point, because while the hero needs advice, he must accomplish his task without supernatural help.

The hero encounters both aid and temptations along the way and must pass several tests. He spends some time in the Underworld, where he comes face to face with his own demons. Frodo traverses the hell of Mordor and comes to realize that he is not that different from Gollum, the creature who desires the One Ring for himself. Luke Skywalker goes into a cave, fights the apparition of Darth Vader, and sees his own face behind Vader's mask. Arjuna looks at the army arrayed against him and sees his beloved uncles and teachers. At this point, the hero may come close to dying or even die outright before being resurrected.

The hero has to confront or pass tests set by a powerful woman/witch/goddess or a powerful man/sorcerer/villain. Sleeping Beauty's prince cuts through the forest of thorns and defeats the witch Maleficent in her dragon form; Harry Potter finds and destroys the horcruxes that are the evil Lord Voldemort's fail-safes against destruction. In a decisive battle or feat of endurance, the hero achieves what he set out to do. Once he has accomplished this single wondrous thing, he is free to return home with gifts or wisdom to share with his people. He is now recognized as the rightful ruler and gets to marry the princess.

Many see the heroic quest as a metaphor for growing up and becoming a mature man. When adolescence begins, the child turns away from the parents and begins to venture through the dangers of the outside world. Most teenagers go through a phase where they reject or find fault with the values and opinions of their parents. During this stage, they rely heavily on the opinions and friendship of their peers. This is a necessary step as the child weans himself from his parents. There is often a wise mentor—a teacher, minister, or coach—who provides guidance during this time.

Eventually, the young man must leave the safety offered by the herd of his peers and the guidance of his mentor as he learns to think and decide for himself. As part of this process, he must face his **shadow** (see box). Once he has acknowledged and integrated his shadow side, he becomes a whole man. Now he has the wisdom to be a leader and a father.

In Campbell's *Hero with a Thousand Faces*, all the stories are about male heroes. One finds women only in their relationships

THE SHADOW

According to C. G. Jung, the shadow is the part of the self that we hide from ourselves. It includes all those traits that we are either unaware of or deny having. These aspects can be positive or negative. As long as we deny that we have negative traits, their power over us becomes stronger. And as long as we deny our positive traits and refuse to use them, we are likely to be both drawn to and envious of those who display those traits.

The first step in defeating the shadow is to accept that it is there. The next step is to actively embrace it as part of ourselves.

In Ursula Le Guin's *A Wizard of Earthsea*, the young wizard Ged spends months trying to run away from the evil gebbeth that he himself created out of pride. The longer he runs, the stronger the gebbeth becomes. Finally, Ged realizes that he can never outrun it—that no one can ever run away from his own shadow. He chooses to turn and face it, calling it by his own name. He claims the shadow as part of himself and so "conquers" it. Now its powers are his again.

to the hero: a mother figure, either his real mother or the World Mother; the Goddess who guides and gifts the hero; the Temptress who tries to distract him from the quest; and the Princess who is his prize for completing the quest. In fact, some think that the entire hero quest story is about a man learning how to integrate his feminine side. Jungian psychologist Lyn Cowan, for example, states that in a society where women are seen as inferior, a man's struggle to learn how to honor his feminine aspects can be so difficult that it may indeed take on heroic proportions.[2]

This perspective may explain why, when people try to write the heroic quest story with a heroine instead, it doesn't quite work. A woman who learns how to integrate her feminine side—and women who have been taught that the feminine is "less" often *do* have to struggle with this work—is not a hero. Dorothy in Frank

Baum's *The Wizard of Oz* follows the quest story exactly as out-lined in Campbell's book and accomplishes the single wondrous thing of destroying the Wicked Witch of the West and bringing back her broom, thus saving the Land of Oz from evil. But she does not return home to Kansas as a hero; in fact, no one believes her when she tries to tell them what happened! Instead, they tell her that she was ill, that she got a bump on the head and dreamed the entire thing. Unlike the hero, she comes into no inheritance and gains nothing new. Nothing changes in her life. (We hope, but do not know for sure, that at least she gets to keep her little dog, Toto.) The entire time that she is in Oz, all she ever says to anyone is that she wants to go home. The message seems to be that girls who long for an adventure will only want to run back home again if they ever find themselves in one.

Steve Blamires, author of several books on Celtic mythol-ogy, said to me once that women don't have to go on the quest for the Holy Grail because they already possess it. In the Arthu-rian legends and many other heroic quest stories, women are the keepers of what men seek. The Lady of the Lake has the magic sword Excalibur that Arthur needs. When Percival finally finds the Holy Grail, it is in the keeping of three women. Campbell says that women in these myths represent "the totality of what can be known. The hero is the one who comes to know."[3]

But what does the hero come to know that women already know? I believe that he comes to know two things: first, that he is a whole man; and second, how to connect to others. These are things few men grow up knowing. Men are constantly under tre-mendous pressure, particularly in Western society, to prove their maleness. Until they can accomplish this feat, they may be denied heartfelt connection to others.

"BE A MAN"

The 2014 documentary film by Jennifer Siebel Newsom, *The Mask You Live In*, explores the damage done to boys by our culture's insistence that being a man means never showing any emotion. In the film, psychologist Michael Kimmer says that this idea of maleness "prevents young boys from ever feeling secure in their masculinity," so they constantly feel the necessity to prove it.[4]

Many boys and young men feel forced to maintain a false front that not only prevents honest communication with others but also fosters a climate in which violence becomes the only acceptable outlet when repressed emotions erupt. This violence may be aimed at others or at oneself; over a thousand adolescent boys commit suicide in the United States every year, and the death rate from violence is five times as high for boys aged fifteen to nineteen as it is for girls.

The consequences persist throughout adulthood as well. Psychotherapist Terrence Real, in his book *I Don't Want to Talk about It*, blames the high incidence of midlife depression and heart attacks in men on the inability to express emotions and connect fully with others.[5]

Anyone who has been around a group of teenage boys will have noticed how quick they are to accuse each other of being less than manly over the slightest slip in behavior, often by calling each other derogatory names for women or gay men. Military officers and coaches challenge those under their command to "man up" and call them "girls" or "ladies" when displeased with their performance. I recently heard a young man say of a male friend that he "got all vaginal" when the friend showed emotion. Almost any show of emotion, other than anger or pride, is feminine—and therefore threatening to heterosexual maleness. But emotion is how we connect with others.

The heroic quest stories are about men who do extraordinary

things, things that test them and force them to grow. Our culture considers logic and strength to be the most masculine traits. Thus, the hero must accomplish things that only a warrior or a wizard can do by using his powers: his wits and his physical strength. The hero wins by acting like a "real man." This exploration of his essential maleness appears to be the key to opening up a man's heart to the feminine. The hero has to learn to trust his maleness, to know that he is truly a man, by *doing* what only a man can do. Once the hero knows absolutely that he is a real man, he can stop fearing betrayal by the feminine side of his own nature and learn how to connect emotionally.

For example, in the *Star Trek* stories, Mr. Spock is the epitome of logic. But he is incomplete—only half a man. Spock is half Vulcan, a race known for being coolly logical at all times, and for many years he struggles to repress his human, emotional self. When Spock dies and is miraculously brought back to life, he is not fully restored until he can answer his human mother's question: "How do you *feel*?"

The whole man is at ease with his emotions and can respond to an appeal for connection. The quest usually ends with the hero coming full circle, back to the land of his origin, and getting married. This is symbolic recognition that the feminine is no longer a threat and that the hero's feminine qualities no longer have to remain in shadow. In *The Lord of the Rings*, when Aragorn becomes king and marries Arwen, the Elven princess known as the Evenstar, Frodo exclaims, "Now not day only shall be beloved, but night too shall be beautiful and blessed and all its fear pass away." The Great Marriage of myth is the wedding of hero and princess where masculine and feminine are united in perfect harmony.

Yin and Yang

Genia Pauli Haddon provides another way of looking at heroes and heroines in her essay on "The Personal and Cultural Emergence of Yang-Femininity."[6] Haddon argues that we might benefit by replacing our Western ideas of masculine and feminine with the Eastern ideas of yang and yin. *Yang* comprises the energies of heat, daylight, conscious thought, power, active forces, and other qualities we tend to think of as masculine, while *yin* contains the energies of cold, receptivity, darkness, intuition—traits we usually think of as feminine. But instead of saying that yang is equivalent to male and yin is equivalent to female, Haddon contends that there are yin and yang ways of being masculine and feminine. She discusses her idea of yang femininity in depth but does not go into much detail about yin females or males of either type; the following is my extrapolation from her original ideas.

The yang male is our idea of the hero, all action and power. He is the alpha male, the superhero, the king, the warrior who leads the charge against evil. In his admirable incarnations, he fights on behalf of others. He is single-minded; he always works toward a goal. He is forthright, upright, morally incorruptible, honest—a perfect figurehead, a strong leader, a protective father.

But every archetype has its shadow side. If a yang male puts his considerable gifts toward serving himself instead of others, he will seek power for its own sake and be corrupted by it. He will become a dictator or a tyrant, feared instead of loved—until a new hero comes along to defeat him.

A yin male can be just as goal-oriented as a yang male, but he goes about achieving his goals in a very different way. He's a multitasker and usually has several plots in hand at once. He doesn't

WORDS AS MAPS

I brought up the concepts of yin and yang men and women to a group of people who are studying archetypal psychology. Several found these ideas are still too polarized, too rigid, too limited for conveying the complexity and uniqueness of individual people.

One woman observed that we are struggling to find a better vocabulary. She likened this search to explorers who had to use incomplete and often inaccurate maps as their guides to a new land. The maps were less than ideal, but they were all the explorers had. Once they reached the new land, they could redraw the maps to conform better to reality.

In the same way, she said, we're using out-of-date language to help us navigate to a place where we can broaden our ideas of men and woman as individuals. As part of this journey, we will discover a better vocabulary for what we are trying to say. We can't get attached to any of the terms we use, for they will change in time.

use force to achieve his goals. Instead, he manipulates the situation, using guile and smooth words to get what he wants, and often using others as well. He may be the power behind the throne of the yang male, or the Trickster who enters on the scene and changes everything. He may be the spin doctor who tells people what to think about the politician, the second-in-command who makes sure the captain's orders are followed, the invaluable aide who knows exactly what wheels need to be greased and when.

Again, the yin male is at his best when he puts his gifts in service to others and at his worst when he manipulates others for his own gain. Many yin males do not seek power at all; instead, like the Aletis, they desire lives where they can simply be themselves instead of having to conform to society's preference for yang males.

The yin female fits the conventional idea of the princess who waits for the prince to rescue her and change her from a maiden to a wife and mother. In her ideal aspect, she represents unconditional love, love that accepts others just as they are without putting any demands on them: the love of a mother for her baby. At the other extreme, she can be clingy and dependent, requiring others to take care of her at the cost of their own lives. A recent example of a yin woman is Bianca in the movie *Lars and the Real Girl*. Bianca is a plastic sex doll. She passively sits and looks pretty while all the people around her project their own issues onto her—a perfect example of what Jung would call an "anima woman." She is not real; yet she serves as a catalyst for change in the movie, allowing others to work through their own issues with women in their interactions with a woman who only "says" and "does" what they imagine. They know (unconsciously or consciously) that she is not truly initiating anything, though, and they eventually learn to "take back" their projections and own those ideas as their own shadows. This "taking back" of projections ultimately heals Lars, his family, and many others in the community.

Women who have yang personalities, on the other hand, find the role of a yin woman to be too limited and passive. But until recently, the only role model they had for how to live a different kind of life was the yang male, and so yang women tried to be like yang men. Many achieved success in the spheres of power, but, as Murdock and others discuss, they later came to feel that this path took as much away from them as it gave. For one thing, women trying to be yang in a masculine way often come across to others as "hard" and difficult and have difficulty with relationships.

A woman in the ideal aspect of being yang expresses herself in different ways from those of a yang male. She is interested in the process as much as in the goal. She enables and facilitates rather than forces; she works with situations and people like a midwife works with a laboring mother to allow a child to be born in the easiest and most natural way. She embodies the power of transformation and often helps others to bring out their own gifts instead of making them do things her way.

The warrior princesses so popular in today's culture often behave like yang men, using force to achieve their ends. Fortunately, filmmakers like Brenda Chapman (*Brave*), Jennifer Lee (*Frozen*), Kathryn Bigelow (*Zero Dark Thirty*), and Joss Whedon (*The Avengers*) are also giving us heroines who understand the ways of yang femininity and put those ways into action. I discuss these new heroines in the last chapter of this book.

The Search for the Heroine's Journey

In a 1980 essay, Campbell stated that myths do not offer any models for how women *individuate*—a Jungian term for the process of becoming a mature, whole person.[7] But Campbell was speaking from the perspective of a man who had spent years studying stories about heroes. Ever since his book on the heroic quest came out, many authors have tried either to reimagine his model in a way that fits women or to find a new model altogether for the heroine's journey. Some of these models look much like Campbell's, while others are radically different. Still other writers are more interested in what truths myths and stories may hold for women in general, whether or not they are heroines.

In 1990, psychotherapist Maureen Murdock published *The Heroine's Journey: Woman's Quest for Wholeness*. Murdock based her book on her own life experience and what she kept hearing in the life experiences of her women clients. She also provides some examples of similar experiences from myths and tales. Murdock's model of the heroine's journey is partially based on Campbell's model of the heroic quest, but she uses different terms for the stages that are more relevant to women.

At the time Murdock wrote her book, her clients were likely of the generation born in the post-World War II "baby boom" of 1945–59. The women of this generation were the vanguard of the Women's Liberation Movement of the 1960s and '70s. Murdock's model begins with the heroine embarking on the traditional heroic quest. That is exactly what many women of this generation did as they followed masculine models for a successful life— a necessary tactic, considering that women who rejected the idea that they were suited only to be wives and mothers had no other role models to follow. If you didn't want to be a traditional woman, your only option, it seemed, was to be as much like a man as you could and become a hard-driving career woman or professional.

Unfortunately, this strategy only brought women pain as "they chose to follow a model that denies who they are," says Murdock.[8] A fictional example of this can be seen in the 1987 movie *Broadcast News*: Holly Hunter plays a woman driven to succeed in the male world of broadcast journalism, which means she works so hard that she begins to have emotional breakdowns, while her intelligence and ambition alienate most of the men around her. Murdock found that the woman who tries to follow the traditional masculine path eventually ends up with "a sense of sterility, emptiness, and dismemberment, even a sense of betrayal."[9] No one applauds such a woman's heroism, as Dorothy found out after returning from Oz. So Murdock's heroines eventually abandon that path to seek one that affirms their own identities and meets their needs better.

I believe Murdock's model represents the journey that many women experienced in the second half of the twentieth century. Women who lived before that time rarely had the option to follow the masculine path, while women in the twenty-first century are challenging the binary idea of their options and forging a new path entirely. Novels by women written in the late twentieth century often follow the pattern that Murdock portrays. In these novels, the turning point for the heroine may be the realization that the masculine model doesn't work for her. Then she experiences a dark night of the soul (see box) that leads to a new beginning.

Murdock's model focuses on the transitions and obstacles in life faced by her clients. Two years after Murdock's book came out, Jean Benedict Raffa, at the time a professor of education, wrote

---

THE DARK NIGHT OF THE SOUL

We've all had them: those moments when we face up to an unpleasant truth we've been avoiding. Although it may have been building for years, the actual moment when we stop denying and let ourselves see the truth can come like a thunderclap. Or, it may be a sudden stillness in which the inner voice finally can speak and be heard.

We may hear this inner voice say, "You need to leave this relationship." We may hear it say, "This job is killing you." Or worse, we may hear the voice say, "This problem you keep encountering is of your own making."

The voice is guiding us to action. But before we can act, most of us have to live through a "dark night" in which we grieve the loss of illusion and wail that we don't know what to do. This dark night may last hours, days, weeks, or even years. I suspect that many cases of depression are rooted in this moment when we realize that the life we've been living does not work for us, but we have no clue of what to do about it.

about her own psychological journey in *The Bridge to Wholeness: A Feminine Alternative to the Hero Myth.* Her model parallels Murdock's in many ways, and she also describes her life as a series of transitions and crises.

I don't doubt that Murdock and Raffa portray these crises accurately. However, I think some aspects of a full life may be left out when one focuses only on turning points. A nonfiction book intended as a guide for others going through similar crises necessarily focuses on those events, but a novelist or biographer is more likely to include details about the periods when life is *not* in crisis. This may be one reason why the pattern I've seen in women's stories has a much broader scope.

Raffa thinks that the journey women follow is circular like the hero's quest but in reverse order. In Campbell's model, she says, the hero leaves home, which is the mother's place, for the outside world, which is the father's place.[10] The hero can only return to the mother's world and be reunited with the feminine after he does something significant in the outside world, the world of the masculine. He has to prove himself a real man *to other men*, in other words. In contrast, says Raffa, the heroine has to integrate her masculine side while still at home; only then is she is able to go out and function in the outer, masculine world.

Joan Gould also puts a psychological spin on the heroine's journey in *Spinning Straw into Gold: What Fairy Tales Reveal about the Transformations in a Woman's Life.* Gould was born in 1927 and matured before the time of birth control and expanded choices for women. This may explain why she sees a woman's life as dictated by the urges of her own body, particularly the drives to pair-bond and reproduce, and why she seems unable to imagine a fulfilling life for a mother after the children are grown and gone.

Annis Pratt, a novelist and former professor of literature, develops a different model for the female journey in *Archetypal Patterns in Women's Fiction*. Pratt uses "archetypal" to mean literary tropes and characters, and her viewpoint is primarily sociological. Men's and women's experiences of society are entirely different, she says, because men represent the norm while women represent "radical otherness." Thus, the primary motivation for a woman is to claim her uniqueness in a culture that refuses to see it, and the goal is rebirth as a new person. Pratt does not take her analysis much beyond the point where the heroine experiences a "plunge into the unconscious," which Pratt calls "a realm of inherited feminine power quite different from patriarchal culture."[11] While she says that women return from this experience greatly changed and empowered, she does not explore where they go from there. And, indeed, most of the novels she covers stop at that point.

Kim Hudson, a scriptwriter, looks at movies to find an alternative to the heroic quest model in *The Virgin's Promise: Writing Stories of Feminine Creative, Spiritual, and Sexual Awakening*. Hudson says this feminine path can also be taken by a man in the sense of embarking on an inner exploration of self rather than a heroic act of fearlessness. She calls the protagonist of such films the Virgin, as the heroine moves from an innocent, dependent position to a self-empowered one. Hudson finds that most of the obstacles the Virgin faces occur at home. Yet Hudson also relies on Campbell's stages of the heroic quest for her model, renaming them as necessary with feminine equivalents, and emphasizing turning points. She sees the stages of the Virgin's journey like movie-plot twists that impel the protagonist forward.[12] I have the same criticism of this argument that I have with the psychotherapy approach:

while focusing only on motifs that move the story forward—on *doing*—is valid in itself, it ignores other motifs critical to the feminine experience, motifs that have more to do with *being oneself* and that occur over and over in women's narratives.

Raffa sees the ultimate outcome of the heroine's journey as wholeness; similarly, Murdock sees it as the integration of the heroine's masculine and feminine sides. But for Hudson, the outcome is transpersonal: the heroine transforms what needs changing in the culture. She gives the example of the movie *Bend It Like Beckham*, in which Jess, the second daughter of an East Indian family living in London, longs to play football (soccer, to Americans). At first she can only play by sneaking out behind her parents' backs, but eventually she wins her parents over and gains not just the right to play but the right to accept an athletic scholarship to an American college—a revolutionary idea for her birth community.

Other writers don't address the heroine's journey directly but look to myths and tales for insights about women in general. One of these is Jungian therapist and storyteller Clarissa Pinkola Estés, who published *Women Who Run with the Wolves* in 1988. Estés analyzes folk tales about women and provides examples from the lives of real women to illustrate the psychological truths of these stories. She agrees with Murdock that women who try to live according to society's ideas for them end up feeling depressed and powerless and are thus unable to be creative. Estés believes the answer to this loss of **eros** (see box) lies in "the simplest and most accessible ingredient for healing—stories."[13] Estés is aware of the problem of men rewriting old stories, but she claims that she can spot these edits and reconstruct the original tales. She

EROS

Eros was the name of the Greek god of love. In modern parlance, it is often used to denote romantic and sexual love.

But, as Clarissa Pinkola Estés and other Jungians use the term, *eros* has a much broader meaning. It connotes not just sexual desire but passion for living. It includes the inner creative spark and intellectual curiosity—anything that feeds our creativity and our engagement with life.

looks at each story as a separate thing, each with particular messages for women in particular situations.

Marie-Louise von Franz, a psychotherapist trained by Jung, pulls equally from her experience with women clients and from her studies of folk tales in her book *The Feminine in Folk and Fairy Tales* and other works. Like Estés, von Franz does not provide a model of women's development but focuses on one specific issue at a time, such as a woman's need to integrate her inner masculine aspects or to wake up from living unconsciously. Sadly, von Franz sometimes expresses negative attitudes toward women, attitudes I believe she unconsciously picked up from Jung.

Allan Chinen is another psychiatrist who lectures and writes about folk tales from a psychological viewpoint. He focuses on the life lessons that these tales hold for both men and women in *Beyond the Hero, Once Upon a Midlife,* and *In the Ever After—Fairy Tales and the Second Half of Life.*

Then there are those who follow the "Great Goddess Matriarchy" theory of history first proposed by anthropologist Johann Jakob Bachofen in his 1861 book, *Mother Right: An Investigation of the Religious and Juridical Character of Matriarchy in the Ancient*

World. Bachofen argues that before written history began, Eastern European civilization was a matriarchal, goddess-centered culture where all denizens were peaceful and held equal status. This utopia was shattered by an invading "dominator" culture that replaced it with a patriarchal and hierarchical system. His ideas have been given new life by art historian Merlin Stone in *When God Was a Woman*, sociologist Riane Eisler in *The Chalice and the Blade*, and archeologist Marija Gimbutas in *The Civilization of the Goddess*.

Recently, scholars have cast doubt on the historical validity of the idea of a lost goddess-based matriarchal culture. Still, it is meaningful that women yearn for such an idea to be true. In *The Goddess: Mythological Images of the Feminine*, Christine Downing insists that "we need the goddess in a culture that tears us from woman, from women, and from ourselves."[14] We see this yearning for the goddess in the popularity of books like Marion Zimmer Bradley's *The Mists of Avalon*, a retelling of the Arthur legends from the standpoint of the female characters, including Morgaine/Morgan le Fay.

Other scholars of folklore take a political or sociological view of heroines instead of a psychological one. Madonna Kolbenschlag, author of *Kiss Sleeping Beauty Good-Bye: Breaking the Spell of Feminine Myths and Models*, finds the Sleeping Beauty story to be a metaphor for how Western society stifles female ambition and creativity and instead encourages young women to do nothing as they wait for a man.[15] Karen E. Rowe, in an essay on "Feminism and Fairy Tales," agrees that many fairy tales teach a girl to believe in an external force—a prince or fairy godmother—that will release her from an unpleasant life if she only waits long enough.[16] Maria Tatar makes a similar argument in *The Hard*

Facts of the Grimms' Fairy Tales. These authors see no evidence of a unique female voice at work in fairy tales, nor do they find any role models that women might follow.

Recently there has been a movement to rewrite old stories with a more active heroine who acts just like a male hero would. Examples include Barbara Walker's *Feminist Fairy Tales* and the anthology *Don't Bet on the Prince: Contemporary Feminist Fairy Tales in North America and England*, compiled by Jack Zipes. Other scholars have looked for examples of stories with strong heroines in the mythologies of other cultures, an effort that has resulted in Ethel Johnson Phelps's compilation in *Tatterhood and Other Tales* and *Not One Damsel in Distress: World Folktales for Strong Girls* by Jane Yolen.

This movement to make heroines more heroic is readily seen in movies and on TV with heroines like Wonder Woman, Supergirl, the Bionic Woman, Buffy the Vampire Slayer, Xena the Warrior Princess, and Kara Thrace, who replaced the old male "Starbuck" in the new version of *Battlestar Galactica*. Beautiful, powerful, and unafraid, these women fight as equals with men. They are not just strong, but logical and intellectual, passionate and loving, even soft and seductive at times.

As empowering as these female heroes may be to a girl's idea of her potential, however, they present some problems. These "she-roes" imply that to break free of society's restrictions, a woman must be like a man—and not just an ordinary man, but the extreme idea of masculinity: the warrior hero. That idea is as restrictive as the idea that a girl should aspire to nothing beyond motherhood. Also, today's girls are often aware that the masculine way doesn't really work for them. It's time we find a middle path, a way to become a powerful woman in a uniquely feminine way.

The Descent Journey

There is another story that speaks to many women and is sometimes intertwined with the Aletis, or wandering heroine, story. In this other story, a woman—or a goddess—is forced to journey underground to a dark and dangerous place. The archetypal images for this story can be found in the mythical descent journeys of the Greek goddess Persephone and the Sumerian goddess Inanna, as well as the story of Psyche, the mythological character whose name now stands for our own deepest self.

In her book *The Long Journey Home: Re-Visioning the Myth of Demeter and Persephone for Our Time*, Christine Downing states that the story of Demeter and Persephone may be "the myth for [women], as the Oedipus myth may be the myth for men."[17] (Freud was convinced that every man secretly desires to kill his own father and marry his mother, as Oedipus does.) Downing finds the Demeter/Persephone story frees women "from being defined by the roles of mother or daughter . . . through the transformed understanding of human relationships and of death" from a female perspective.[18] The first and primary task for a young woman is to get free of her mother so that she can become an adult—and the primary task for a loving mother is to let that daughter go.

Sylvia Brinton Perera, author of *Descent to the Goddess: A Way of Initiation for Women*, believes that Inanna's descent to the underworld realm of her powerful and dangerous sister Ereshkigal also provides perspective on the full meaning of life. To embrace femininity entirely means to embrace the dark, wild, and dangerous aspects as well as the queenly, loving, and mother-like aspects. Perera thinks the story speaks to men, too: she says that the story of Inanna and Ereshkigal gives us all "a description of a pattern of psychological health for the feminine, both in women and in men."[19]

Betty Meador expresses a similar view in *Uncursing the Dark: Treasures from the Underworld*. Inanna's story, she says, "seemed to me the very substructure of the meaning of femaleness, the rock-bottom facts of women's relationship to the primal material world."[20] Meador thinks that the story shows how a woman can learn how to love herself and how to live in a way that honors that self.

Although the ultimate outcome may be the same, the Aletis follows a very different path from that of Inanna or Persephone. What is the difference between a journey out into the wilderness and the journey down into the Underworld? Why do some women seek out the goddess in the cave, while others go looking for the witch in the forest?

Part of the answer, I believe, lies in different experiences of childhood. We expect, when a girl child is born, that her life is going to follow a certain path. She will remain at home, protected by good parents, a virgin in body and in experience, until she and they feel that she is ready for the next step in life. She may choose college; she may choose to marry; she may choose to enter the workforce. She has control over her own sexual initiation, which is not traumatic, and marries for love. Children usually follow, and this experience, too, is enjoyable for the most part. Her pains and sorrows are part of the norm, as well—difficult teens, marriage squabbles, deaths in the family, hopefully in that order.

But obviously, not every girl grows up in such ideal circumstances. The girl who doesn't often finds that her wishes for her life are not honored by others when she is young. Such a girl is not protected and cherished during childhood; her sexual initiation often comes too early, violently, or without her consent; and she may not choose her (first) husband. She has no control over her life until the moment when she has had enough—and leaves.

My view is that, in their quest for wholeness, girls who grow up in the first, ideal sort of setting often become attracted to the descent story of the goddess, while girls who are forced to grow up in less than ideal circumstances are more likely to follow the pattern of the wandering heroine. Both seek a full experience of life by seeking out (perhaps unconsciously) the very experiences they have been denied. But because what has been lacking in their lives is very different, their paths are different, too—the first being downward and the second, outward.

In support of this argument, I have found that women who write about the goddess descent often report that they had supportive parents. Chris Downing told me that she had what Estés calls a "too-good" mother. Her mother was loving and supportive of Chris throughout her life and gave her a wonderful role model of feminine strength to call upon. Meador states in her book that her childhood nanny, Liz, was "a good mother" to her who "lived from the feminine."[21] Dara Marks, a mythologist and Hollywood "script doctor" who conducts workshops on the descent journey, has stated that she was fortunate to have received good parenting as a child.[22] I have no doubt that these girls were princesses in their homes.

When I asked why she was so drawn to the descent story, Downing replied that she reached a point in her life where she needed to know more about "the depth of things." At this point she had a dream (which she describes in her book) that told her she needed to go looking for "Her" in a cave underground.

Meador describes this search for the dark goddess as "a down-going excursion away from the intact emotions of 'normal' life, a ride on waves of disorientation, despair, and chaotic turmoil."[23] What women are seeking in this descent experience, I believe, is the fullness of life: not just the positive face of the feminine that they saw in their mothers while growing up or reflected back in their fathers' eyes as those fathers gazed with love upon their daughters, but the entire range of possibilities open to a woman, both the beautiful and the horrible. They seek to integrate those "dark" feminine qualities and thus move past polarity to wholeness.

The Aletis, in contrast, and as I discuss further in chapter 5, does not receive optimal parenting. Instead, she is usually left to get through whatever childhood troubles she might face on her own. And often those troubles are terrible ones: incest, abuse, death of loved ones, loss of family and home. At a young age, the Aletis becomes fully acquainted with the dark reality of life and death. She feels alone and unfriended and trapped. In other words, she *grows up* in Ereshkigal's cave; from a tender age, she knows it intimately.

Again, these very different experiences of childhood explain, I believe, why some women are drawn to the descent story while others write or love to read Aletis stories. Those who know the benign, loving face of the feminine, but lack experience of those darker aspects that are feared or repressed both by society and in themselves, instinctively seek out those experiences later in life. But Aletis girls have no need to go looking for the dark goddess, being so well acquainted with Her from an early age. What they need instead is what the more sheltered girls have always been able to take for granted: the freedom to be themselves—the freedom to get out of the cave of an oppressive childhood, and often a sub-sequent stifling marriage, and be the queen of their own lives.

The Aletis's lack or loss of protective parents who softened every blow provides a two-fold incentive for her to undertake her journey. First, she has to go out into the world to find support for her uniqueness, for she does not have it at home. Second, she is prepared by *how* she was parented to handle the rigors of a solo journey.

For the daughter of the too-good mother, on the other hand, going by herself into the unknown may be too terrifying to con-template; and why, after all, should she even attempt it? Downing said to me that the idea of going anywhere by herself was terrify-ing; even when she craved a new adventure, she essentially had to be "abducted" to have one, just as Persephone is abducted by Hades. Perhaps this is why nice girls are so drawn to the "bad boys" their parents warn them against—they are instinctively seeking a kind of abduction away from the safe home they've lived in until now. It is in the underworld realm of the bad boys that these girls will have the chance to find their real strength.

But to the Aletis, who from an early age has had to endure many trials, the idea of leaving is less frightening than the idea of staying. Those who have been abandoned by parents or by fate have nothing to fear from being alone. Those who have never been supported in their dreams may believe that their best hope for the future lies elsewhere. Leaving may be an act of desper-ation, but it is also an act of hope. The Aletis does not need to be abducted anywhere. She steps out boldly into her new life by herself.

The "descent" story may also appeal to those women who have found themselves, without warning, in the Underworld. The death of a child or husband, a life-threatening illness or accident, financial reversals, rape, divorce, a family member who becomes addicted to drugs or alcohol or commits a crime—many things can cause a sudden catastrophic change in a woman's life. For example, Lydia Rowe, the heroine of Lynne Sharon Schwartz's *Disturbances in the Field*, had a happy childhood and seems to have a perfect life with a passionate marriage, fulfilling career, and four delightful children. But when tragedy strikes she is forced to reevaluate everything. The stories of Persephone and Inanna may have powerful meaning for a woman like Lydia who has been abducted "underground" against her will.

Finally, some women may identify not with Inanna or Persephone but with bitter Ereshkigal. A single mother tied down by the claims of her children can understand Ereshkigal's pain and jealousy of Inanna who is free to go where she wants, has a husband, and better yet, has loyal servants who help her out of difficult moments. Inanna spends three days in the cave, but Ereshkigal *lives* there—and there are many women who feel that they, too, are trapped forever.

Ereshkigal may also be relevant to women who identify more with their fathers than their mothers. (I discuss these "father's daughters" in the next chapter.) In her book *Addiction to Perfection*, therapist and writer Marion Woodman calls such women, only half in jest, "Ereshki gals" because they tend to despise feminine women or see them as competitors.[24] Like Ereshkigal, they do not love their sisters. Even if they reign in their own domains as successful professionals or businesswomen, they may resent women who appear to "have it all" without having to work for it. This resentment can also be a trap that keeps a woman from moving forward.

The hallmark of the Aletis is that she refuses to be trapped, either by others or by her own resentments and fears. She moves forward. But before tracing that movement, we must first look at how the wandering heroine is unlike the traditional hero, as well as at the forces in her early life that give her the resolve she will need to escape.

CHAPTER 4

The Aletis Story

My experience is, "Oh, I'm never really going to get it right.
I'm never going to get it done. But that's not the point here."
The point is the journey.

—Melissa Etheridge

THE CHARACTER of the wandering heroine or Aletis has always been before our eyes, yet she has been largely invisible. To see her, we have to stop thinking in terms of the heroic quest and look for a different pattern. Lois McMaster Bujold, a multiple award-winning fantasy author, realized when she wrote *Paladin of Souls* that "The Hero's Journey is just the wrong shape for the Heroine."[1] We have to stop looking for a heroine who acts like a hero and look instead for a different kind of bravery.

The Aletis Is Not a Hero

The following list provides some of the basic differences between Campbell's heroic quest story and the Aletis story:

→ The heroic quest is almost always about a *male* hero, while the Aletis is almost always *female.*

→ The hero is applauded for *accomplishing* the "single wondrous thing." But the Aletis rarely accomplishes anything that others think important. If she does, it is not seen or she is not believed. What she does is not acknowledged. Her bravery takes the form of *refusing* to do what others want her to do or to be what they want her to be.

→ *Doing* is the theme of the heroic quest. But *being* is the theme of the Aletis story: she seeks the freedom to be herself.

→ The hero is seen as different by his community, often to the point of being an outcast or *isolated*. He is the odd man out, the youngest son, the dreamer. But the Aletis is *immersed* in her family or community, often to the point of being invisible to others and denied a separate, unique identity.

→ While the hero must go away and accomplish deeds to *prove his masculinity*—to prove that he is a real man—the Aletis's femaleness is never in doubt. In fact, her gender is the very thing that keeps her trapped. When the heroine breaks free, it appears to society that she wants to *defy her femininity*.

→ The hero's challenges occur *away from home*, on the road of trials. But the Aletis undergoes most of her greatest challenges and trials *at home*, before she ever leaves it.

→ The hero is *expected*. Prophesies foretell he will come, or the need for such a hero is apparent to the community. The young man has only to prove that he is the hero they have waited for. In contrast, the Aletis must fight to overcome the community's expectations of her. What she does is completely *unexpected*.

→ The heroic quest is a *circle back to home*. The hero leaves home, proves himself, and returns home when he is ready to be the king. But, as Bujold came to realize, "the successful female (in exogamous cultures, which most are) goes out and keeps on going, never to return."[2] Once the Aletis finally does leave home, the path of her story is not as easily defined as that of a hero's. It spirals, follows blind alleys, or goes off on tangents. The Aletis wanders, moving on again and again, occasionally revisiting a former home briefly, before finding or creating her true home *somewhere altogether new*.

→ The movement of the hero is always *toward* something. The movement of the Aletis, in contrast, is almost always *away from* something. She leaves when the place she is in becomes intolerable and goes to find a new place where she can be more fully herself.

→ The hero's mentor *seeks him out and travels with him*. The old man, the wise guide, shows up early, teaches the hero necessary lessons while accompanying him, but then disappears without warning—often to the distress of the hero, who may not feel ready to face his challenges alone. The Aletis, on the other hand, *finds and then leaves* her teacher, the old wise woman who lives in the woods. The heroine goes to the witch for lessons and leaves when she has learned what she needs.

→ The hero *transforms himself and restores or preserves the community*. He is changed by his journey into a whole man who then saves the community from evil or restores or finds the lost thing necessary to the well-being of the collective. But the Aletis *transforms the community while preserving herself*. She shatters old ideas of what it means to be female as she gets in touch with who she really is. Once she has established her identity, she brings forth the gifts within herself to share with the community. And, as a consequence, she often changes that community forever.

Thus, the Aletis story is not just a matter of replacing a male hero with a female heroine and following the same plot. It is a different story entirely. Both stories are about someone becoming a whole person, but the paths are not the same.

To Be a Woman

Girls are not under the same pressure to prove their femaleness as boys are to prove their maleness: quite the opposite! From baby-hood onward, most girls are made very aware that they are female. They cannot lose this identity no matter what they do. Thus, they are free in a way that boys are not to experiment with taking on the traits of the opposite gender. They may be condemned for doing so, and some may even say they are unfeminine, but the underlying theme of even these negative messages is not that "you have stopped being female" but rather that "you are female and so should not be doing these things."

Nowadays—in the West, at any rate—women can wear male clothing and do jobs traditionally reserved for men, and no one will blink. An athletic or outdoorsy girl may be called a "tom-boy," but this word does not carry the same weight of shame and accusation as the names leveled at boys and men who fail to appear properly masculine. A woman can climb Mount Everest or become a fighter pilot with less risk to her gender identity than a man who takes a sewing class, while world-class female athletes are still seen as sexy enough to be photographed for *Playboy* magazine.

Historically, the expectations placed on most women were low: look as pretty as you can, be nice, get married, have babies. Few people looked beyond that. Until the late twentieth century, most women were expected to stay at home and keep the house while the man went out of the house to work, to war, or to go on quests. "They also serve who only stand and wait," a line from a sonnet by the seventeenth-century poet John Milton, was used in World Wars I and II to celebrate women who waited for their soldier husbands and sons at home (although they weren't just sitting around passively waiting; they were holding the home together and doing all the chores they'd always done in addition to all the chores their absent husbands had done as well).

Many myths and fairy tales reflect the idea of female passivity. Penelope waited for Odysseus for twenty years while he fought the battle of Troy and then had adventure after adventure— including seven years as Calypso's lover—before getting back to his wife. Snow White did nothing except sleep in a glass coffin, waiting for a kiss to awaken her. Sleeping Beauty outdid Snow White by sleeping for a hundred years. In a typical heroic quest, the princess waits at home while the prince does all the work. She is his reward for battling the bad guys. Apart from marrying him and giving him babies, she has nothing to do.

But in real life, happily ever after rarely happens. Prince Charming turns out to be a frog, the castle needs endless housework, and the balls and pretty dresses are quickly a thing of the past. To get what she really wants from life, the princess has to leave the castle. There is no task to accomplish before she can be free, no omen, no prophecy, no strange wizard knocking on the door to call her to this journey. Neither is there any promise of a reward. On the contrary, the Aletis knows that to leave will probably mean losing everything she has valued up until now. Yet she has no choice. She embarks on the journey because she knows her soul will die if she stays.

The Aletis moves on to another place that seems better at first, but the change process is still going on. Soon she will find she must leave again—often, over and over again—until she finds the place where she can simply be herself. Instead of accomplishing tasks to prove her worth to herself and the world, the heroine travels deeper and deeper into her own psyche as she comes to see and value the uniqueness of her being.

The pivotal moment for the hero is when he does the single wondrous thing that proves his worth to others. But the pivotal moment for the heroine is when she says to herself and then to the world, "*This is who I am.*" She must learn to know herself first, and then she must have the courage to live as herself in the world. And, as I discuss in the last chapter, that act of courage can enable others to change as well.

While the heroic quest is a circle that begins and ends at home, the Aletis pattern is one of always moving forward, always seeking to be born anew. Ironically, the symbol for a male is an arrow, while the symbol for a female is a circle. To become balanced and whole, it seems each must learn the opposite shape: the hero must trace a circle while the Aletis must follow the arrow's flight.

Éowyn's Journey

THERE ARE FEW WOMEN *in J. R. R. Tolkien's* The
Lord of the Rings, *but one of them is a match for any of
his heroes. Éowyn, niece of the King of Rohan, is a tall,
strong woman who can ride and fight as well as any man.
Yet she has been relegated to the role of caretaker to her ail-
ing uncle. While her cousin and brother ride out to defend
the kingdom, Éowyn is stuck in the sickroom. When Gandalf the Wizard heals the king, Éowyn is released from her
role as nurse, but no one includes her in their plans for war.
She falls in love with Aragorn, the rightful High King of
Gondor. If Aragorn would only love her back, she thinks,
he will take her with him, away from Rohan where no one
sees her for herself.*

*But Aragorn rejects her, for his heart is already given
to another. As the men prepare to ride, Éowyn is told by
her uncle to stay at home—to mind the house. Desperate,
Éowyn disguises herself as a warrior and rides with the
men. She does not care if she lives or dies; all she wants is to
do one great deed, to be a hero.*

*And she does just that. In the great battle of the Pelen-
nor Fields, she faces the Witch-King, the evil undead sorcerer in command of the enemy's armies. Prophecy has
long foretold that "not by the hand of man" will the Witch-
King fall. When the sorcerer taunts her with this prophecy,*

Éowyn tears off her helmet, letting her long golden hair shine in the sun, and replies, "But no man am I! You look upon a woman." As the Witch-King hesitates in sudden doubt, Éowyn, helped by Meriadoc the Hobbit, slays him.

Éowyn is seriously hurt in the fight and is taken unconscious to the Houses of Healing. She is healed there of her injuries, but her heart remains dark. She has achieved the heroic quest, yet there is no prize for her. In this despairing mood she meets Faramir, son of the Steward of Gondor. Faramir has nothing to offer her except his heart. But, unlike everyone else, Faramir sees into Éowyn—sees the person she really is—and loves her. When she understands this, Éowyn's heart is healed. She lets go of her fantasy about Aragorn and vows to become a healer and a lover of growing things. She and Faramir marry. Aragorn makes them Prince and Princess of Ithilien, a land now freed from the enemy, and together Faramir and Éowyn turn Ithilien into a beautiful garden.

CHAPTER 5

Parents

> What we cannot see, that has come before—what our
> parents have seen and been and done—are the hand-me-
> downs we begin to wear as swaddling clothes, even as we
> ourselves are naked. The flaw runs through us, implicat-
> ing us in its imperfection even as it separates us, delivers us
> onto opposite sides of a chasm. It is both terribly beautiful
> and terribly sad, but it is, finally, the fault in the universe
> that gives birth to us all.
>
> —Katherine Min, *Secondhand World*

WOMEN WHO WRITE the Aletis story often spend several chapters on the young heroine's life with her family, for the Aletis faces many of her most difficult trials while still at home. Jane Austen takes seven chapters in *Pride and Prejudice* to get Elizabeth Bennet out of her home and off to Netherfield Park where she and Mr. Darcy can embark on their extended mating dance. Charlotte Brontë gives us four chapters on Jane Eyre's unhappy childhood at Gateswood and several more on her life at school. In *Middlemarch*, George Eliot needs ten chapters to describe Dorothea Brooke's home life and the restraints others wish to place about her before sending her to Rome on her honeymoon.

Toni Morrison starts *Beloved* in the middle of the story of Sethe's life, but in classical epic style, spirals back to Sethe's beginnings to explain the forces that pull on her. Margaret Atwood uses a similar device in *Cat's Eye*, introducing us to her heroine Elaine after she has become a successful artist, then taking Elaine and her readers back to childhood and adolescence to uncover the wounds that still pain her heroine.

Women who have lived the Aletis story tend to describe their childhood and adolescence at length in their autobiographies. Maya Angelou requires an entire book to talk about her life at home in *I Know Why the Caged Bird Sings*, as does Jill Ker Conway in *The Road to Coorain*. Nancy Mitford devotes nine chapters in her fictionalized autobiography *The Pursuit of Love* to describe her life with her parents. Katherine Hepburn expends four chapters on her childhood in her autobiography, *Me: Stories of My Life*, while Margaret Mead takes seven chapters in *Blackberry Winter*.

In contrast, in hero stories little attention is given to the conditions of childhood or home life other than to establish the hero's uniqueness. Perhaps we know that he's the youngest boy (usually the third or the seventh son) or an orphan; we may be shown that he isn't wanted or that he doesn't fit in. That's all we need to know to be prepared when he answers the first important motif of the heroic quest: the Call to Adventure.[1] We know nothing about Beowulf's life before he appears in answer to King Hrothgar's call for help against the monster Grendel. We barely meet Luke Skywalker in the first *Star Wars* movie before the robot R2D2 appears and plays him part of a call for help from a young woman, a siren call that sets Luke off on a quest to find her. Likewise, young Arthur in T. H. White's *The Once and Future King* is enticed into the woods in the very first chapter. There he meets the wizard Merlin, who will guide him to his destiny.

The Lost Golden Time

Some girls find life at home suits them just fine. This is more likely if a girl has confident and loving parents who see and support her uniqueness. As discussed in the last chapter, such a girl may feel no need to embark on a journey of self-discovery (until she decides that it is time to encounter the dark goddess). But authors rarely write stories about people whose lives go smoothly. In Aletis stories, girls who do have a happy home with loving parents in their early years inevitably experience a change of fortune. Vasilisa the Beautiful of Russian folklore is the pampered only daughter until her mother dies and her father remarries—a common motif in folk and fairy tales. The Dashwood girls of Austen's *Sense and Sensibility* are protected from the world by two loving parents and plenty of money until their father dies. Actress Katherine Hepburn admired and loved her parents and never lost her attachment to her childhood homes—to one of which she returned for extended stays throughout her life—but the shocking death of her beloved older brother when she was fourteen changed her forever.

The Misfit Girl

In most Aletis stories, however, the heroine feels that she doesn't fit in at home. She may feel this way even as a young child, but it's more likely that her discomfort begins when she begins to grow up. Adolescence is the time when the Aletis comes under increasing pressure from family, friends, and the culture she lives in to conform to an ideal of womanhood that doesn't suit her. Home or school can then become a war zone where she has to fight battles for what she wants instead of accepting what others think is best for her. If her original home is happy, she may, like Margaret Hale of Elizabeth Gaskell's *North and South*, be "abducted" away to another place where she will feel that she is a misfit.

The sense of not belonging can come on slowly for those who are not abducted away but remain at home. There is often no distinct event, no obvious change, that turns the young heroine's situation from happy to conflicted. Her family and friends are not the ones who change; they continue to be the same as they always were. Therefore, they may think that the girl is "creating" a problem where none existed before and blame her for it. This only increases the misfit girl's sense of alienation.

For example, Dorothea Brooke of George Eliot's *Middlemarch* becomes aware of the terrible living conditions of the poor tenants in her neighborhood when she returns home after being away at school. Wanting to help the tenants, she researches designs for cottages to replace their unhealthy hovels. But when she tries to convince her uncle and the local squire to implement her plans, they dismiss her ideas as nonsense and urge her to forget them. Her uncle and neighbors make it clear that she is destined for nothing greater than being a mother and a decorative wife to the squire. Such expectations did not matter to Dorothea when she was a child. It is only as she comes to adulthood that Dorothea begins to imagine a different life and finds herself in opposition to those she loves.

Dorothea is motivated by empathy and compassion. Her society expects and approves of these feelings in a wife and mother— *if* she extends them only to her own relations and friends. But Dorothea's compassion is so great that she cannot ignore the reality of the tenants' living conditions. This refusal to keep her feelings "at home" sets her up for conflict with others in her social set. And that conflict causes Dorothea to realize that she is different. Her friends and family don't understand her and refuse to try. They don't want her to be unique. They are uncomfortable whenever she shows any spark of individuality.

That spark of individuality is precisely why the Aletis doesn't fit in. It takes a lot of work to get to know someone as a unique personality, and most people—like the families in these stories—are not willing or able to work that hard. They would rather expend their effort monitoring how well the girl fulfills her expected role as daughter and wife. Her real self is invisible to them, and they don't want to hear from her. Even as a child, writer Judy Blunt understood this. In her autobiography, *Breaking Clean*, she says, "At thirteen I stood where the world I knew ended, imagining no future beyond my ordained leap into the abyss at my toe tips, vanishing into the station of woman, wife, and mother—storytellers with no story of their own."[2] She could see no path around the abyss before her.

A girl may spend years trying to fit in, trying to find peace with the life assigned to her, trying to reconcile being invisible with her own sense of self while her wishes and desires, her unique qualities, all the things that make her a person, are not honored. She is expected to do what others think she should do and not have any thoughts of her own. But eventually it is too much to bear. Through Jane Eyre, Charlotte Brontë complains that:

> Women are supposed to feel very calm generally: but women feel just as men feel; they need exercise for their faculties, and a field for their efforts as much as their brothers do . . . and it is narrow-minded . . . to say that they ought to confine themselves

to making puddings and knitting stockings, to playing on the piano and embroidering.

Lyndall of Olive Schreiner's *The Story of an African Farm* laments that "we fit our sphere as a Chinese woman's foot fits her shoe . . . the parts we are not to use have been quite atrophied . . . we know that we are compressed, and chafe." This feeling of being confined is echoed in Gandalf's explanation of Éowyn's character to her loving but baffled brother in *The Lord of the Rings*:

> My lord, if your sister's love for you, and her will still bent to her duty, had not restrained her lips, you might have heard . . . what she spoke to the darkness, alone, in the bitter watches of the night, when all her life seemed shrinking, and the walls of her bower closing in about her.

These girls long for larger lives. They want to do more, understand more, see more of the world, and to have the chance to make their mark on that world. Eliot describes Dorothea as being an idealist who thinks deeply about things, which is why she doesn't fit in:

> With such a nature, hemmed in by a social life which seemed nothing but a labyrinth of petty courses, a walled-in maze of small paths that led no whither, the outcome was sure to strike others as at once exaggeration and inconsistency.

The inconsistency lies, not in Dorothea herself, but between her great-souled nature and the tiny life that others expect her to embrace.

Jane Eyre's vivid imagination is laughed at or condemned by all those around her, even at Thornfield where she is *not* imagining that eerie laughter or the strange events in the night. Dorothea begins to realize just how out of step she is with those around her when her sister Celia downplays Dorothea's earnest attempts to draw plans for decent cottages as nothing more than a passing fad. She starts to wonder "what was life worth—what great faith was possible when the whole effect of one's actions could be withered up into such parched rubbish as that?" Dorothea's attempts to explain her thoughts and values to Celia are futile in the face of such a contemptuous dismissal.

Therapist Patricia Reis says in her book *Daughters of Saturn* that misfit girls fight "against a living death, a cultural mummification that works to stifle their thoughts, silence their voice[s], confuse their mind[s], and halt their speech."[3] The misfit girl is the ugly duckling, the changeling switched at birth, the fish out of water. She is not seen, not heard, not understood, and certainly not valued as a unique person. A crisis is inevitable. One day the misfit girl will break free in a way that upsets and startles her friends and family—the first step in becoming an Aletis.

Problematic Parents and Guardians

Many psychologists and others believe that good parenting is necessary if children are to grow up with a strong sense of self. As clinical psychologist Mary Pipher puts it in *Reviving Ophelia: Saving the Selves of Adolescent Girls*, "Good fathers are nurturing, physically affectionate and involved in the lives of their daughters. Good mothers model self-sufficiency and self-love."[4] But these are usually not the kind of parents one finds in the Aletis story.

James Hillman argues in *The Soul's Code* against the cause-and-effect attitude toward parents expressed in the above paragraph.

He believes that every child has within them the "acorn" of their destiny that will drive their choices in life far more directly than any childhood trauma may do. He calls the idea that how our parents raise us determines how we will live our lives the "parental fallacy"[5] and gives as part of his argument the example of identical twins separated at birth and raised by different parents. Both men grew up to be obsessively neat in their habits, a characteristic for which they each blamed their respective mothers. However, one mom was a "neatnik" while the other mom was slovenly!

Hillman wants us to step beyond the parental fallacy for two reasons: first, so we can start seeing every child as unique and honor the "acorn" that wishes to grow into the oak of the person's life purpose, and second, so we can stop blaming our parents, especially our mothers, for everything we do or don't do in life. I hold to the idea expressed in the last chapter that no matter what kind of childhood we may have—whether we were surrounded by loving support or exposed to neglect and abuse, whether we blame or absolve our parents for what they did or did not do—as we grow to adulthood we each will naturally seek whatever we feel is needed to make us "whole." We desire a full experience of life. The Aletis story is one of a girl whose quest is toward the light, toward experiences that will empower her. The story requires that authors give their heroines difficult childhoods to explain this need.

Many fictional heroines, like Jane Eyre and Dorothea Brooke, have no parents at all. The story of the orphan girl was a popular formula of short stories published in women's magazines of the nineteenth century. This "orphan Ann" genre inspired Lucy Maud Montgomery's *Anne of Green Gables*, Kate Douglas Wiggins' *Rebecca of Sunnybrook Farm*, and the comic strip *Little Orphan*

Annie. The orphan girl is usually treated like a servant until she is miraculously reunited with the supposedly lost parent (as in Frances Hodgson Burnett's *The Little Princess*), is discovered to be an heiress, or comes under the protection of a wealthy benefactor. Some girls have parents who have deliberately abandoned care of their daughters to others. Hermione Granger of J. K. Rowling's *Harry Potter* books, for example, is sent away to school for most of her childhood. Her parents love her but have no idea how to deal with a daughter who is so different from them. In Susan Warner's 1850 novel *The Wide Wide World*, Ellen is sent to live with her aunt even before she is orphaned. Tenar, the heroine of Le Guin's *Earthsea* books, is taken by the local temple to be a priestess when she is only five years old. There she has no identity of her own; even her name is taken away from her.

Some guardians may be kindly and well-meaning but have no experience of being a parent. They may do well enough when the girls are children but fail to cope with trials of adolescence and young womanhood. Neither Dorothea's Uncle Brooke or the Rev. Villars of Frances Burney's 1778 novel *Evelina* have any idea how to guide their wards once the girls reach young womanhood. When Dorothea and Evelina run into difficulties, their guardians do little more than talk and let events take their own course.

More often, the foster home is difficult or hostile. In Austen's *Mansfield Park*, Fanny Price is sent by her parents to live with rich relations so that they will not have to bear the cost of raising her. Her parents do not seem to know or care that their daughter's position in her aunt's home is little better than that of a servant, or that Fanny is denied the comfort of a fire in her bedroom in winter. Jane Eyre's uncle welcomes his orphaned niece, daughter of a much-loved sister, to his home. But after he dies, his resentful wife and children make Jane's life a torment. When she is sent to school, her new guardian is the harsh Mr. Brocklehurst, who looks for reasons to punish Jane at every opportunity.

Children whose parents fail to provide love and support are, in essence, orphans. They have lost the parent they should have had, and the emotional fallout for them is much the same as if the parent had died. Unfortunately, if the parent is still living, they are not able to grieve the loss, a necessary prerequisite to healing. Instead, they may spend much of their energy trying to get the love they need and want from the unresponsive parent. Or they may become stuck in anger and blame, both at the parent for withholding love and at themselves for not being lovable. It is only with great effort (and usually, years of counseling) that such "orphans" can gain enough insight to let go of blame, grieve their loss, and learn how to take care of and love themselves.

Problematic guardians make the reader uncomfortable. Those who ought to be responsible for and protective of the children are shirking their responsibility. Their failure reinforces the feeling that the heroine is friendless, alone, and adrift. The reader pities the girl and may even hate the fictional guardian. When the heroine finally asserts herself, we rejoice and our pity turns to admiration. We're almost glad that she had such a difficult guardian because it forced her to show us the real strength of her character. However, this silver lining is more difficult to see when it is a parent who is the problem.

To do something heroic means to dig down inside oneself and find a strength one did not know was there. For many people this occurs only in extreme circumstances, such as the woman who finds the physical strength to lift a car off a child. But children who have difficult childhoods learn to find their strength early. The Aletis taps into that deep place of strength over and over as she forges her own path instead of the one prescribed for her by others. At every step she must choose, and then choose again and yet again, to trust herself. The Aletis may be forced onto the journey because of her upbringing, but her upbringing also prepares her for it.

The Problematic Mother

The first person a girl looks to for a role model is her mother. Girls who have positive, confident, loving mothers are less likely to seek out lessons from others on how to be a whole woman. But women novelists who write the Aletis story rarely give their heroines such a mother. If they do, it's unlikely that the mother will still be alive when the daughter nears adulthood. Estés argues that a "too-good" mother *must* die in the story so that the girl will be forced to develop her own internal guide for living.[6] It seems that the only mother who can be allowed to live in an Aletis story must be problematic in some way.

The Weak or Absent Mother

Often the mother is missing altogether from the story. If she is present, she may be weak or silent, offering little help to her daughter. This is unfortunately too often true to life. Weak mothers do not just fail to give their daughters a positive role model to follow; they also may fail to keep their children safe. As a child, the poet Mary Oliver says, she could not understand why her mother never protected her from her sexually abusive father.[7] It took Oliver decades to get over the trauma and find her strength on her own.

A weak mother cannot protect because she is not an equal partner in the marriage. Mrs. Hale of *North and South* does not question her husband's decision to leave his comfortable position as a vicar, nor does he seem to think there is any reason to consult her. Judy Blunt gives many examples of how her mother silently acquiesced to her father and made it clear to her daughter that she must do the same.

Some mothers are silly or ridiculous. Mrs. Bennet of *Pride and Prejudice* is hysterical and a hypochondriac with no sense of how to behave properly in public. The job of trying to teach her younger daughters a sense of decorum falls on Elizabeth and Jane, but their mother constantly undermines their efforts with disastrous results. Likewise, Mrs. Dashwood of *Sense and Sensibility* is unable to handle her own finances or rein in her middle daughter Marianne's emotional excesses. Her oldest daughter, Elinor, has to take over running the household and do her best to prevent Marianne from running headlong into trouble. But Mrs. Dashwood, like Mrs. Bennet, sabotages Elinor's efforts until Marianne nearly dies. Such mothers are an obstacle, not a guide, to their daughters.

The Discontented Mother

Many heroines have mothers who are unhappy with their own lives. Often these women live in Ereshkigal's cave. They may have lacked loving guidance and support as children themselves and have no model for how to give those things to their own children. Lily Owens, the heroine of Sue Monk Kidd's *The Secret Life of*

Bees, has a mother who became profoundly depressed and left when Lily was only four. Although she later attempts to retrieve Lily, she is killed before she can do so. Lily grows up believing that she must be unlovable, or why would her mother have left? The truth is that Lily's father was abusive, and Lily herself runs away from him ten years later. But understanding why her mother left does not help her feelings of abandonment.

The artist and naturalist Beatrix Potter had an unhappy mother. Biographer Linda Lear draws a picture of Beatrix's mother as a controlling, insecure, demanding, and social-climbing snob who despised "tradesmen," although both her fortune and that of her husband were inherited from fathers who were in trade. Helen Potter had no interests outside of achieving a place in society, not unusual for a Victorian woman of whom little was expected beyond correct behavior and appearance. Her "pretentiousness was a reflection of her personal powerlessness," says Lear.[8] Mrs. Potter was unable to understand her daughter's yearning for a larger life and tried to make Beatrix conform to her own limited views.

Jill Ker Conway draws a detailed portrait of such a mother in her childhood memoir, *The Road from Coorain.* Her mother was an intelligent and capable woman who became a nurse and was running a hospital by her late twenties. Then she fell in love, married, and moved to the Australian outback to help her husband run a sheep ranch. Widowed fifteen years later and further bereft by the death of a much-loved son, she became increasingly unhappy and demanding of her daughter. "My mother's devotion to me, the self-denial that had sent her to work to educate me properly, her frequent references to the fact that I was her consolation for all her tragedies, weighed on me like the Ancient

Mariner's albatross," says Conway.[9] When Conway discovered Carl Jung's essay on "The Positive and Negative Aspects of the Mother Archetype," she was shocked to find her mother rising up from the pages:

> I needed no convincing that we were Demeter and Persephone, and that my mother would indeed turn the world around her into a desert of grief if she were to lose me. It was a comfort to see my life situation so well described, but alarming to realize it was even more elemental than I had supposed.[10]

Eventually, Conway's mother became addicted to prescription medicines and alcohol. Conway "tried to rescue her, stimulate her interests, get her involved in charities, anything to harness her energies creatively,"[11] but all her attempts to help her mother find a new life failed. She could not stop her mother's downward slide.

This failure and her own encounters with the entrenched misogyny of Australia in the 1950s led Conway to flee the country so that she could pursue her life work of studying women's roles in society, which she acknowledges was a "sublimated expression of my own guilt, generalized towards caring for all frustrated and angry older women."[12] She *had* to leave her mother to live her own life, but it was a wrenching experience that haunted her for years. The only way she could justify her abandonment of her mother was to work tirelessly on behalf of other women.

The Evil Stepmother

In fairy tales, the heroine often has a stepmother who is controlling and unsympathetic. Cinderella and Snow White are well-known victims of such evil stepmothers. Vasilisa the

Beautiful also has a hostile stepmother. The evil stepmother is the mother who is not really a mother, who puts her own needs and interests above those of her daughter, perhaps even opposes or sabotages the daughter. As with Beatrix Potter's mother, such a woman need not be a literal stepmother; she can be a biological mother who does not value her daughter as an individual. For example, in the Russian fairy tale "Frost," the scheming mother prefers her two eldest daughters and treats the youngest badly, to the point of leaving her out in the freezing night in hopes that she will die.

In some stories this non-mother is an older sister who takes over when the mother dies. Anne Elliot of *Persuasion* suffers for years from being under the thumb of her snobbish older sister Elizabeth, who unites with their father to keep Anne from living life as she would wish. Elizabeth treats Anne almost more like a servant than a sister and does all she can to prevent her from marrying Captain Wentworth, just as Cinderella's stepsisters conspire with their mother to keep Cinderella in the kitchen and out of the way of Prince Charming. The function of the evil stepmother and stepsisters is to keep a would-be heroine in her prescribed place and prevent her from expressing her real character. They may represent both the external and internal voices that tell a girl she is worthless and should not aspire to any kind of life of her own.

The Dominating Mother

Some heroines' mothers are dominating characters. Such mothers may be beautiful and sexy as well as intelligent; in many ways they are positive role models, but they cannot be trusted. The young heroine must learn to stand on her own two feet without their guidance. For example, Lyra Belaqua of Philip Pullman's *The Golden Compass* believes for years that she is an orphan. She chafes under the restrictions placed on her by her guardians, a group of professors at a university, and perfects the art of eluding them as much as possible. When she is twelve, she meets her mother, Mrs. Coulter, and is charmed by her sophistication and apparent concern for Lyra's happiness. But Lyra very soon realizes that Mrs. Coulter is deceitful and dangerous. Using the skills she learned at Jordan College, Lyra runs away from her, too.

Molly in *The Golden Notebook* reminds her friend Anna of her mother because she is "somebody strong and dominating, whom Anna had had to fight." But Anna's mother died when she was a baby, so Anna cannot have really known what her mother was like. Lessing implies that Anna instinctively knows she must learn how to overcome the domination of the mother so that she can be herself.

The ideal mother gives her daughter a positive role model of femaleness. She is also the most likely person to offer unconditional love and nurturing. At the same time, she will expertly guide her daughter into independence. When mothers are absent or less than ideal, the girl is abandoned to her own devices. Figuring out how to be a confident and fulfilled woman becomes the major task of her life.

The Problematic Father

A father plays an important role in a daughter's life not only as a parent but as her initial experience of the male sex. Suzanne Fields, author of *Like Father, Like Daughter*, says, "The parent of the opposite sex carries a special responsibility: the child's first guide to dealing with the opposite half of the human race is the crucial one."[13] Linda Schierze Leonard, writing in *The Wounded Woman*, agrees:

> [The father] is the first masculine figure in [a girl's] life and is a prime shaper of the way she relates to the masculine side of herself and ultimately to men. Since he is "other," i.e., different from herself and her mother, he also shapes her differentness, her uniqueness and individuality.[14]

Through her father, the girl has her first experience of knowing herself as an individual who is unlike someone else. The father's attitude toward that difference is crucial to how she perceives herself. If a father likes and supports a girl in her femininity, she is much more likely to be comfortable in her body. If he likes and supports her individuality, she has permission to explore her uniqueness. When people asked Ziauddin Yousafzai how he fostered the strength and poise of his daughter Malala, the girl who defied the Taliban to attend school and was shot for it, he replied, "Don't ask me what I did. Ask me what I did not do. I did not clip her wings, and that's all."[15] A good father lets a girl be herself.

At the same time, the ideal father provides a girl with a sense of being cherished and protected. He also serves as a strong role model for those traits society labels as masculine: power, responsibility, decision-making, logic, and discipline. All of these are traits that the daughter will need in adulthood.

Fathers play key roles in most Aletis stories; their authors explore all the varieties of the father-daughter relationship and the effect of each on a daughter's life. Unfortunately, all too often the father-daughter relationship is heavily influenced by societal attitudes toward women. A good father who desires to bolster his daughter's self-esteem is hard put to compensate for the messages our culture gives women. Fathers who agree with those messages do not even try.

The Dominating Father

At one extreme are the abusive and incestuous fathers. These fathers violate their daughters in multiple ways. A father should be the primary protector of his daughter's physical well-being. He violates this obligation if he batters her; he violates it even more if he breaks the taboo against incest.

Western society equates virginity with purity. Traditionally, it is the father's job to protect this purity. A girl who has lost her purity is still considered damaged goods in many communities where potential husbands believe they have the right to sole possession of her body. Even if she was forced, she may be considered a slut or a whore because she must have "invited" the attack somehow. The incestuous father is the one who breaks the covenant he has with society, yet it is the daughter who bears the consequences (and literally so, if he impregnates her).

A virgin is also wild in a sense because she has not yet been "tamed"—that is, she has not yet been forced to submit to the will of anyone else. Thus, a virgin is a girl who has not yet had to submit her body—or her heart, mind, and soul—to another. In the cult of Artemis in ancient Greece, adolescent girls were raised apart from men for several years to allow them to develop a sense of self before they married. Sadly, few girls since then have been given the time and space to develop such a sense of self.

If a girl is physically violated before she has any real idea of who she is, she may develop ideas about life that she will later have to erase and replace if she is to function well, and this can be difficult. Poet Mary Oliver, who was abused as a child, was in her seventies and had undergone five years of therapy before she could say in an interview:

> I finally feel healed—kind of late in life . . . I'm now able to understand, one, that it happened, which a child fights and doesn't want to acknowledge, and two, that it affected certain things in my behavior. . . . What I have done is learn to love and learn to be loved. That didn't come easy.[16]

When she was raped at the age of eight, Maya Angelou wondered why God had let such a terrible thing happen. After a horrendous trial where she was mercilessly badgered by the defense attorney, Angelou felt so guilty that she decided to stop talking and did not speak again for over a year. "Sounds came to me dully. . . . Colors weren't true either," she wrote of that time in her life.[17] Everything had been distorted by her experience.

But it was out of this experience that Angelou began to understand the power of story. She began to heal when a sympathetic neighbor gave her books to read and asked her questions about them. Angelou found to her amazement that she could reply, and that "To be allowed, no, invited into the private lives of strangers, and to share their joys and fears, was a chance to exchange the Southern bitter wormwood for a cup of mead with Beowulf or a hot cup of tea and milk with Oliver Twist."[18] Talking over the stories with the neighbor also helped to her feel that "I was liked, and what a difference it made."[19]

In *The Color Purple*, Celie's stepfather first rapes her when she is fourteen. When she cries, "He start to choke me and say 'You better shut up and git used to it.' But I don't never git used to it."

Abused girls face a long struggle to overcome the effects of these early violations. Such a trauma is "disabling" and "short-circuits normal maturation,"[20] laments Jungian therapist Marion Woodman, who was sexually abused by both a family friend and her own brother in childhood.

In contrast, there are the overly protective, dictatorial fathers. Judy Blunt's rancher father, in the best feudal tradition, decided that his daughter would marry an older man who owned the land next door. He punished her when she sneaked out to date a boy she liked from school. When Blunt defied him and saw the boy again, her father beat up the boy, threatened to charge him with statutory rape, and told his daughter he would take her out of school and restrict her to the ranch for a year unless she obeyed him. She had no option but to comply.

This protectiveness is not from love. Domineering fathers, says Leonard, "are quite often exiled from the vitality of life, cut off from their own feminine sides . . . they are not open to the unexpected, to the expression of creativity and feelings."[21] When they encounter such "feminine" traits in others (women or men), they are often enraged by them. For example, the only reaction to his daughter that T. Ray, the father in *The Secret Life of Bees*, seems capable of is anger. Lily can hardly say or do anything without being yelled at or hit.

These dominating fathers are otherwise distant and uninterested in the daughter as a person. Blunt makes this clear in a telling passage:

Dad seldom intruded on our upbringing, partly because he was seldom around the house to observe it, but partly because raising kids simply wasn't his job. . . . Facing him across the supper table . . . I would feel his gaze drift over me and away, ready to notice what wasn't there but never quite seeing what was.[22]

Blunt's father did not see her as she was; he looked at her only to make sure she was not doing what he would forbid. What such fathers primarily look for in a daughter is obedience to their rules. Blunt's father fiercely protected her virginity, but only as part of his obligation to society in the person of his chosen future son-in-law, not out of any concern for her own well-being. If he ever saw his daughter cry, his only response was to tell her to toughen up.

The Indifferent Father

Then there are the fathers who don't think about their daughters at all. In Jane Austen's *Persuasion*, Anne Eliot's father is vain, shallow, and extravagant and "had no affection for Anne." Her mother "had been an excellent woman, sensible and amiable . . . she had humoured, or softened, or concealed his failings." But after her mother dies, those failings of her father come to the fore and cause more and more problems for Anne. When Captain Wentworth asks for her hand in marriage, her father cares only for how the match will reflect on him personally; the happiness of his daughter means nothing to him.

In *North and South*, Mr. Hale is intelligent and highly moral, and he loves his family. But it does not occur to him to consider how his wife and daughter Margaret may suffer as a result of his decision to leave the Church (thereby losing his home and income) over a point of doctrine. He is so lacking in a sense of protectiveness that he never enquires into Margaret's activities. He is unaware when she puts herself in physical danger or when she damages her reputation by escorting her brother to the train station late at night, something their father ought to have done. He is surprised when a friend suggests that there might be an attraction between Margaret and John Thornton—and does nothing about it.

Such fathers in these women's narratives either do not care about or are too weak to further their daughters' well-being. To the dominating father, a daughter is a possession, a thing, not a person in her own right with her own desires and needs. The girl interprets this as the reality of a woman's life. An abused girl may believe that anyone has the right to hurt her. But the message to the daughter of an indifferent father is just as bad: that she is of no value to anyone.

The Seemingly Good Father

Most girls connect first with their mothers. But if a mother is absent or weak, the daughter may try to connect more with her father. She may seek his approval by behaving more like a man than a woman. In time, this identification with the father can become the critical problem of her life.

This is not all bad. Girls who identify with their fathers may learn to use their intellect and discipline, traits that do, after all, work well in a masculine world. In a perfect world, these qualities would be balanced by qualities such as empathy and compassion: qualities that give the girl a sense of herself as a nurturing, loving person. Without these feminine qualities, the girl may succeed in material ways—in *doing*—but miss out on the deeper aspects of relationships.

There is another danger when a father trains his daughter to think and behave like a man instead of a woman. Sometimes, a girl with a strong father may turn so much to him that the mother is shut out entirely. Murdock calls such women *father's daughters*,[23] as does Woodman.[24] Writer Jean Shinoda Bolen calls them *Athena women*, after the Greek goddess who sprang fully grown from her father Zeus's forehead.[25] Leonard calls them *armored Amazons* because they often adopt an armor of competence and self-sufficiency that keeps others at a distance. While this may help them professionally, she says, such armor can work both ways and cut them off from their femininity. As a result, they can "become alienated from their own creativity, from healthy relationships with men, and from the spontaneity and vitality of living in the moment."[26] Unless these women also have strong role models for how to use feminine traits successfully in the world, they may live a kind of half-life, cut off from their female selves.

One of the ways this problem manifests is dishonesty—or perhaps *pretense* is a better word. In *Leaving My Father's House*, Marion Woodman laments that despite being her father's favorite, she could never tell him about the sexual abuse she suffered as a child. She assumed he would judge her and reject her if he knew the truth.[27] But she was hiding the truth from the very man that society had charged with protecting her sexual self. If she confronted him with this failure, who really stood in danger of losing their "special" status? Was she protecting herself, or him? And what about her mother?

One of the most beloved women characters in literature is a father's daughter. Elizabeth Bennet of *Pride and Prejudice* is no great beauty, but her wit and charm more than make up for this. Her uniqueness is seen and appreciated by most of those around her, particularly her father. When a father sees and values a girl's uniqueness, she learns to value it as well. Thus, a father's approval can give a girl powerful protection against many of the forces that might try to repress her. When Elizabeth overhears Darcy say that she is only "tolerable," she has the self-confidence to turn it into a joke against Darcy. Caroline Bingley, the voice of censorious society, also has no power over Elizabeth. Elizabeth sees Caroline as her father would: ridiculous and not worth listening to.

But here is the paradox and the trap. While Mr. Bennet regards his daughter with love and approval, he tends to be judgmental and dismissive of most other people—particularly Elizabeth's mother. Mrs. Bennet is indeed quite silly, but Mr. Bennet never tries to reason with her or overrule her in questions of parenting; instead he retreats to his library or makes fun of her. He has abdicated his responsibility as a husband and father, leaving much of the burden on his two oldest daughters. Hence, Elizabeth grows up with a model of parenting and marriage that is far from ideal.

Mr. Bennet's attitude also unconsciously teaches his daughter that his love (and, perhaps, the love she can expect from her own husband) is conditional on her *not* being like most women—particularly her mother. Like many father's daughters, Elizabeth reacts by trying to live up to her father's standards so that he will continue to love her and not abandon her emotionally, as he has her mother and younger sisters. She, like Marion Woodman, protects her father from his own shortcomings so that he won't be angry with her.

Such dishonesty is difficult to maintain. Eventually Elizabeth tries to caution Mr. Bennet about the dangers facing her youngest sister, Lydia, who has received the worst of her mother's ideas of parenting. He dismisses Elizabeth's fears. Life, though, has a way of making us see what we try to refuse to see, even if others aid and abet us in keeping our illusions. After Lydia is seduced by Wickham, Mr. Bennet acknowledges the truth to Elizabeth:

> "It has been my own doing, and I ought to feel it."
>
> "You must not be too severe upon yourself," replied Elizabeth.
>
> "You may well warn me against such an evil. Human nature is so prone to fall into it! No, Lizzy, let me for once feel how much I have been to blame. I am not afraid of being overpowered by the emotion. It will pass away soon enough."

Sure enough, Mr. Bennet does not change; he continues to make fun of his wife and younger daughters just as before.

People who think they have to be perfect to be loved tend to be harshly judgmental of themselves and others, and Elizabeth is no exception. She is easily prejudiced. On very little evidence she decides that Mr. Darcy is selfish and careless of the feelings of others and despises him for it. She rejects Mr. Collins's proposal because she thinks he is shallow and stupid, and she is shocked when her best friend Charlotte finds Mr. Collins acceptable and marries him. Charlotte tries to tell Elizabeth that her own expectations of marriage are far less exacting than Elizabeth's:

> I am not romantic, you know; I never was. I ask only a comfortable home—and considering Mr. Collins's character, connections, and situation in life, I am convinced that my chance of happiness with him is as fair as most people can boast on entering the marriage state.

Charlotte is pragmatic. And in fact, her marriage turns out reasonably well; Charlotte is every bit as happy married to Mr. Collins as she expected to be.

But Elizabeth can't imagine how anyone can settle for a less than perfect marriage. When her sister Jane defends Charlotte's actions and suggests that Charlotte may even see virtues in Mr. Collins, Elizabeth protests:

> To oblige you, I would try to believe almost anything, but no one else could be benefited by such a belief as this; for were I persuaded that Charlotte had any regard for him, I should only think worse of her understanding than I now do of her heart. My dear Jane, Mr. Collins is a conceited, pompous, narrow-minded, silly man; you know he is as well as I do; and you must feel, as well as I do, that the woman who marries him cannot have a proper way of thinking.

Elizabeth is not just blind to Mr. Collins's virtues; she is blind to how her best friend and her sister think. She dismisses their attempts to explain themselves to her in insulting terms: in one breath she accuses her beloved sister of hypocrisy and her dearest friend of poor judgment. It is easy to see her father's attitudes about the intelligence of most women reflected in this speech.

Margaret of *North and South* is another father's daughter. Although she loves her mother, she has learned from her father to treat her mother as someone to be protected, even kept ignorant at times for her own good. Margaret comes in time to treat her father the same way, keeping him ignorant as well of things she suspects will upset him. Like Elizabeth, she is quick to judge and decides that the Hales' new landlord, wealthy John Thornton, is "not quite a gentleman" and has only the qualities one would expect from a lower-class tradesman. Her attitude is obvious to Thornton, who tells his mother that "she treated me with a haughty civility which had a strong flavour of contempt in it."

Such women, while often respected and even admired by others, tend to feel lonely and isolated. Their judgmental attitudes prevent the free and open communication that is the hallmark of female friendship. They lack the feminine flair for emotional connection that most girls learn from their mothers, because their fathers have taught them to despise the gifts of the mother.

Therefore, girls who have been abused, abandoned, neglected, or simply not valued as female by fathers tend to have trouble not only in relationships but also in their ability to accomplish anything. A father who protects and guides his daughter correctly will help her find her own strengths. But, as with mothers, one rarely finds a father in women's narratives who is still alive and useful to his daughter. Perfect literary fathers, like perfect literary mothers, tend to die young.

CHAPTER 6

Other Relationships at Home

*I would rather walk with a friend in the dark, than alone
in the light.*

—Helen Keller

PARENTS MAY BE THE FIRST, but they are not necessarily
the most significant, relationships in the childhood life of the Aletis. Parents in such stories, as discussed in the prior chapter, are
usually either missing or do not provide adequate guidance. But
that does not mean the Aletis lacks role models.

Often, girls who lack ideal parents turn to other girls for guidance. These may be positive and supportive sisters or friends, or
they may take the form of the mean girl, a corrective model. Some
girls have "frenemies" who combine the characteristics of a friend
and a mean girl. The budding heroine may also have an adult
mentor who helps to make up for the lack of parental guidance.

The Sweet Sister-Friend

The Aletis usually has a female friend who provides comfort and
help. The role of such a friend has been surprisingly overlooked

by many literary analysts, even those who study women's lives
in general. Nor is this lack only found in literary studies. My
own research turned up more scholarly works on relationships
between female baboons and monkeys than on human female
friendships!

Janice Raymond offers a rare examination of women's friendships in *A Passion for Friends: Toward a Philosophy of Female
Affection*. In the introduction to her book, she argues that female
friendships in books are often invisible even to those looking for
them. Raymond believes that this is because society relies on
masculine ideas of friendship.[1] Just as masculine definitions of literary style have prevented people from appreciating how women
write, friendships between women in books go unnoticed.

Yet female friendship is a staple feature of women's novels.
Elizabeth and Jane in *Pride and Prejudice,* Elinor and Marianne
in *Sense and Sensibility,* and Celie and Nettie in *The Color Purple*
are examples of sisters who band together to deal with the vicis-
situdes of life. Margaret Hale is close to a female cousin when
she lives in the south of England and forms a strong friendship
in her new town with Betsy, a mill hand. Jane Eyre is befriended
at Lowood School by Helen Burns. Anna and Molly's friendship
lies at the heart of *The Golden Notebook,* as Nel and Sula's friendship does in Toni Morrison's *Sula*. We see Nancy Mitford's Linda
in *The Pursuit of Love* only through the eyes of her friend Fanny.
They are so close that after Linda dies in childbirth, Fanny adopts
Linda's bastard son.

Pratt theorizes that women form alliances in novels by authors
such as Austen, Brontë, and Eliot to "outwit their lords and masters."[2] She also suspects that some of these alliances may mean a
lesbian attachment. It is true that the servant Rachel helps Helen

of *The Tenant of Wildfell Hall* to escape her abusive husband, while Elizabeth colludes with her friend Charlotte in *Pride and Prejudice* to avoid the boring company of Mr. Collins. And there is no denying that a percentage of women in any era are lesbians or bisexual. But there are other reasons for female friendships besides shared oppression or sexual attraction. I think it more likely that these authors drew on their own relationships to their sisters (Anne and Charlotte Brontë with each other and Emily; Jane Austen with Cassandra; and George Eliot with Chrissey Evans) rather than repressed lesbian feelings when they depicted close female relationships.

One of the strengths of such close attachments, in fact, can be the *lack* of a sexual element. Like the parent-child relationship, it is both comforting and relaxing to be able to touch and hold another person with love and affection without the pressure to provide anything else. While sex can and ought to be imbued with love and affection, it is also about pleasing and being pleased and hence can be demanding. It is revealing how often movies and television shows make fun of women's desire to "cuddle" instead of having sex—to connect on another level instead of the purely physical, to have contact without an agenda.

Also, an asexual friendship allows for more "virgin time" in a girl's life. With a sister or a friend who is like a sister, girls may be free to be themselves in a way that may be impossible with anyone else. This is something the Aletis in particular needs, especially if she has been sexually violated.

There is another, more prosaic reason for the intense bond formed between sisters and friends in nineteenth-century novels. Well-born men and women of these authors' time lived almost entirely separate lives. Lucy Jago, who researched the lives of upper-class women during the early 1800s for a television "reality" show where people tried to live as if they were in that time, found that those women spent most of their time with each other. They interacted with men—even their husbands, who often slept in separate rooms or were gone for long periods of time—primarily at meals and social occasions.[3] It is no wonder that their closest relationships were with other women. Friends can be a safe outlet for people to complain about the trials and disappointments of their relationships—and provide comfort and support when relationships fail altogether. "Friendship is certainly the finest balm for the pangs of disappointed love," Jane Austen tells us in *Northanger Abbey*.

In a study of college women, Ana Martínez Aléman found that female friendships can help women develop their intellectual capacities and become better scholars.[4] Writer Vera Brittain reveled in the intellectual freedom of her women's college at Oxford. She fell in love with her first fiancé (who died a soldier in World War I) primarily because he loved such discussions as much as she did. But the person she turned to most often to talk over ideas was her good friend and sister author, Winifred Holtby. Brittain devotes the second volume of her autobiography, *Testament of Friendship*, to her relationship with Holtby. Jane Harrison, a nineteenth-century British classical scholar who attended and taught at one of the first colleges for women at Cambridge University, believed that "marriage, for a woman at least, hampers the two things that made life to me glorious—friendship and learning."[5] Harrison never married, became one of the leading figures in modern studies of Greek mythology, and had strong, life-long friendships with both women and men.

Mary Pipher relates a story about Caroline, a girl who seemed to have the deck stacked against her: an abusive father, a weak mother, a horrible school that had little to offer and where she was an outcast. But she made friends with another girl like her in high school. When the friend was invited to live with an aunt and uncle so she could attend a better school, she insisted that Caroline come with her. Both flourished with each other's support and looked forward to earning scholarships to college.[6]

Female friends can help a woman to know who she is instead of accepting others' ideas of who she ought to be. When a woman does not know how she fits in the world, she may find help by connecting with other women who are also trying to find their way. Talking with friends allows a woman to see herself in a new way, through the eyes of those who love her just as she is.

THE SPRING FLINGETTES

Since the late 1970s, I have been part of a circle of women friends. It began when we were poor students. Once a year, we would splurge on dinner at a nice restaurant and tickets to the ballet or the symphony.

As our fortunes improved over time, our Spring Fling grew to an annual getaway. Now we rent a vacation home in a beautiful place, usually on the water and with a hot tub, and leave the partners and spouses and kids at home. We talk, eat, take long walks, talk, eat, read, talk, and eat some more.

In the past thirty-odd years, we have stood by each other at weddings and divorces. We have celebrated the birth of children and mourned the loss of siblings and parents. We have encouraged each other to pursue higher education and careers. We have worked in each other's gardens and helped clean and remodel each other's homes.

The Spring Flingettes keep me grounded and sane. They have rescued me, listened to me, and, most importantly, laughed at me to let me know they love me warts and all. They are my family of choice, my true sisters, the home to which I can always return.

Friendship with someone who is of the same sex requires, to some extent, love of self. Like so much in women's lives, it is a spiral: women friends help each other to love themselves, and loving oneself allows one to find loving friends. Each reinforces the other. Like the bonds formed between people who have fought in war together, friendships formed as young women help such women to overcome negative messages about their self-worth and can endure for life.

From an archetypal viewpoint, friends and companions in stories often represent qualities that the hero or heroine needs but may not yet have developed internally. Sweet, pious Helen Burns teaches impulsive, rebellious Jane Eyre to be more patient and to trust in God. Elizabeth Bennet is given guidance in how to be more objective by her pragmatic friend, Charlotte Lucas, and how to be more trusting and accepting of others by her compassionate sister, Jane. While Elinor Dashwood does her best to curb her sister Marianne's excessive emotionality, Marianne encourages Elinor to be more open about her own feelings. It could be argued that each of the March women in *Little Women* represents qualities of a whole woman: Marmee is wisdom and motherliness, Meg stands for fecundity and flexibility, Jo embodies anger and independence, Amy provides beauty and creativity, Beth represents connection and compassion, and let us not leave out the fearsome power of Aunt March!

Sometimes the friend or sister represents the woman's own true self. In *The Color Purple*, Celie cannot save herself from her father's abuse and the life he has planned for her, but she manages to save her sister Nettie. This act gives her life meaning. Nettie's success as a teacher is Celie's greatest joy, and Nettie saves Celie's children in return. Thus friends and sisters can provide a safe anchorage for the Aletis during her journey.

The Mean Girl

While heroes have to fight powerful men or supernatural beings, other women are often the villains of women's stories. As a girl approaches womanhood, she is judged by other women on every aspect of her appearance and behavior. If she passes muster, she is accepted into the ranks; if not, she is as good as shunned. The ugly stepsisters of early tales turned into snobbish characters such as the Misses Branghton in *Evelina*, Caroline Bingley in *Pride and Prejudice*, and Blanche Ingram in *Jane Eyre*. In twentieth-century novels, they have further morphed into the mean girl who dominates social life in high school, such as Cordelia of Margaret Atwood's *Cat's Eye*. The mean girl's role is to punish the Aletis for not conforming to societal expectations. Her cruel remarks confirm the girl's sense of being an outsider or rebel.

The challenge offered by the mean girl is not one that can be resolved through physical strength (although some mean girls can be physically violent). Primarily, the mean girl threatens the young heroine's sense of self. Pipher argues that in our current culture, adolescent girls often face a terrible choice; they "can be true to themselves and risk abandonment by their peers, or they can reject their true selves and be socially acceptable."[7] It is the mark of the heroine that she stays true to herself, even if this trait invites attack from others.

Parents may be oblivious to a girl's uniqueness, but her peers—particularly other girls—notice any differences immediately.

And those girls often respond by trying to make the heroine fit in and stay invisible. A girl who is "different" triggers shadow fears of calling attention to oneself in a bad way and not being accepted. This threat must be controlled, and the mean girl is the chief enforcer of this effort.

The mean girl looks like the epitome of what the family and community wish a young woman to be. She is pretty, fashionable, and desirable to males—both because she is sexy and because she flatters their egos and does not challenge them. Although she seems to stand out, there is little to her personality. She is admired because she *looks* like the ideal of what is expected; she has power because agreeing with her and trying to look like her confers invisibility and therefore safety upon her followers. The mean girl perverts the feminine tendency to seek connection to others; she offers safety by inclusion to those who agree to fit in and obey the rules. But when the mean girl encounters a girl who is too different, she isolates and separates that girl, turning her into a social outcast.

Even girls who try to fit in but don't do it correctly may be attacked. Judy Blunt's initial attempts to use makeup gave her a clown face, a fact pointed out to her cruelly one day by two cheerleaders who talked about her loudly in her presence. Looking back, Blunt could see that "this first sharp lesson was a mercy, delivered . . . in the privacy of the girls' bathroom" instead of in public.[8] Blunt hid in the bathroom the rest of the day until she could go home and scrub the stuff off. From then on she managed to look and act enough like the other girls to avoid negative attention.

The Aletis usually defeats the mean girl in time by one of two methods. The first is to win the mean girl's support. If the heroine can connect in a heart-felt way to the mean girl, that girl may become a friend and ally. She may still act like a mean girl in public—she's not about to give up her power entirely—but in private she may become helpful. Fanny Thornton, although she never stops thinking that Margaret Hale is a snob, is touched by Margaret's attempt to protect John Thornton from an angry mob of strikers. She assumes that Margaret loves her brother. Although she does nothing to advance the match, her attitude toward Margaret softens, and, instead of her former sniping, she begins to make overtures of friendship. Cordelia, the ruling queen of the high school in the television show "Buffy the Vampire Slayer," becomes an ally to Buffy after Buffy saves her from an attacker. But she never loses her snide and condescending manner, especially when others are around.

The second method for defeating the mean girl is to make her look ridiculous. Elizabeth Bennet replies to Caroline Bingley's sneers in a calm, disinterested tone of voice instead of reacting as Caroline hopes. This refusal to engage drives Caroline to more and more outrageous attacks until Mr. Darcy himself rebukes and embarrasses her—an event that gives us another reason to consider Mr. Darcy worthy of Elizabeth: like her, he is not taken in by the mean girl and what she represents. Similarly, Jane Eyre ignores the jibes of the beautiful and supercilious Blanche Ingram, who is then humiliated by Mr. Rochester.

Sometimes the battle takes place entirely within a young woman's psyche. Rebecca of Daphne du Maurier's novel of that name is a mean girl whose power can be felt from beyond the grave. The new Mrs. de Winter, whose first name we never learn, is controlled by Rebecca's image as promoted by Mrs. Danvers, the housekeeper. Mrs. Danvers mentions Rebecca's beauty, social graces, and charisma at every opportunity in a way that comes across as a rebuke to the new, unsure wife. Eventually, the second Mrs. de Winter becomes convinced that her husband Maxim cannot possibly love her because she is so unlike Rebecca. She does not understand that he wants her precisely because she *is* different. In this case the victory over the mean girl happens when the heroine realizes that Rebecca was never the perfect wife; Maxim actually despised her—and that the true mean girl in the house is Mrs. Danvers. The new Mrs. de Winter now finds the courage to assert her authority over the housekeeper (who resorts to burning down the house when she realizes that she cannot destroy the marriage).

One of the problematic issues in feminism is a romantic belief in "sisterhood." This belief is challenged whenever women sabotage or behave unkindly to each other, but most feminists are at a loss as to how to explain such behavior. Recent books on the phenomenon of mean girls offer some answers, such as Rosalind Wiseman's *Queen Bees and Wannabes*. Mean girls and their followers, says Wiseman, are

> a platoon of soldiers who have banded together to negotiate the perils and insecurities of adolescence. There's a chain of command, and they operate as one in their interactions with the environment. Group cohesion is based on unquestioning loyalty to the leaders and an us-versus-them mentality.[9]

In other words, the mean girl is the collaborator within the oppressed group whose loyalties lie with the oppressors. She enforces the rules against her own gender.

Because connection to others is vital for girls, social ostracism can cripple the isolated girl's emotional development. Girls who have been victimized by mean girls may suffer from self-esteem problems for a long time. Years later, Wiseman says, she was still so intimidated by the memory of her school's mean girl that she bolted without thinking when she caught sight of that girl, now an adult, in a grocery store.[10] Anthropologist Margaret Mead, who was ostracized for being "different" at the first college she attended, says in her autobiography *Blackberry Winter* that such treatment can cause permanent damage to a girl's self-esteem.[11] But, she adds, the mean girls harm themselves even more. Female friendship helps women become strong individuals, and the mean girl is no one's friend. If same-sex friendship is based upon and reinforces one's ability to love oneself, the girl who hates other girls may be acting out her own lack of self-love by turning against those like her.

Sadly, many mean girls continue in the role as adults, trying to hang on to the power they had in high school, unable to understand how their former victims have managed to move on and create vibrant new lives. We also see these adult mean girls playing the enforcer for religious and political organizations. For instance, Phyllis Schlafly, the mouthpiece in the 1970s for those who opposed the Equal Rights Amendment, always looked perfectly dressed and very feminine—as part of the message that "women's libbers" were primarily unattractive women and therefore to be despised—while she fought to deny women equal rights with men. (Schlafly recently said that women prefer not to be paid as much as men for the same work, because they'd rather marry men who earn more than they do.[12]) Her modern-day counterparts include Ann Coulter, a political commentator who has stated that women are too stupid to think for themselves, so women who don't have husbands to advise them should be denied the right to vote—including herself, apparently, as she is not married[13]—and Michelle Bachmann, a Congresswoman who has gone on the record as saying that wives should be submissive to their husbands.[14]

The Frenemy

A "frenemy" is a friend who behaves at times like an enemy. Such girls can be sweet sister-friends in one situation but turn into mean girls in another. The heroine does not know when or if she can trust this friend. Although the term *frenemy* is of recent use, examples can be found in earlier novels. Cecelia of *Middlemarch* is one; she loves her sister and defends her to others; but she is not above being a bit brutal with the truth, as when she points out that Dorothea has misunderstood the attentions paid to her by Sir James:

> I thought it right to tell you, because you went on as you always do, never looking just where you are, and treading in the wrong place. You always see what nobody else sees; it is impossible to satisfy you; yet you never see what is quite plain. That's your way, Dodo.

Anna of *The Golden Notebook* realizes that her friend Molly, while usually supportive, is often critical of her:

> What Molly had said was pure spite. . . . Once I wouldn't have noticed: now every conversation, every encounter with a person seems like crossing a mined field; and why can't I accept that one's closest friends at moments stick a knife in, deep, between the ribs?

Another example is Cordelia in Atwood's *Cat's Eye*, a mean girl who poses as the main character Elaine's "best friend" while encouraging her other friends to tease her.

The frenemy loves to point out the contradictions in the heroine's character, as Celia does with Dorothea. This forces the heroine to look at her own behavior—a process that, while painful, can also be clarifying. Sometimes, the criticism of such a friend provokes the heroine into standing up for herself. The frenemy can also act as a sort of contrary muse. Both Anna and Elaine develop their creativity in response to the goading of the frenemy.

Mentors

Even though their parents or guardians and others around them may not understand or may even work actively to undermine them, girls who are destined to become heroines do find help along the path. Mentors serve as guides and protectors for a while. At Lowood, Miss Temple clears Jane Eyre of the charge of lying and educates her. Elizabeth Bennet can turn to her Aunt Gardiner for sage advice as needed, and her aunt is the first person to discern Mr. Darcy's real worth. Margaret Hale learns about the realities of millworkers' lives from her friend Betsy's father. Anne Elliot finds motherly counsel and friendship from Lady Russell. As a child, Ursula Le Guin's Tenar is taught most of what she needs to know by the patient priestess Thar and the kindly eunuch Manan.

Mentors can be either female or male. Beatrix Potter grew up surrounded by male mentors. Her father was an amateur artist and photographer who took her on photography expeditions and encouraged her "eye" for the natural world. His friend, the painter

Sir John Millais, encouraged Beatrix to draw and paint. Naturalist Charlie McIntosh guided her in the study of fungi and lichens. Her uncle Sir Henry Roscoe taught her how to conduct experiments with scientific rigor. When her experiments on the propagation of lichen contradicted the theories of some of the leading botanists in England, Sir Henry got her paper presented to the prestigious Linnean Society. Her paper was dismissed as the work of an uneducated amateur, but her theory was proven correct, and a hundred years later the Society issued a formal apology for how she was treated.

Mentors also help the heroine in another way. The heroine usually can disobey or dispute with her mentor without undue fear of punishment. Thus she can express herself freely and discover some of her own abilities and limitations. Adolescents need to rebel, for defining what they are *not*—rejecting those attitudes and values that don't fit them—is the first step to finding out who they *are*. For example, Beatrix Potter's art teacher insisted that Beatrix learn to use oil paints instead of her preferred water colors, which Beatrix chafed at, and which her biographer Linda Lear sees as a positive thing:

> Rebelling against Mrs. A.'s methods, Beatrix was challenged to move ahead in her own experiments with light and colour, and so develop her own style. Like many creative people, Beatrix made the most progress when she had something to push against.[15]

In *Persuasion*, it is only after disagreeing with her beloved Lady Russell over what qualities constitute a suitable husband that Anne Elliot gains the courage to stand up to her father, reject Mr. Elliot as a suitor, and do all a lady can do (and a little more) to assure Captain Wentworth that she would not reject a second proposal.

Dorothea of *Middlemarch* really wants a mentor, not a husband. Before she marries Mr. Casaubon, she sees him as "a man who could understand the higher inward life, and with whom there could be some spiritual communion; nay who could illuminate principle with the widest knowledge." She imagines her life with him as that of a student: "I should learn everything then." Unfortunately, as she soon finds out, Mr. Casaubon wants neither a wife nor a student, but unquestioning adoration from a live-in personal servant.

Menial Work

Being a servant to others is often expected of the Aletis. Toni Morrison's Sethe is a slave, and Alice Walker's Celie is treated as a drudge by her father and then her husband. Maya Angelou grew up helping her grandmother in her store. Judy Blunt and Jill Ker Conway were expected to work as farmhands whenever their fathers needed help and to help their mothers in the house at all other times. Ellen of *The Wide, Wide World* is likewise required by her aunt Fortune to spend all her time doing chores and is denied the education she longs for.

Even those born into the upper classes rarely escape drudgery. Jane Eyre's education is solely for the purpose of turning her into a teacher or governess to others. Such work was almost the only way a woman from the upper classes could earn a living, but it turned her into a pariah—too "good" to associate with the servants, but not good enough to join the family at the dinner table.

Anne Elliot is supported by her father, but she is expected to have no concerns of her own and to do whatever her sisters or father ask of her. For example, when her father and sister Elizabeth leave for Bath, Elizabeth hands Anne a long list of chores to be done before their house is ready for the new tenants. Having accomplished these chores, Anne is then sent to her sister Mary's house, where she becomes a *de facto* nursemaid to her nephews. When their father dies, the Dashwood girls have to take on most of the work formerly done by servants. Similarly, Vasilisa the Beautiful and Cinderella are put to work by their stepmothers as soon as the father is out of the picture.

Menial work humbles the heroine. But it also teaches her useful skills and patience, and toughens her up. Blunt observes:

> I am sometimes amazed at my own children, their outrage if they are required to do the dishes twice in one week, their tender self-absorption with minor bumps and bruises. . . . For a moment I want to tell this new generation about my little brother calmly spitting out a palm full of tooth chips and wading back in to grab the biggest calf in the branding pen. I want to tell them how tough I was, falling asleep at the table with hands too sore to hold a fork.[16]

Blunt chose not to raise her children as she had been raised, but her pride in her own toughness is obvious.

Thus, the Aletis undergoes many trials while still living at home. These trials help toughen her up. Their lessons will serve her well on her journey, for more arduous tasks lie ahead. First, she must encounter the trials of marriage.

IDYLL

Dorothea's Journey

DOROTHEA BROOKE, heroine of George Eliot's Middlemarch, is an orphan girl born into the landed gentry of England. She and her sister have been raised by a kind but easily distracted uncle and sent to school for "finishing." But Dorothea is not content to live out the typical life of a woman in her social sphere. She has no interest in fashion; instead, she longs to do some good in the world, to make a difference to those whose lives are not as easy as hers, and she suffers great guilt over how her path has always been smoothed for her.

When her attempts to help the local peasantry are balked by her uncle and the neighboring squire, Dorothea begins to seek a way to escape her present life. The opportunity comes in the person of the Reverend Casaubon, a learned gentleman twice Dorothea's age. Everyone else sees Casaubon as a pedantic, dried-up old stick, but Dorothea sees him as a wise teacher who could expand her horizons and help her understand life in a new way. She listens eagerly to Casaubon's platitudes and encourages him to talk. Flattered, the older man proposes and Dorothea accepts, much to the distress of her family and friends.

But the marriage is a failure. Casaubon turns out to be just what Dorothea's friends saw him to be. Moreover, he is threatened by Dorothea's innocent desire to be of help *in his work, for he secretly knows that he is a fraud and his great work, the "Key to All Mythologies," is hopelessly muddled and out of date. So he shuts Dorothea out and treats her coldly. The situation is exacerbated when Casaubon's young cousin Will Ladislaw visits; Will not only knows the truth about Casaubon's work but is attracted to Dorothea. Dorothea is oblivious, but Casaubon sees and is jealous, which makes him treat his wife with even more suspicion.*

After a crisis in which Casaubon tries to get Dorothea to promise to be guided by him in everything, even after his death, he suffers a heart attack and dies. Dorothea has a long struggle with her guilt, but eventually realizes that she must refuse Casaubon's last request and make her own decisions about how to live her life. She finds ways to help her community by working with a local physician who has innovative ideas about how to treat fever. Meanwhile, Will Ladislaw has been treading his own path from dilettante student to a responsible aspiring attorney. In time Will and Dorothea marry and move to London, where Will, with his wife's support, does good work.

CHAPTER 7

The Wrong Husband

I disapprove of matrimony as a matter of principle. . . .
Why should any independent, intelligent female choose to
subject herself to the whims and tyrannies of a husband?
—"Amelia Peabody" in Elizabeth Peters's
Crocodile on the Sandbank

THE WRONG HUSBAND shows up in many women's narratives. He may be a man whom the heroine marries in the hope that he will change her life for the better. She may think he is her knight in shining armor, her ticket to a more fulfilling life or true love. Or she may marry him because she has no other options or is pressured or forced to do so. Sometimes the wrong husband is just a man that she marries almost unconsciously, without getting to know him or giving much thought to what marriage will be like. Sometimes he is the man that others have picked for her.

THE KNIGHT IN SHINING ARMOR

The Knight in Shining Armor is a powerful archetypal image. He represents one face of the animus, which Jung describes as "all woman's ancestral experiences of man." In other words, he represents those so-called "masculine" traits that a woman does not consciously believe are hers to use.

The Knight in Shining Armor usually appears in stories—or daydreams—when a heroine is stuck or in danger. He comes charging in and rescues her. He has all the traits that are needed to get one moving or to stand up to a threat. What the heroine learns is that these traits are *within* her and, thus, always available to her.

In novels before the twentieth century, marriage to the *right* husband is usually the end of the story. Finally the heroine has found the right partner, a worthy man who loves her as she truly is and will "allow" her to be that person after they are married. But in twentieth-century novels by women, marriage rarely symbolizes the evolution of a young woman into a new, more powerful self and equal partner with a worthy man. Instead, marriage is more likely to be an *obstacle* the Aletis must get past. Some earlier novels—such as Eliot's *Middlemarch* and *Daniel Deronda* or Anne Brontë's *The Tenant of Wildfell Hall*—are ahead of their times in this regard. Widowhood or separation and divorce in these novels often become a rite of passage to a freer life.

Marrying a Fantasy

Marianne Dashwood of *Sense and Sensibility* is convinced that George Willoughby is her soul mate. They meet under romantic circumstances: Marianne falls and hurts her ankle, but before her younger sister Margaret can go for help, Willoughby appears out of nowhere, takes Marianne up in his arms, and carries her all the way back to the Dashwoods' cottage. She falls instantly in love. "I have not known him long indeed," she says to Elinor a few days later, "but I am much better acquainted with him than I am with any other creature in the world. . . . It is not time or opportunity that is to determine intimacy; it is disposition alone." Marianne is so sure of their being meant for each other that when she finds out that money means more to Willoughby than she does, she falls ill and nearly dies.

In *The Tenant of Wildfell Hall*, Helen marries for love despite being warned that her intended, whose name is Arthur, is a dissolute wastrel. Her fantasy is that their mutual love is so strong that she will be able to change him for the better:

> I think I might have influence sufficient to save him from some errors, and I should think my life well spent in the effort to preserve so noble a nature from destruction. He always listens attentively now, when I speak seriously to him . . . and sometimes he says that if he had me always by his side he should never do or say a wicked thing.

Today we might label Helen as having a "rescuer" mentality. She is not blind to her fiancé's faults. Even before they marry, she begins to realize that "his very heart, that I trusted so, is, I fear, less warm and generous than I thought." Still, she remains convinced that she can improve him, so she goes ahead with the wedding.

Her disillusionment is swift. Arthur begins to display his true self on their wedding night when he tells Helen about having sex with other women. Soon he has slipped back to drinking and carousing with his friends every night. But Helen is also trapped by her own pride. After fighting to marry Arthur in the teeth of her relatives' fears and warnings, she cannot bring herself to acknowledge that everyone else was right and she was wrong. Two months into her marriage, Helen admits to herself that her husband "is not what I thought him at first, and if I had known him in the beginning, as thoroughly as I do now, I probably never should have loved him." But rather than admit that publicly, she sticks it out for several more years while Arthur becomes worse and escalates into outright abuse. Like many abused women, Helen silently bears what he does to her. She is only driven to break free when he begins to harm their child.

In *Middlemarch,* Dorothea Brooke's fantasy is of a different kind. She marries Mr. Casaubon because she expects that he will open up a wider world for her, the world of intellect, and "deliver her from her girlish subjection to her own ignorance." She day-dreams about the wonderful life she will have once she is married to him:

> I should learn everything then. . . . There would be nothing trivial about our lives. Everyday-things with us would mean the greatest things. It would be like marrying Pascal. . . . And then I should know what to do, when I got older: I should see how it was possible to lead a grand life.

Like Helen, her disillusionment is swift and bitter. Within a few months it is clear to her that she has married not Pascal but an elderly, querulous, and suspicious man who has no intention of allowing her to pursue her dreams. In fact, he restricts her far more than the family she married him to escape ever did.

"Marry in haste, repent at leisure" goes the old saying. If Helen had not been so eager to marry Arthur and prove her relatives wrong, or if Dorothea had shared her ideas about marriage with Mr. Casaubon before the wedding, they both might have realized their mistakes in time. But they believe in the "happily-ever-after" of fairy-tale marriages in which the girl waits until she is found or saved or fought for by a prince among men and then enjoys per-fect harmony and love with that prince for the rest of her life. It never occurs to Dorothea, as it does not occur to Sleeping Beauty or Cinderella, to look carefully at her intended. Nor does it occur to Mr. Casaubon or the charming princes that their chosen ladies might have minds of their own.

Scarlett O'Hara of Margaret Mitchell's *Gone with the Wind* is another believer in the knight in shining armor. She clings to the illusion that Ashley Wilkes is her true love even after he marries another woman and tells Scarlett to her face that he is wrong for her. Linda Radlett in Nancy Mitford's *The Pursuit of Love* marries for love despite opposition from both her family and her new husband's parents. She falls into the same trap as Helen; her pride will not let her admit her mistake. "Linda's marriage was a failure almost from the beginning," says her friend Fanny, but like Helen, Linda puts up a good front for years.

Clarissa Pinkola Estés sees "Bluebeard" and similar fairy tales as warnings to girls about the dangers of marrying men they do not know.[1] But for some girls, making such a mistake is the only way to learn. Recognition that one has married the wrong husband, painful as it turns out to be, can help the Aletis grow up and overcome her immature belief that things are as they appear to be on the surface. Sadly, all too often a young woman has to be forced into consciousness. Once her illusions are stripped from her, the young wife learns to see things as they really are.

She also has to swallow her pride and learn humility: necessary steps for surviving on her own. But some girls refuse to learn this lesson. Linda Radlett never grows up; instead, she finds "true love" again and again—and loses it every time. She ignores the example of Fanny's mother, who is nicknamed "the Bolter" for her lifelong habit of jumping from one failed relationship to another. When Fanny says to the Bolter that the man Linda was in love with when she died bearing his child was "the great love of her life," her mother replies, in a sad voice, "One always thinks that. Every, every time."

Estés likens this refusal to learn from experience to that of an addict who keeps taking more and more of a drug in a vain attempt to recapture the high it initially provided. Unless the woman can let go of this illusion, she is doomed.[2] Linda Leonard calls the woman who hangs on to the illusion an "eternal girl."[3] The eternal girl, no matter how old she is, refuses to take on adult traits such as responsibility. The result is a woman who is terrified of attempting anything new or living on her own. Such a woman is also unable to work out problems with her partner. The eternal girl believes in true love and perfect soul mates. The only responsibility she thinks she has is to pick the right person (or be chosen by that person) to marry. If she is not happy, it must be because she is with the wrong person. But because she is afraid to be on her own, she only leaves the bad marriage after she finds someone else upon whom to pin her picture of the ideal partner. Some, like Linda Radlett, manage to hold on to the illusion of a soul mate or true love for years, despite repeated experiences to the contrary.

Novels by women in the twentieth century may be more likely to contain eternal girls because "serial monogamy" became possible for women during that century. When one knows one can always leave a marriage or stop living with someone, one may be less cautious about entering into the relationship in the first place. In the nineteenth century and earlier, women novelists often warned their readers to be more careful and thoughtful about their choices, as the consequences were likely to be lifelong. But eternal girls existed then as well; Emma Bovary of

THE ETERNAL BOY

Men can also buy into the illusion of the perfect partner and the perfect marriage. Like the eternal girl, the eternal boy assumes that all he has to do is find the right woman and everything will be perfect from then on. When trouble arises in the marriage, he dances away and finds a different woman—and is surprised when the same problems occur with her.

Gustave Flaubert's *Madame Bovary* is one example, forever seeking to fulfill her fantasies until they all shatter. Because she lacks the inner resources to deal with reality, her only recourse is to commit suicide.

Marrying Unconsciously

Despite the freedom to leave a marriage, the process of disillusionment seems to take longer in women's novels of the later twentieth century. This may be because the husbands aren't really the problem. These wives seem to have good lives: nice houses, enough money, and healthy children. But over time they come to realize that something essential is missing, although it usually takes them a while to put their finger on what that something is. For example, Beth in Marge Piercy's *Small Changes* marries her high-school sweetheart, Jim. Several years later, she realizes that she spends much of her time daydreaming. When she stops fantasizing, she becomes conscious of what her life is really like and how tired she is of all of it, including her husband. Fantasy has kept her from seeing the painful truth until it becomes too painful to bear. Once Beth realizes the depth of her discontent, she also realizes that unconsciously she has been thinking about leaving Jim for some time. Only later does she recognize that she is attracted to women, not men.

Beth's marriage is an example of what Annis Pratt calls the "complicity" theme often used by American women novelists of the middle 1900s. In such novels, she says, female protagonists "will-lessly" accept what they don't really want because they can't see any alternative.[4] For example, Helen in Joyce Carol Oates's *Wonderland* gets married because society expects her to, despite the fact that she hates the very idea of having sex with a man. Estés sees the same theme in folk tales where the bride falls for promises that she would know were false if she were properly cautious.

This complicity is not conscious. Too many girls are taught from an early age to ignore their own intuition and believe the fantasy of the happily-ever-after story. But something pushes certain girls (Estés calls them the "feisty" ones)[5] to face up to reality, to encounter the dark fullness of life. On some level, such a girl knows that she needs her eyes to be opened and so arranges for something to shock her awake. In fairy tales, the shock can be quite graphic, as when Bluebeard's naïve wife unlocks the door into a room full of the bloody corpses of her predecessors. In real life, it often takes the form of violence against the wife or children, a shock that forces the wife to realize that she has sold herself for an illusion.

Author Judy Blunt married an older man at eighteen because she felt she had no choice. Despite her good grades and praise from her high school teachers, there was no family support for going to college. The only jobs in town were menial ones. "My options were as frightening as they were simple," she says in her autobiography about her upbringing in rural Montana. "I could marry, or I could leave."[6] But at that age she didn't have the resources to leave. She stood in the kitchen with her mother as the man she would marry asked her father's permission, panicking: "I wanted her to grab my cold hand and tell me how to run. . . . I wanted her to tell me what I could be." But her mother said nothing except, "He's a good man."[7]

Soon after her wedding, Blunt fell into a deep depression, sleeping up to sixteen hours a day. She eventually emerged from this stupor only to begin a long, futile struggle with her husband to get him to see her as an equal partner in the marriage. The final straw came when she asked for the right to sign checks:

> "Don't think you're going to run this ranch," he said, and for once the truth lay between us, flat and unmoving. In the stillness that followed, his expression never moved, and my gut twisted with the finality I read in those clean straight lines.[8]

This shocking moment of clarity about her marriage enabled her to leave shortly after "with three scared kids and some clothes piled in the back"[9] of her old car. She started college the next day and put her training as a ranch hand to use by becoming a construction worker to support herself and her children.

Nancy Miller observes in her book *The Heroine's Text* that while romantic fantasies are more common in novels by English and American women, French women tend to write stories in which women are disappointed by men and men by women.[10] The French accept with a shrug that men and women can and will irritate and frustrate each other, and that most romantic fantasies are not realistic. People do not fantasize about an experience that they can easily have; instead, they go do it. If they think the experience can never happen any other way, they resort to fantasy.

But it is one thing to fantasize about an impossible thing (for example, being able to fly like a bird) while being aware that it's just in fun, without any expectation that it could actually happen. The trap is when one starts to believe the fantasy, or can't get past wishing that it would come true. Women need to see their romantic fantasies as just that—fantasies that could never actually occur. If a woman clings to her dream and ignores reality, she sets herself up either to dream her life away or to be in for a bitter awakening. The Princesse de Clèves in the 1678 novel of that name (presumably written by Madame de Lafayette) is an example of the realistic French attitude. As Nancy Miller says, "She never dreams . . . for she knows that love as she imagines it is not realizable. What is realizable is a counterfeit she does not want."[11] Fantasies are a drug she refuses to numb herself with.

A woman who has believed in the romantic fantasy of happily-ever-after does not always grow up when she is disillusioned. She may, instead, think of herself as a victim and refuse to take responsibility for her own life, either by blaming others or by waiting passively for someone else to fix her problem. Lily Bart of Edith Wharton's *The House of Mirth*, for example, is undone by clinging to the illusion that she can find true love with a wealthy man. She evades the attentions of the man who loves her because he is not rich enough and instead trusts a wealthy, married man whose attentions bring her to social ruin.

Women who don't take responsibility for their own lives are often doomed to live out their lives as Ereshkigals, forever bemoaning their lot, forever stuck in a cave they could walk out of at any time. Recognizing one's own unconscious behavior, naiveté, and complicity is the key to finding one's power. Women might take a lesson from the French here and say, "Well, if I can't have what I want romantically, that's sad and makes me angry, but perhaps I should be thinking more about what else I want out of life that I *can* make happen." This is what the Aletis does. She does not remain passive; she does not whine; instead, she takes responsibility for herself and takes action. She leaves.

IDYLL

Inez Haynes Irwin's Journey

INEZ HAYNES, my great-aunt, was born in 1873, the daughter of Gideon Haynes, one-time actor and later a noted prison reformer, and his second wife. Inez was one of seventeen children. As she grew up, she observed the toll that running such a household took on her mother (who bore ten of those children). She resolved to have a different life. She attended Radcliffe College and became an ardent suffragist as well as an author. She later moved to Europe with her second husband, Henry Irwin, and worked as a war correspondent through World War I.

The Irwins returned to the United States after the war. Inez continued to be active in women's rights and served on the National Advisory Council of the National Women's Party. She wrote The Story of the Woman's Party *in 1921 and* Angels and Amazons: A Hundred Years of American Women *in 1933. She also wrote over thirty novels, including a fantasy novel,* Angel Island, *and the* Little Maida *series of children's books. She won an O. Henry Award for one of her short stories, "The Spring Flight." She never had children.*

I only met my great-aunt Inez once, shortly before her death in 1970. She was still sharp, a remarkable and inspiring woman.

CHAPTER 8

Leaving

To stay at home, I knew, would be my demise.

—Linda Schierse Leonard

SOONER OR LATER, the Aletis realizes that she has to leave her home. This difficult act may involve departure from the childhood home or the home a young woman goes to when she first marries. In these places she has lived by the rules laid down by others. She leaves when she can no longer comply with those rules.

The hero, according to Joseph Campbell, receives the call to depart when a character who represents "the opening of a destiny . . . appears suddenly as a guide, marking a new period, a new stage."[1] This herald must be followed, as Arthur follows the white hart into the beginning of the quest for the Holy Grail. But this herald character rarely appears in heroine stories. Instead of being called out of the home by someone or something from outside, the Aletis is pushed out by forces *within* the home.

She doesn't leave, however, until she has been forced to question the values she was raised with, the messages she receives from society, and even the love offered to her by others. She has to reach the point where she admits that the people around her are not going to let her be a unique individual. Rather, they will do all they can to force her to conform to society's or their own ideas about her role in the family—as they always have done. Once she sees this clearly, she realizes that there is no home for her where she is.

A girl will often passively accept repression for years without question. But once she becomes aware of a dissenting inner voice, the girl begins to wake up and dream of getting free. Although it may have taken her years to get to this point, once the Aletis reaches it, she leaves as soon as possible to seek a future life where she can be true to herself.

At this point the girl has become aware that she is *other*, different, a misfit. This new awareness is painful, but it also triggers questions. If she is not what others want her to be, then who or what *is* she? What is her purpose in life? What does she *want* from life? Thus the Aletis doesn't just travel away physically; she also travels within her psyche to a new place of self-understanding.

THE EGO AND CHANGE

The heroine must also overcome her internal resistance to change. Many people think of "ego" as pride or arrogance. But I believe that the real purpose of the ego is to protect the emotional self and the physical body. The ego functions like an over-protective mother, always on the watch for danger.

This is can be a good thing; the ego keeps us from doing things like jumping off the roof to see if we can fly. But the ego is very suspicious of anything new or different. Even if life is bad, it warns us that change could be worse.

Yet if we are ever to accomplish anything, we have to override this voice by an act of will; we have to say, "*I am* going to do this, even if it scares me."

Some heroines manage to separate themselves from their former lives and see everything differently without actually moving away from home. Virginia Woolf was fond of writing about this style of leaving: both Mrs. Ramsay of *To the Lighthouse* and the title character of *Mrs. Dalloway* go through a mental shift in the course of one day that alters everything for them. They remain at home, but the reader understands that their lives will never be the same.

Joan Gould took as her inspiration the example of the poet Emily Dickinson, who learned how to find and express her creative voice without leaving home. Gould never left her home or marriage, either. Instead, she found a place within herself where she could, as she said, "discover my Self . . . find my true potential in all its masculine and feminine strengths, and . . . make peace with all that I truly was, whether it was valued by the world nor not."[2]

All heroic journeys happen internally as well as outwardly, but heroines seem to be more aware from the beginning that the real battle is inside. The Aletis seeks not only to know herself but also to reclaim those parts of herself devalued by society. Rejecting internalized negative cultural ideas about women is the first barrier she must overcome before she can go on. It is sometimes a long process to discover in just how many ways such ideas hold power over us, even after we are sure that we've rejected them.

For many women, these negative ideas are also given voice by the people around them, and so the only way to overcome them is to leave them behind. In *Women Who Run with the Wolves*, Clarissa Pinkola Estés talks at length about the motif of escape in folk tales and adds, "In outer reality we find women planning their escapes, too, whether from an old destructive mode, a lover, or a job."[3] Yet Doris Lessing points out that "we give little attention to the people who leave."[4] It is difficult to understand how anyone can study women's narratives and fail to see how many heroines are, in fact, people who leave.

Leaving is hard, especially when a woman cannot see any other possible paths open to her. Often, the first thing the Aletis tries, instead of leaving, is to refuse to comply with others' plans for her. But at certain point, the heroine has to say "no." This word will not be heard or believed—or allowed—at first, so she must keep saying it. If it works, if others will honor her refusal, then she may be able to stay. If it does not work, she must follow up her refusal with action.

Refusing the Wrong Husband

In many women's novels, the heroine confounds the expectations of her family or community by refusing to marry a particular man (or to marry at all). Like the Princess of Cleves, she refuses to settle for a "counterfeit" marriage. Another early example occurs in the 1788 novel *Emmeline,* where Charlotte Smith has her title character declaim, "Tell him therefore, sir [that she] disclaims the mercenary views of becoming, from pecuniary motives, the wife of a man she can neither love nor esteem." Such a refusal was a radical act in times when women had almost no means of supporting themselves other than inheriting or marrying money. It was also radical because unmarried women were usually pitied or despised by most of the people around them.

Jane Austen herself refused at least one proposal, and she likes to have her heroines do the same. Elizabeth turns down Mr.

Collins's proposal with the words, "You could not make *me* happy, and I am convinced that I am the last woman in the world who could make you so." Mr. Collins doesn't believe her, and it takes some time for Elizabeth to convince him that she truly does not want to marry him. "It is always incomprehensible to a man that a woman should ever refuse an offer of marriage," snorts Emma Woodhouse of *Emma*; "a man always imagines a woman to be ready for anybody who asks her." Emma follows up this statement by rejecting the suit of Mr. Elton. Fanny Price of *Mansfield Park* refuses Henry Crawford, while Catherine Morland of *Northanger Abbey* is baffled by John Thorpe's attempts to propose after she thinks she's made it clear that she doesn't like him.

When she refuses to marry Mr. Collins, Elizabeth shocks the people around her. They cannot understand how she can turn down marriage to man who can support her and is of her own social class. Also, they cannot believe that she is willing to risk not just her own future but that of her mother and sisters (if Mr. Bennet dies, Mr. Collins will inherit their home and might turn them all out). When Elizabeth finally does say yes to marriage, she challenges the social hierarchy again by marrying above her station. This idea is hardly limited to Austen; many fictional heroines refuse to go along with society's ideas and marry either "up" or "down" to please themselves.

Refusing the wrong husband was a popular idea in nineteenth-century America as well. For example, in Caroline Lee Hentz's 1850 book, *Linda*, which was very popular at the time, Linda finds herself hounded by her stepmother and stepbrother to marry a man she does not love and cannot respect. Her father has recently died and cannot protect her, so she runs away, has many adventures, and nearly dies of fever before gaining permission to marry the man she has loved all along. In Hentz's *Eoline*, published two years later, the heroine also runs away from the marriage her father wants to force her into and becomes a music teacher instead.

To provide contrast to the heroine's refusal to settle for anything but love, Austen also likes to write secondary characters who marry for the wrong reasons. Charlotte Lucas in *Pride and Prejudice* marries the boring Mr. Collins to have a house and future security, while Lydia Bennet runs away with Wickham primarily to score one over her older, unmarried sisters. Mr. Elton, after failing to win Emma's hand in *Emma*, marries a woman he hardly knows—and who turns out to be a garrulous, small-minded snob—because she has money. Both Maria Bertram in *Mansfield Park* and Lucy Steele in *Sense and Sensibility* marry men they do not love for money and to increase their standing in society. Charlotte arranges her married life so as to avoid her husband as much as possible, and Austen tells us that the affection between Lydia and Wickham is short-lived, while Maria eventually flees her unhappy marriage, losing her reputation in the process. (We are left to make our own assumptions about the future happiness of the Eltons or Lucy and Robert Ferrars.)

Refusing the House

Sometimes the refusal is not of a particular man, but of a situation. George Eliot's Dorothea refuses to comply with her dead husband's will and gives up the house and income he left her to marry Will Ladislaw. Like Elizabeth Bennet, Anne Elliot of *Persuasion* refuses to marry the man who is to inherit her father's estate and loses her chance to be mistress of the family home, despite the advice and pleas of her friend Lady Russell, who wants to see Anne take her mother's place.

Austen also creates male characters who refuse the house. In *Sense and Sensibility*, Edward Ferrars refuses to obey his mother's command to jilt Lucy Steele and so loses his inheritance; ironically, Lucy then breaks their engagement, which frees him to marry Elinor. Mr. Knightley in *Emma* realizes that the only way he can marry Emma is to agree to move into her home instead of bringing her to his own, much larger estate. In each case, society is horrified.

Refusing on Principle

Jane Eyre's refusal is one of principle. Although she loves Rochester and is convinced he loves her, she is aware that he unconsciously despises his former mistresses. She fears that "if I were so far to forget myself... to become the successor of these poor girls, he would one day regard me with the same feeling." All Rochester's pleading is to no avail: "One drear word comprised my intolerable duty—'Depart!' " She chooses to leave because "*I* care for myself. The more solitary, the more friendless, the more unsustained I am, the more I will respect myself... I will hold to [my] principles.... If at my individual convenience I might break them, what would be their worth?" Jane values self-respect over love.

Similarly, Anna in *The Golden Notebook* will not have an affair with Richard, Molly's ex-husband. When Richard criticizes Anna for this, she tells him, "Perhaps what it is you don't like is that I do know what I want. . . . [I] never pretend to myself the second rate is more than it is, and know when to refuse." Anna, like the Princess of Cleves, will not settle for second best.

Doris Lessing is speaking through her character here. When Lessing was a girl, she was extremely resistant to the prospect of marrying, having children, and living the life she saw her mother living. As a young woman, though, Lessing lost her will to refuse. She married and had children, but eventually she abandoned them. Joan Gould, writing about Lessing in *Spinning Straw into Gold*, says Lessing believed "that if she had not walked out she would have had a nervous breakdown; she would have become an alcoholic and in time a bitter, dried-up woman."[5] Lessing saw the danger and refused to take the path to Ereshkigal's cave. She did marry again later and had another child, but by then her career as an author had begun, and a husband and child no longer represented obstacles to the life she longed for.

In another real-life example, Mary Ann Evans refused to comply with society's expectations of women in almost every way she could. Not only did she work for her living, she wrote books that were a far cry from the romances expected of women writers of the time, using the pseudonym "George Eliot" so that readers and reviewers would not judge her work by her gender. She lived out of wedlock with a man for many years in a society that condemned and shunned women for such behavior.

Evans's refusals began when she became a religious dissenter and rejected the teachings of the Church of England. After a period of intense piety in her teens, she read some historical accounts of the Bible that convinced her that the scriptures contained as much fiction as truth. One day she refused to accompany her father to church. Her father stopped speaking to her; when that had no effect, he threatened to throw her out of the family home. Eventually they reached a compromise: Mary Anne agreed to keep going to church while reserving the right to her own opinions, and her father let her stay—a rather self-serving favor as she kept house for him.[6] But it was a significant victory for a young woman dependent upon her father, and it may have sowed the first seeds of her later rebellions against society's strictures on the behavior of unmarried women.

Dinah Morris of Eliot's *Adam Bede* insists on her right to preach her Dissenter faith publicly, despite public suspicion of women preachers. Religious refusal also lies at the heart of the novel *Juliette*, published in 1869 by American author Harriette Newell Baker. Juliette is forbidden by her father to profess her faith, but, instead of agreeing, she runs away and makes a new life for herself where she can express what she thinks. Emily Dickinson wrote about her refusal to comply with the religious norms of her community in poem 236: "Some keep the Sabbath going to Church—I keep it, staying at Home."

Such refusal is never easy. Great courage is required of any woman who refuses to bow to the authority of a husband, a priest, or any other representative of patriarchal society. Speaking up, as Mary Ann Evans did, can lead to shunning or isolation—or worse, attack. In *Middlemarch*, Dorothea accepts that once she marries Will Ladislaw she will be cut off not just from her first husband's money but also from her friends and family. (She does not foresee that after a couple of years, her sister will refuse to comply any longer with this embargo.) Dickinson reported in her letters that certain friends never stopped hounding her to behave in accordance with their ideas of a good Christian. The only safety lies in being silent. But if one is silent too long, one may choke to death on all those unsaid words.

Refusing Obligations

Perhaps the most difficult refusal for a woman is to refuse familial and societal obligations that require her to sacrifice herself to the needs of others. A woman in search of her authenticity almost inevitably will be called "selfish" by others. For example, in Miles Franklin's semi-autobiographical novel *My Brilliant Career,* the heroine Sybylla's desire to pursue a writing career leads her mother to describe her as "an abominably selfish creature, who would not consider her little brothers and sisters. I would never be any good, as all I thought of was idleness and ease." When a girl's real "job," according to others, is to take care of others, anything she chooses to do instead—no matter how difficult—will be seen as not just selfish but lazy. Sybylla also drew censure for refusing to marry (Franklin herself never did). She knew that marriage would bring a new set of obligations: to her husband, to her eventual children, and in terms of all the duties expected of a wife.

In Kate Chopin's 1899 novel, *The Awakening,* Edna Pontellier marries unconsciously. But she eventually rebels and moves into her own house, abandoning her husband and children, because "every step which she took toward relieving herself from obligations added to her strength and expansion as an individual." Only then could she begin to explore her own creativity.

In *Persuasion,* Anne Elliot's father tries to shame her into going

with him to curry favor with a distant cousin who is a viscountess
instead of visiting an impoverished friend:

> Upon my word, Miss Anne Elliot, you have the most extraordi-
> nary taste! Everything that revolts other people, low company,
> paltry rooms, foul air, disgusting associations are inviting to
> you. . . . A mere Mrs. Smith, an every day Mrs. Smith, of all
> people and all names in the world, to be the chosen friend of
> Miss Anne Elliot, and to be preferred by her, to her own family
> connections among the nobility.

But Anne is resolute, for she enjoys conversations with her friend
and despises the stupid and uninteresting Lady Dalrymple, who
has nothing to recommend her apart from her rank.

When Jill Ker Conway made up her mind to leave Australia
and pursue higher education in the United States, her hardest battle was with her guilt over leaving her widowed mother. "I was
haunted by my knowledge of the silence that would enfold the
house when I left. I could see my mother, already aged beyond
her years, becoming more stooped and skeletal as she forgot to
eat and lapsed into greater eccentricity," she writes in *The Road to
Coorain*.[7] Conway chose to bear this guilt as the price of having
her own life.

Stealing Away

In the folk tale "The Seal Wife," a man traps a seal-woman on land
by hiding her sealskin so that she cannot swim away and forces
her to become his "wife." But after many years, she finds the sealskin and returns to the sea without a backward glance, even for

her child. Like the Seal Wife, says Gould, the woman who has had enough of unwanted responsibility "slips into her original skin and makes a break for freedom . . . as if a woman is a person who has a right to disappear into the distance alone."[8] So Jane Eyre runs from Thornfield Hall the morning after her disastrous near-marriage, with very little more than the clothes on her back. Helen Huntingdon lays careful plans for her own escape in *The Tenant of Wildfell Hall*, but she must wait for the right moment and, when it comes, act quickly and go in secret. None of them know what really lies ahead. They only know that they must get free, as soon as possible.

IDYLL

Allerleirauh's Journey

ALLERLEIRAUH RUNS AWAY *into the forest after her widowed father tries to rape her. She disguises herself by covering her face and hands with soot and wearing a mantle made from all kinds of fur. She also takes with her three beautiful dresses so fine that they can be packed into a nutshell.*

The king of the neighboring land goes out hunting one day. He finds Allerleirauh in the forest. In her disguise, she appears to him as an exotic beast. Finding that she can speak, he does not kill her but instead has her taken back to his castle and put to work in the kitchens.

Allerleirauh quickly proves to be a better cook than the royal cook. The cook takes the credit, but, in trade, allows Allerleirauh to go watch when there is a ball. The next time one of these events occurs, she takes off her furs, washes herself, puts on one of her fine dresses, and goes to the ball. Her beauty catches the eye of the king, who dances with her. But at the end of the ball she eludes him, runs back to the kitchen, and disguises herself again.

The second ball is just like the first. Allerleirauh takes off her furs, washes herself, dresses in another of her fine garments, goes to the ball, and dances with the king. Again, she escapes back to the kitchen without anyone seeing and puts on her fur disguise.

The third time, the king manages to slip a ring on to her finger as they dance. He already suspects that it is she who cooks so well, so he goes to the kitchen after she disappears. He sees the ring on the finger of the "beast" and tears off the fur mantle to reveal the woman. She becomes his queen.

CHAPTER 9

Into the Wild

I wish I were out of doors! I wish I were a girl again, half savage and hardy, and free. . . . I'm sure I should be myself were I once among the heather on those hills.

—"Cathy" in *Wuthering Heights*, by Emily Brontë

EVERY CHANGE IN OUR LIVES requires us to spend some time in liminal space, the space *between* the old life and the new, the person we were and the person we are going to become. It is not enough to leave the known place; we must also leave behind the trappings of the old life. Initiates into a new life or new career often go through a process of divestiture where they strip off their old clothing and put on plain garments that express their status as people in between one life and the next, like prospective soldiers who must take off their "civvies" and walk naked through testing stations before being given the uniforms that mark them as trainee warriors.

The liminal space is a time out, a time away, a time when nothing is certain. The past is irrelevant here. Life is a blank slate; anything can happen. The initiate must open both mind and heart to new ideas, new experiences—to the possibility of an entirely new and different future. If the Aletis can open herself in this way, she will learn and be forever changed.

Fairy tales frequently have a heroine who goes into the forest all alone—Vasilisa, the Handless Maiden, Rapunzel, Snow White, and Beauty, to name just a few. This motif is also common in narratives by women. Cathy of Emily Brontë's *Wuthering Heights* constantly runs away from home to be out on the moors. Hetty Sorrel in George Eliot's *Adam Bede* runs away from her village when she discovers she is pregnant and later abandons her baby in the wilderness. Jane Eyre runs away from Thornfield and becomes lost on a moor, where she sleeps under bushes and nearly starves to death. Harriet Beecher Stowe's Eliza of *Uncle Tom's Cabin* and Sethe of Toni Morrison's *Beloved* run away from slavery with their children and survive in the wild for months.

Elizabeth Bennet's wilderness journey is on a smaller scale: she tramps three miles across country from her parents' home to the Bingley estate at Netherfield to take care of her sick sister. Trivial as this act seems, Mr. Bingley's sisters, the judgmental voices of society, are horrified:

> "I shall never forget her appearance this morning. She really looked almost wild."
>
> "She did, indeed, Louisa. I could hardly keep my countenance. Very nonsensical to come at all! Why must *she* be scampering about the country, because her sister had a cold? Her hair, so untidy, so blowsy!"
>
> "Yes, and her petticoat; I hope you saw her petticoat, six inches deep in mud, I am absolutely certain."

A woman who cares about society's opinion would never behave as Elizabeth does. When she sets out from home for Netherfield, she is refusing to go along with the idea that a woman should stay at home and make herself look perfect to attract a husband. This refusal is precisely what piques the interest of Mr. Darcy.

The woman who goes into the wilderness is unprotected. For one thing, she is no longer under the aegis of society's approval. She is also vulnerable physically—to the weather and to attack. To claim a new life for oneself is to take a huge risk both physically and psychologically. As I discuss in chapter 4, many women are unwilling or afraid to take that risk and will only go into the wilderness if they are abducted or forced into it. But the Aletis seeks it out consciously.

"Leaving" as a literary device involves loss, but it opens up the future for the protagonist. Not only does it provide new opportunities for her, it also allows her to redefine herself. In a new situation and with new people around who do not judge us by our past, as Eliot says in *Middlemarch*, "one can begin so many things"—even become a different person.

Disguise

The girl who leaves runs many risks. The wilderness is dangerous. But the heroine is conscious of what she is doing, and she is aware of the danger. Many heroines of fairy tales who venture into the forest disguise themselves to avoid rape and other violence. Often they dress in rags or the skins of animals. Their beautiful hair is hidden away under a cap or hood.

Heroes sometimes put on disguises, but usually so that they can spy on others or get into a guarded place. They do not fear violence as women must; indeed, they often welcome a challenge to prove their heroism. They may even puff themselves up as being more than they really are, like the valiant tailor who kills seven

at one stroke and brags about it—omitting the salient fact that it
was only flies he slew—so that all around him become convinced
he is a fearsome warrior. His bravado carries him through many
trials until at last he wins the hand of the princess. But the heroine
cannot resort to such tactics. Nor does she wish to; she is not out
to claim power over others.

Disguise can also be a form of refusal. In nineteenth-century
novels, heroines sometimes insist on dressing plainly to avoid
unwanted attention or to establish their rejection of what others
expect of them. Jane Eyre, Dorothea Brooke, and Dinah Morris
all choose "Quakerish" plain dress to indicate that they are seri-
ous-minded individuals uninterested in fripperies and baubles.
Being plain or disguised may be a device the heroine uses to make
her life on her own terms. We all tend to judge people by how
they dress. The heroine uses this fact to her advantage: dressing
unremarkably allows her to pass unremarked.

Dressing and behaving like a man does not just offer safety
from attack; for women before the twentieth century, it was a way
to expand one's options. If a woman wants adventure, she must
dress the part. Silvia, the heroine of Aphra Behn's epistolary seventeenth-century novel, *Love-Letters between a Nobleman and His
Sister*, puts on men's clothing so that she can travel freely across
Europe without a female chaperone. Behn herself worked as a spy
for England and may have done the same. In the nineteenth century, Frenchwoman Aurore Dudevant, who wrote under the pen
name of George Sand, was infamous for dressing like a man and
frequenting male-only establishments. Estimates of how many
women dressed as men to serve in the American Civil War go
as high as four hundred. They did not just dress as soldiers, they

became soldiers in fact. (Many of these women were publicly celebrated on their return home to their communities, yet the military firmly denied that any women had fought in the war.)[1]

In the twentieth century, dressing unattractively, refusing to
hide the signs of aging, cutting hair in a masculine style, or gaining or losing weight often served as protective coloring or sig-
naled a woman's rejection of society's rules. In Doris Lessing's *The
Summer before the Dark*, the protagonist, Kate, realizes that her
real self is invisible to others, including her family. All her family sees are the things she provides for them; all others see is her
outward appearance that she has labored to keep attractive. Defi-
antly, she stops coloring her grey hair and deliberately becomes
old and thus invisible to the gaze of men. She tests this idea out by
changing her appearance and walking repeatedly past a group of
construction workers: when she dresses "attractively," they whis-
tle and hoot; when she dresses unattractively, they do not even
see her. And for the first time in her life, she feels free.

Reclaiming "Virgin Time"

The Aletis's decision to run away into the wilderness has another
dimension. As well as running away from the life she does not
want to seek an unknown but potentially preferable alternative,
the Aletis also goes into the woods in search of the "virgin time"
she may have been denied in her prior life.

Wilderness is often equated with virginity. We speak of a
virgin forest, for instance, to mean a forest that has not yet been
touched by the hand of man. It is the place of Artemis, the virgin goddess who not only hides from men but punishes any man

BREATHING SPACE

Toward the end of my marriage, I began suffering from attacks in which I could not breathe. A specialist diagnosed me with asthma and put me on medication. Soon after, I moved to a high valley on the east slope of the Cascade Mountains and lived there with my dog for a year. I had no job and no obligations; the pass between my past life and me was a mile high and blocked by snow all winter; my time was entirely my own.

The hours I spent hiking or horse riding or skiing through the forests of aspen and ponderosa pines were healing in a way entirely unlike the healing I had received through counseling and the support of my friends. I instinctively knew that I needed something more, a real "time out"—not just time away from all demands others might place on me, but time *out* in a literal sense, out in the wilderness where my soul could breathe.

After three months of breathing the mountain air, I threw the medicines away.

who presumes to look upon her. But virginity concerns more than remaining unmolested. It also connotes self-containment, a period during which a girl can focus on her own thoughts and needs without having to answer to others. In an essay on the Sleeping Beauty fairy tale, Ursula Le Guin writes of the dreaming castle hidden away in the forest of thorns and the girl asleep within it:

> It is the secret garden; it is Eden; it is the dream of utter, sunlit safety; it is the changeless kingdom.
>
> Childhood, yes. Celibacy, virginity, yes. A glimpse of adolescence: a place hidden in the heart and mind of a girl of twelve or fifteen. There she is alone, all by herself, content, and nobody knows her. She is thinking: *Don't wake me. Don't know me. Let me be. . . .*[2]

Eventually, the prince slashes his way through the thorny wall and claims the princess, but, as Le Guin says, "at least she had a little while by herself, in the house that was hers."[3] The Aletis runs away to the wilderness in search of that house, that place that is hers alone and where no one else can intrude.

The Forest

Many see the forest or wilderness as representing woman's untamed feminine nature. The forest, says Marie Louise von Franz, is "the place of unconventional inner life, in the deepest sense of the word. Living in the forest would mean sinking into one's innermost nature and finding out what it feels like."[4] Simone De Beauvoir observes that "it is when she speaks of moors and gardens that the woman novelist will reveal her experience and her dreams to us more intimately," for she is writing about her deepest self.[5]

The wilderness is often where a woman first and most vividly experiences her true self, and its allure never ceases. For the Aletis, the flight to the forest can be a spiraling back to an earlier stage of life, just as someone who has gotten lost will backtrack until they know where they are and then try again. She goes to where she was free and starts anew.

Joan Gould relates the real-life example of Eleanor Roosevelt, the plain girl who adored her handsome husband until she found out he was unfaithful. In her shock and anguish, Eleanor became anorexic. For months she sat for hours each day in Rock Creek Park. After this time out, Eleanor transformed herself into a teacher and celebrated social activist. She founded a school where she also taught, built herself a separate home on the Roosevelt estate, and created a new family of friends who shared her ideas and outlook on life—including journalist Lorena Hickok, with whom she had a thirty-year relationship.[6]

The wilderness also represents the terra incognita *between* paths. Even the most difficult path is a path made by others first. Changing paths requires leaving the one you are already on and crossing uncharted territory that is full of obstructions and dangers, without any guarantee that you will strike another clear path. In a word, one is lost. We see this in the myth of Psyche and Cupid. After the shock of finding out that her husband is a god and then losing him, Psyche wanders by herself in the wilderness, not knowing where to go but unwilling to stay where she was or return to her childhood home.

When one is lost in the wilderness, one is not going anywhere; one is simply *there*. Cheryl Strayed, who walked the Pacific Crest Trail from Mexico to Oregon, wrote in her book *Wild* that her journey was not about getting to the end; rather, she went for the express purpose of experiencing the wilderness on its own terms. "It had only to do with how it felt to be in the wild," she says.[7] This is in stark contrast to the hero, who, Campbell tells us, is always on his destined path even while he wanders in the wilderness for a while. The hero is goal-oriented. But for the Aletis, it is the process, the experience of being alone in wilderness, that matters.

If the girl goes into the wilderness unconsciously, says von Franz, she will need to be rescued by a hero, who von Franz thinks represents her *animus* or ability for logical reasoning.[8] But if a prince has to go into the forest to rescue the lost or sleeping princess, I believe that means it is *his* story, and the princess more likely represents his repressed feminine side that he needs to retrieve from his own unconscious. A female character, unlike an *anima* figure, is entirely conscious when she chooses to leave the path; she gets herself through the forest and out again without any need for a hero. For example, Vasilisa the Beautiful goes into the forest in search of the fearsome witch Baba Yaga, dwells with her for three days, and wins her release all on her own. She does not need the assistance of a prince or anyone else.

In the past, many women became wives or tried life in the masculine world first before venturing into the woods. But in fairy tales, the girl makes the wilderness journey early on, and that is now becoming the model for young women of today, who seek out adventures first before settling down to marriage and careers. The "gap year" that many students (both male and female) now take in the middle of their college experience and spend traveling or working, often abroad, is often time spent in the liminal zone.

Outside the confines of society, one becomes an outsider. Time in the liminal space can help a woman see the form and shape of the trap she was stuck in before. She can detach and become objective about the world she lives in. This sets her up for the next stage in her development, in which she learns to trust her own judgment. But more than that, the wilderness is a place without distractions or rules—a place where one can and must come face to face with all of oneself, including the wild, unruly parts.

The Uncharted Place

The liminal space can also be a kind of negative space. Artists sometimes use a technique whereby they draw everything *around* a thing instead of the thing itself; the negative space that is left is an outline of the thing that is sought. Similarly, when teenagers

LEAP OF FAITH

When I quit my job at midlife and sold my house to fund my return to school, my niece gave me a picture I treasure. A person is walking out from a cliff on a tightrope—while holding on to the other end of the rope. That is just how I felt at the time. I knew that I had to make that leap off the edge of the world, but I had no idea what would happen next. All I could do was trust.

reject what others tell them to think or be, they are, in a sense, outlining what it is they want to be. The liminal space is a place apart from the old life where one can begin to define oneself. In women's narratives the forest, the desert, the wilderness, or even a big city stands for the *terra incognita* where the heroine can go to find out who she is.

When women venture into the wild, there are no longer any rules or expectations they must meet. The hero's journey is mapped out: pass the threshold, meet the guardians, endure the trials, descend to the Underworld, etc. The heroine who leaves has no such map to follow, no role models to emulate. She can go where she wants, do what she wants.

Such freedom is both heady and terrifying. "The future of a woman alone in the world in the 1950s was a blank page, because no one I knew had lived that way," says Jill Ker Conway, "so I experienced my leave-taking as a farewell to the known, a jump off the edge of the world."[9] The frightening jump into the void seems to be a requirement for many who seek to free themselves from an unwanted life.

In the real world, finding such a space usually requires money. In *A Room of One's Own*, Woolf talks about how an annuity from an aunt freed her, not just from having to earn a living, but from "hatred and bitterness," because with that money she could follow her own path.[10] Beatrix Potter used the money she earned from her books to buy Hill Top Farm in the Lake District, where she would live out the rest of her life.

Fictional women rarely get such windfalls that allow them to create a private place in the context of their current lives. Instead, they go into the woods until they come to a special place that they enter *into*—a magical cave, perhaps, or Baba Yaga's hut on legs. Because these images come from our own unconscious, a place we visit only in dreams and disbelieve in most of the time we are awake, they can seem fantastic or frightening. But this is where we can find our own deep truth.

We do not take this step alone. The Aletis is about to meet her teacher.

IDYLL

Vasilisa's Journey

VASILISA, *a popular heroine of Russian fairy tales, is the only daughter of a man and a woman who love her very much. She is pampered and fussed over as a child. But sadly, when Vasilisa is still quite young, her mother takes ill. Despite all the efforts of the best physicians, it becomes clear that she will die. When the mother understands this, she calls Vasilisa to her and gives her a doll. "This doll will protect and guide you just as I would have done," she tells her daughter. "Always keep it in your pocket. If you are ever in trouble, take it out and ask the doll what to do." She dies soon after.*

The father mourns his wife for several years. But as Vasilisa grows up, he begins to feel that his daughter needs a mother. He marries a woman who has two daughters near Vasilisa's age. As long as he is in the house, every-thing seems fine. But then the father takes a long trip for his business and is lost at sea. Now the true natures of the stepmother and her daughters reveal themselves. To save money, the stepmother fires all the servants and moves the family to a small cottage on the edge of the woods. The work that had been done by the servants is now all done by Vasilisa, who is treated with contempt by her stepmother and stepsisters.

One night, the stepsisters decide to get rid of Vasilisa forever. They blow out the candle that is their only light. Then they tell Vasilisa that she must go into the forest to find the witch Baba Yaga and get a light from her. Vasilisa goes outside but at first is too terrified to go on. She takes out her doll. The doll tells her not to be afraid, for as long as Vasilisa has the doll there is nothing to fear—not even Baba Yaga.

So Vasilisa goes into the forest and walks all night and all the next day. At nightfall she comes to Baba Yaga's hut standing on legs in a clearing. Baba Yaga soon appears and asks why she has come. When Vasilisa replies that she has been sent by her stepsisters to fetch a light, Baba Yaga snorts and replies, "Oh, yes! I know them." She invites Vasilisa in and tells her to make dinner, which Vasilisa does. After the witch gorges herself, she tells Vasilisa that the next day she must clean the hut, make dinner again, and also pick out all the black seeds from a sack of millet before Baba Yaga returns. Baba Yaga then goes to sleep.

In despair, Vasilisa takes out her doll and asks it how she can possibly do all these tasks in one day. The doll tells her to go to sleep and not worry about it. When Vasilisa awakes, it is day and Baba Yaga is gone. But also, the hut is spotless, dinner is on the stove, and the doll is just picking the last of the black millet seeds out of the sack. When Baba Yaga returns, she tries to find a speck of dust in the house or a black seed in the millet, but finally has to say, grudgingly, "You have done well." Then she gives Vasilisa a similar task to complete the next day, and again the day after that. Each time the doll performs all the tasks.

At the end of the third day, Baba Yaga lets Vasilisa go and gives her a lantern made out of a skull for her light. Vasilisa returns home with this lantern. As soon as its rays fall upon the stepmother and stepsisters, they are burned up in an instant!

Vasilisa leaves the cottage and moves into the town again, where she lodges with a kind old lady. Vasilisa needs to support herself, so she weaves some linen cloth out of flax and gives it to the old woman to sell. The cloth is so fine that the old woman takes it to the tsar. When he sees and feels the fine cloth, the tsar is pleased. He asks the old woman to make it into shirts for him. The old woman takes the cloth back to Vasilisa and tells her to make the shirts, which Vasilisa does. The tsar recognizes that these shirts have been made by someone truly gifted and asks to meet the maker. When Vasilisa is brought before him, he immediately sees not just her beauty but her great worth and makes her his tsarina.

CHAPTER 10

The Woman of Power

They say you lurk here still, perhaps
in the depths of the earth or on
some sacred mountain . . .
you lurk here still, mutter
in caves, warn, warn and weave
warp of our hope.

—Diane di Prima,
"Prayer to the Mothers"

THE HERO IS GUIDED almost from the outset of his journey by an old wise man—a wizard like Merlin in the Arthur legends or Gandalf in *The Lord of the Rings*, or a revered figure like Virgil, who takes Dante through the circles of Hell and Purgatory. This wise man represents Logos, the power of logic and rational discernment. When the hero is ready, the old wise man disappears. But the Aletis is not guided by a similar figure. She makes her own way to the wise woman and, once she has learned from her, goes away again. The witch remains in the forest, waiting for the next girl to find her.

Heroic quest stories, like the cultures they reflect, tend to split the feminine into good and bad. The archetypal female characters with whom heroes deal are often polarized: on the "bad" end of the spectrum are the temptress who tries to get the hero to commit a sin or the sirens who lead him to his destruction, while on the "good" end we find the princess/goddess whom he saves, serves, and marries. But there are also many stories in which, as Joseph Campbell says, the hero has to realize that it is his own ignorance that causes him to see women in a polarized way.[1] Once he can get beyond this blindness, he can look upon even the ugliest witch with compassion and see beyond the superficial to the real and all-encompassing beauty of the feminine.

Women have the same problem; they may have internalized a negative societal view of the feminine on a level so deep that it's not obvious to their conscious minds. This can lead to confusion and contradiction. For example, more than one woman who thinks she is strong and independent has been perplexed and ashamed to realize one day that she is in a relationship with an abusive man. She can't understand how she of all people "let" this happen; she thinks she knows better. But something deep within her has agreed to this situation, something that she may not even be aware is part of her psyche—something which tells her that she as a woman either deserves or should expect such treatment. She cannot free herself completely from the situation until she brings that part of herself into the light of day and releases it. This can take some digging, for the roots of these negative attitudes go deep.

Like the hero, the Aletis needs to encounter and deal with those aspects of the feminine that have been relegated to the dark places. However, she does this in a very different way. For the hero, the feminine is something *other*, something unlike him. He marries the goddess or embraces the loathsome witch as a metaphor for learning how to respect and even love those traits he considers feminine. Yet he still considers them foreign, unlike him. But for the heroine, these feminine traits are not *other*. She doesn't have to marry anyone; instead, what she has to do is learn to take pride in who she is. The voice she must learn to listen to is her own voice.

So the Aletis must spend time with the goddess in the cave or the witch in the forest—negative archetypal images of the feminine. (Later I discuss how she may also encounter the madwoman in the attic or the coldhearted bitch in the office.) Many authors refer to these figures as images of the "dark feminine," but we should be calling them the *darkened* feminine. They are only dark to our eyes because they have been kept in the dark, hidden away, treated as something shameful or dangerous.

Many heroic tales cast the witch as an enemy instead of someone who might be helpful or informative. We see examples of this in the Disney movies of old tales where the hero must fight Maleficent the witch or Ursula the Sea Hag to win the princess. But the Aletis turns this attitude on its head and deliberately seeks out such darkened feminine figures to see what they have to teach her.

Marginalization is a two-edged sword. Those who are pushed off into the corners of society are usually isolated and disenfranchised. But such a corner can also be a sacred space where one can develop without interference, without having to bow to the expectations of others. What many call the witch or the bitch often turns out to be a woman who has stopped obeying those voices in her culture that say certain traits or behaviors are forbidden to "nice" women. Those who manage to stop listening to such voices are then free to learn how to call upon *all* their inherent qualities. Once they can do this, they may teach other women how to do the same. That is why the heroine goes to the witch Baba Yaga's hut in the forest or descends to the goddess in the cave.

When she finds such a mentor, the Aletis must approach

her with humility. Ereshkigal, says Sylvia Brinton Perera, "rages when she is not met with respect. She is proud, but she does not mount an offensive, nor does she transgress her own boundaries. She simply demands recognition as an equal power."[2] The same is true of Baba Yaga, the witch in the woods, says Clarissa Pinkola Estés: "She does not hurt Vasilisa as long as Vasilisa affords her respect. Respect in the face of great power is a crucial lesson."[3] Respect means recognizing the worth of the darkened feminine and honoring it. Women who do this can then learn how to claim that power for themselves. Once a heroine demonstrates that she values the worth and power of the denied feminine, she can begin to value and manifest her own denied worth and power.

Some psychologists trace this fear of the powerful woman to the infant's perception that the mother has absolute rule over the entire world. A baby is completely dependent upon its mother. If the mother responds appropriately to a baby's cries, the baby feels safe; it also feels like it has some control over the mother and, thus, the world. But if the mother is inconsistent in her responses—or worse, neglects the child for long periods of time—the baby comes to realize that it has no control over anything. This is terrifying, for the baby knows that if others do not choose to take care of it, it will die.

This infantile fear of what the uncontrollable mother may or may not do is not easily outgrown. As we grow up, we continue to want mother's support and guidance. But we also resent the guiding hand, for we have an equal urge toward autonomy. Children want mother to be there when they need her but not to interfere when they step out on their own. The perfect mother knows when to allow freedom and when to offer a safe haven. But few mothers are perfect, and most err on one side or the other, either

IT NEVER ENDS

"I'm fifty-five, and my mother still tells me how to put up an ironing board," laments a head nurse at a major hospital. "To her I'm perpetually fifteen years old and can't do anything without her help."

"When she needs me, she wants me to drop everything and come running," says another woman of her college-age daughter. "It doesn't occur to her that I have a life, too. It's as if she assumes that I just sit around waiting for her to call."

For many mothers and daughters, the struggle to find a balance between dependency and autonomy can be lifelong.

neglecting the needs of the child or being a "smother mother" who does not teach the child how to be independent.

The polarized view of women that is so pervasive in our culture may have its roots in this eternal push-pull in our own psyches between our need for dependence and our desire for autonomy. Ideally, children will be given just the right amount of freedom to explore the world, along with help when they really need it. If they are given both in the right balance, they will become capable people who connect well with others. But if they are either neglected or smothered, they will have trouble knowing what to do. As with any shadow aspects of the psyche, humans tend to project this inner struggle onto the nearest appropriate person: in this case, Mom. Some will project their anger over their inner confusion not just at the mother but other women, too—even *all* women.

This tendency is problematic enough for those men who become misogynists and avoid women as much as possible. But a *woman* who distrusts women is cut off from her own essential self. We all have traits that society associates with being masculine or feminine. If a man represses all the aspects of himself that he associates with the *other* gender, his feminine side, it takes a considerable bite out of his own being. That's bad enough. But if a woman represses not just her masculine traits but the part of herself that is *not* "other" because society tells her those traits are worthless, what is left? Sadly, too many women have been taught to reject or repress so much of themselves that they have no idea who they are at all.

Thus, the "war between the sexes" takes place primarily in our own psyches, and the costs of that war are seen every time a person is unable to love her- or himself whole-heartedly. The victims of this war include every man who yearns for connection with the feminine while despising himself for this weakness or blaming women for not "giving" him what he thinks will fill that need; every woman who feels she must hide part of herself to please others; and every person who feels let down by a partner for not living up to the ideal of the *other* promulgated by our culture. The other is *within us*, and until we can love that other, we will fail at loving anyone else.

When a woman attempts to integrate those aspects that she has been taught to fear or despise, she must first become conscious of the shadow figures of the wild feminine such as the witch in the hut, the underground goddess, and the madwoman. Like all archetypes, the number of possible images and names for these figures is beyond counting. As a woman identifies more and more faces of the wild feminine, she starts to understand those aspects in herself and learns how to unlock the gifts they hold for her. This is the first step to beginning to trust and use that power.

A REAL BITCH

I lived for fourteen years with a female German shepherd. She taught me that a real bitch has very clear boundaries; always knows exactly where she is and what's going on around her; and is intelligent, strong, and loving. She is fiercely protective of those she loves, but only when there is a real threat; otherwise, she is calm and relaxed—but never obsequious. She gives her heart to very few and only after they prove themselves worthy of her love and respect.

The Witch

The witch represents a form of wisdom that defies rational, logical understanding. The witch sees and understands in ways that have nothing to do with the conscious mind. It is an intuitive wisdom, but not in the sense of a vague hunch or a feeling. She discerns what is important through *knowing* on a deep level what deserves attention and what should be ignored or discarded.

Like the witch's wand or the goddess's scepter, this form of wisdom is sharp and directed with purpose. It is completely objective and brutally honest, and so it frightens women who have always been taught that they must be "nice." So many women go in fear of being thought unpleasant: a bitch or a witch! But that is precisely where power lies. The witch's fearsomeness is necessary. Many a fairy-tale heroine has been too nice to those who would oppress her (like her stepmother and stepsisters, the mean girls). The Aletis needs to learn how to take a risk, to get past her fears of what others may think or do if she does *not* try to placate them or even dares to stand up to them. She needs a role model.

The first step is to find the witch. The second is to stand before her with confidence. The heroine must demonstrate respect, not just for the witch, but for herself. This is exactly how, in *Pride and Prejudice,* Elizabeth Bennet stands up to the powerful Lady Catherine. She does not attack, but neither does she placate; she answers honestly and as herself. When Lady Catherine tries to browbeat her into promising never to see Mr. Darcy again, Elizabeth replies, "I am not to be intimidated into anything so wholly unreasonable." By refusing to be intimidated by the witch, she gains equal power as mistress of Pemberley.

Aunt March, the crotchety widowed aunt of *Little Women,* has power over the March family because she has money. For much of the story, her relatives cater to her whims without complaint. But Aunt March wants something else from them. Alcott tells us that the old lady "possessed in perfection the art of rousing the spirit of opposition in the gentlest people, and enjoyed doing it." She forbids Meg to marry John Brooke, knowing full well that this is the only way to get Meg to stand up for herself. Meg does so and "hardly knew herself, she felt so brave and independent." This

---

THE DEMANDING TEACHER

"I'm having trouble with my professor," a young woman earning her master's degree told me. "I don't want to use the method she's requiring for this paper; I think it's wrong. I want to do it another way, but I can't even get her to discuss it."

I explained about the witch in the woods and advised her to write the paper the way her professor wanted. A few weeks later, I heard back from her. Not only had the young woman found value in the method her professor required, but the professor now seemed more open to hearing the student's point of view. "And she said I should go on to get my PhD!"

The student now saw her professor not as an enemy but as a source of wisdom and an ally.

is a necessary step for Meg. Before she can marry and become a mother, she has to take on some of the power she has heretofore abdicated to the older generation. After all, Meg is the oldest daughter and may in time step into Aunt March's shoes as the matriarch of the clan. It is time she begins her training for that position.

Miranda Priestley of Lauren Weisberger's *The Devil Wears Prada*, a fictionalized account of Weisberger's stint as assistant to *Vogue* magazine editor Anna Wintour, seems to be the boss from hell. Miranda demands the impossible and refuses to accept that it can't be done; she is harsh and insulting to her staff. But Andrea—the character based on Weisberger— is told that if she can take the heat for just one year and win Miranda's respect, she will gain a formidable ally. Andrea sticks it out and proves her worth, and Miranda helps Andrea land her dream job.

Women often have to prove their worth to other women in positions of power before those women will consent to mentor them. This can be upsetting to some women, especially if the aspiring woman assumes that women ought to be "nicer" than men while performing the same job. Instead of seeing the situation as a challenge she can meet, she may blame or dislike the more powerful woman for being demanding instead of taking care of her. But the woman of power is not her mother and has no time to baby anyone. She has herself learned from the witch. The powerful woman will only consent to teach if the prospective student makes it clear to her that she will not be wasting her time.

Gayle Holmes, founder of a mentoring service, says that women should not think in terms of compatibility when seeking wisdom from a more experienced female colleague. "If you're matched with someone like you," she said in an interview with

Cheryl Dahle, "the potential for discovery is negated. You should pair with someone who, by her very nature, will challenge you."[4] The witch challenges; when the heroine meets the challenge, the witch turns into a helpful—and powerful—guide.

The Madwoman

Sometimes an aspect of a woman's self has been not just devalued but so confined and denied that she goes insane, like Bertha Mason does in *Jane Eyre*. Insanity is, for some women, the only way they can refuse to abandon themselves. A classic example is Charlotte Perkins Gilman's protagonist in *The Yellow Wallpaper*, who is not allowed to pursue her desire for "congenial work, with excitement and change" because her logical, cold physician husband (who calls her "little girl") thinks it is bad for her. He confines her to an upstairs room, from which she "escapes" by going mad.

Bertha Mason's madness manifests as an urge to destroy those men and those structures that would confine her. She tries to kill her husband and her own brother, but while she steals into Jane's bedchamber and looks at her, all she does there is shred Jane's veil, the symbol of the false marriage Rochester has offered Jane. She never touches Jane herself. Indeed, Bertha seems to consider herself Jane's ally. Joan Gould points out that "every time Jane's feelings are violated . . . Bertha erupts with knife or teeth or fire."[5] Furthermore, each time Bertha erupts, a moment of honest connection between Jane and Rochester follows.

Yet Jane runs away after she finally meets Bertha face-to-face. She senses that Bertha represents *eros*, passion, but she has no idea how a woman ought to manage this aspect of life. Bertha is hardly a good role model, and as a child Jane got into trouble whenever she gave in to her own passionate feelings. She has only seen what happens when eros is repressed until it explodes. It's no wonder that Jane fears to let her own eros loose. She rejects Rochester's plea to let passion rule her and instead retreats to the logos-dominated home of St. John Rivers, who does his best to reason Jane into a loveless, dutiful marriage and very nearly succeeds.

But as soon as Jane contemplates a life entirely without passion, her whole being rebels. Rochester's voice speaks in her mind. Once she ran from eros; now she runs back toward it, or rather, to the one man who is her equal in logos *and* eros, intellect *and* passion alike. And her ally Bertha has been at work in her absence; she has burned down the house of confinement and jumped to her death, freeing Rochester and Jane to be together.

Fire represents the insanity of repressed feelings, particularly repressed sexuality, in many women's stories and poems. In *Rebecca*, Mrs. Danvers has been driven mad by her own unsanctioned love for the dead Rebecca. She uses fire to destroy Manderley, which she considers Rebecca's house, rather than allow the socially acceptable but dishonest relationship between Maxim de Winter and his second, childish wife to flourish there.

Unlike Jane Eyre, the new Mrs. de Winter does eventually confront the madwoman. She loses her innocence—which her husband laments—and becomes an equal partner in her marriage. However, her change may have come too late. The last pages of du Maurier's novel describe a passionless marriage in an enervating climate where the most exciting moment is reading the results of sports matches in the English papers that arrive days after the fact. One is left with the impression that Rebecca and Mrs. Danvers took all the fire with them into the dark.

The darkened feminine desires to come into the light, to be seen and understood, ultimately to be welcomed and embraced. If we can get past our fear of her and let her teach us, we return out of the woods with powerful gifts. Vasilisa comes back from her time with Baba Yaga bearing a skull whose eyes shine with the light of truth. When this light falls upon the stepmother and stepsisters who would deny Vasilisa her selfhood, those women are burned up in an instant. The power held by the darkened feminine is dangerous indeed to those who would repress it. But those who can face it with courage and respect can learn to wield that power themselves in the world.

CHAPTER 11

The Time of Learning

*Don't try to comprehend with your mind. Your minds are
very limited. Use your intuition.*
——Madeleine L'Engle, *A Wind in the Door*

ONCE THE ALETIS has reached the hut of the witch, her
apprenticeship in the ways of feminine power begins. She must
not question; she must not refuse or shirk any task; she must
do all that the fearsome wise woman asks of her without complaint, completely and thoroughly and within the allotted time.
This is how she shows her new-found respect for the disavowed

---

OBJECTIVITY

Those who remember their grammar lessons will remember that the subject is the one who acts. The object is the thing that the subject acts upon.
So if I kick a ball, I, the subject, have done something to a ball, the object.

"Objectivity" means to take the subject out of the picture. The thing
that is acted upon—or being thought about—is what matters. For centuries, Western science has taught that the subject has no role in knowledge.

But recently, scientists have had to acknowledge that you can't get rid
of the subject. There is increasing agreement that no matter how objective
someone tries to be, the fact that they are studying something affects that
thing. *We* kick the ball. We can't take ourselves out of the equation.

feminine. But more importantly, as we will see, doing the assigned tasks schools her in how to use feminine ways of knowing.

Jung's theory of typology is based on the idea that people relate to others and the world around them through what he called *functions*.[1] The *thinking* function is our ability to reason. The *feeling* function is about not emotions but our ability to know what we really value. The *sensation* function has to do with our five senses, the physical capacity to comprehend the world around us. The *intuitive* function is the ability to "know" things in a nonrational, non-sensing way—an ability we still do not understand and that many dismiss.

Jung paired up these functions and said that people tended to prefer one function over the other in each pair. For example, some people rely more on thinking than on feeling when making a decision. Such people use logic and make lists of pros and cons to decide what to do; they are very intellectual about how they choose. Other people cite reasons for choosing one thing over another that are more emotional than logical. "This house is much cheaper and closer to work," a thinking type might say, to which a feeling spouse may reply, "Yes, but the other one is charming and I like the neighbors."

When it comes to understanding the world around us, some people prefer to use their senses. To such people, something is not real unless they can see, touch, hear, smell, or taste it. But other people rely more on their intuition. They get hunches or have a "gut feeling" about people or things, although often they cannot explain why. The sensing person demands proof; the intuitive person depends upon an inner certainty. "I think Joe may be thinking about leaving Mary," an intuitive type may say. "Why do you think that? Did he say so?" her sensing friend may respond. "Well, no, but I just have a feeling," the first person will reply.

Jung also noticed that some people are *extraverted* and some are *introverted*. While many people think of extroverts as more friendly and outgoing, and of introverts as shy and reclusive, this is not how Jung uses the terms. Extroverts essentially get energy from social interaction, while introverts charge their batteries through time alone. Some introverts can be as friendly and engaging as any extrovert—for a while. But eventually they have to go off and be by themselves.

Recent studies have found that this difference may be a matter of brain chemistry, not personality. Introverts tend to be oversensitive to the brain chemicals released by social stimulation and "burn out" quickly, while extroverts feel better the more stimulation they get. It's like the difference between people who get wired on even the smallest amount of caffeine and those who require four shots of espresso in their morning latte just to get going.

Jung's typology was later expanded by the mother-daughter team of Katherine Cook Briggs and Isabel Briggs Myers, who created the popular Myers-Briggs personality test. They added another pair of functions: *judging* versus *perceiving*. *Judging* types have the ability to focus only on what is relevant; if it is not relevant, they ignore it or cut it out. *Perceiving* people ignore nothing; they find all information, relevant or not, to be equally interesting. "Get to the point!" growls the judging type as the perceiving type wanders off on yet another fascinating—to them—tangent. But the perceiving person may notice things that the judging type doesn't even see.

In the prior chapter, I talked about how humans seesaw between attachment to and separation from parents, especially the mother, as they grow to adulthood. Western culture takes a linear view of things. If we start out attached and learn over time how to separate, then the "separated" viewpoint must be better. As a result, our culture thinks of abstract, logical, objective thought as the mature and preferable way of looking at things.

Although many of the authors who discuss heroine stories use such terminology, polarized dualities do not fit the witch's way of knowing. The witch teaches the Aletis to discriminate between alternatives and make decisions in a way that combines elements of all of Jung's functions. And, in fact, this is how most mature adults behave. As we age, we (hopefully) learn to call upon the skills of our less-favored functions until we are balanced, able to employ all of them as needed.

Research on decision making finds that women tend to rely more on experience than on abstract concepts.[2] Those who believe that objective logic is the highest form of discernment sometimes dismiss this kind of thinking as subjective and inadequate. Yet it is also pragmatic because it tends to focus on what will actually work or what is actually needed in the situation instead of some abstract ideal.

In *Women's Ways of Knowing*, Marie Field Belenky and her colleagues show how women go through a progression of stages as they learn to trust their own thinking. In the first stage, young girls and women, particularly those who are from disadvantaged backgrounds, are often silenced; they do not feel that they have the right to say anything. They often fear words, as their experience has been that words express or cause anger.[3] Celie, the abused protagonist of *The Color Purple*, is, for most of the book, emblematic of a woman in this stage of development. "I don't even look at mens," she says. Instead, she remains silent, never venturing an opinion, fearing men when they speak to her, fearing to draw their attention.

At some point the girl or young woman may start to pay attention to people that she considers intelligent or knowledgeable. The young woman wants to know *what* to think and looks to others to tell her. In *Middlemarch*, Dorothea Brooke does this in the early stages of her relationship with Casaubon:

> This accomplished man condescended to think of a young girl, and take the pains to talk to her, not with absurd compliment, but with an appeal to her understanding, and sometimes with instructive correction . . . she looked as reverently at Mr. Casaubon's religious elevation above herself as she did at his intellect and learning.

Like Dorothea, a young woman at this stage reveres those she thinks know more than she does and accepts their words without question.

More often than not, these idols turn out to have feet of clay. When this happens, the young woman may feel betrayed and stop trusting anyone else. As part of this distrust of what others say, she may start to see reason and logic "as alien territory belonging to men," according to Belenky and her cohort.[4] As a result, the woman avoids that territory and begins to hear and trust her own intuition instead. "My gut's my best friend," said one woman in Belenky's study, "the one thing in the world that won't . . . lie to me."[5] As an example of a woman at this stage, Jane Eyre repeatedly expresses her unshakeable trust in her own idea of what is right. St. John Rivers tries to sway her to his point of view, but

Jane refuses to bend; she will be guided by herself and no one else—especially not the logical man.

In fact, it's not just women who make decisions this way. Despite the expressed preference for logic in our society, recent studies conclude that most people—men included—give more weight to feelings than logic when making decisions. People of either sex also call upon their gut feelings from prior experiences to guide them to the right decision.[6]

But it is not enough to trust our intuition and rely on feelings. All of us need to learn how to integrate the thinking and sensing functions as well. And for this, we need a teacher who will hold us to a higher standard. The thinking function develops best when it is challenged.

In *Pride and Prejudice*, Charlotte Lucas challenges Elizabeth when she suggests that her friend take what George Wickham has told her about Darcy with a grain of salt. Elizabeth rejects this advice because she is confident that her intuition is always right. But Charlotte is eventually proved to be correct, and Elizabeth is forced not just to rethink her ideas about Darcy but to become aware of how her own biases have kept her from being objective about him or Wickham.

Many of the women in Belenky's study talk about their mentors. One of the women interviewed, a student, understood what her teachers at college were trying to do: "They're teaching you a method, and you're applying it for yourself."[7] Belenky's group calls this "procedural knowledge."[8] Procedural knowledge enables us to confront and work through a problem. The woman who masters procedural knowledge learns to see the world as a complex, interrelated web of interactions that extends far beyond her personal experience.

But that is not the end. The ultimate goal is learning how to think critically, to move beyond inherited biases and the influence of others and become able to think for oneself. Estés says that a young woman must develop "the hooded eyes of the watchful" when it comes to relationships, so that she will not be taken in by someone who could harm her.[9] This is an ability that we also need when listening to politicians or anyone who wants to sway us to their point of view! Critical thinking also involves reflexivity: the ability to look objectively at oneself and see how one's own biases, fears, and hopes may be coloring one's view.

Stories in which women learn how to exercise a more objective kind of judgment are not necessarily perpetuating the societal bias for rational detachment. Rather, these writers are often trying to imagine a new way of decision making that occupies a middle ground between rational, detached objectivity and emotional, attached subjectivity. Such an approach reflects Jung's concept of the *transcendent* function, which he defined as a dialogue between the unconscious and the conscious mind that allows us to get beyond a stuck point and rise to a new level.[10] Jung advised people facing a difficult decision to delay deciding as long as possible. The longer one can put off the decision—the longer we can hold the tension of not knowing what to do—the greater the chance that another and better way will reveal itself. Jung believed that this third option does not come from our rational mind but from the unconscious psyche, which can only speak when the mind quiets enough to give it space. Holding the tension can provide this space.

What the heroine learns to do at the feet of the witch is to hold the tension in another way: to call upon her intuition *and* her objectivity at the same time. The senses and the intuition are not split but work together, creating an embodied capacity for discrimination. This capacity allows the Aletis to make the right decisions.

Sorting the Seeds: Learning Discrimination

Learning how to integrate such different ways of perceiving and thinking is not easy. At first, it may seem impossible. In the stories, the first thing the witch does with her new pupil is to set her an impossible task. This task often takes the form of "sorting the seeds." Cinderella must pick lentils out of the ashes; Vasilisa must remove all the black millet seeds from a mixture of seeds; Psyche must separate wheat, millet, and poppy seeds from one another. Such a task, Sylvia Brinton Perera says, teaches the heroine how to see what the witch sees: "not what might be good or bad, but what exists before judgment." The witch combines the intuitive, sensing, and perceiving functions to see *everything*. What she sees is not freighted with emotional reactions. It is not sorted into categories and labels by the rational mind, but neither does it appear chaotic. She sees and accepts the world as it truly is. And once she can do this, Perera adds, the heroine can move beyond what the rational mind sees as chaos and find meaningful patterns (which sounds remarkably like what quantum physicists do).[11]

But it is not enough to see things as they are. The sorting task also teaches the Aletis how to discern which seeds should be planted—that is, allowed to grow. The witch, who after all is an avatar of the Great Mother, teaches women not just how to mother but how to choose what should be mothered in their lives. And as an avatar of the force of destruction that is inextricably combined with the force of creation, the witch teaches us what must die and be discarded.

In most women's novels, the heroine sorts out her *own* feelings by opening herself to seeing as the witch does, without judgment. She learns to suspend her feelings so that she can perceive even the information that contradicts her prior assumptions. For example, Elizabeth Bennet comes face to face with her own prejudices after reading Darcy's letter telling her the true story of his dealings with Mr. Wickham:

> [Elizabeth] grew absolutely ashamed of herself. Of neither Darcy nor Wickham could she think without feeling that she had been blind, partial, prejudiced, absurd. . . . "I, who have prided myself on my discernment! I who have valued myself on my abilities! . . . How humiliating is this discovery! Yet, how just a humiliation . . . I have courted prepossession and ignorance, and driven reason away. . . . Till this moment I never knew myself."

When Elizabeth learns how to see others clearly, she sees herself clearly as well. This is true objectivity.

Many women's novels warn women against letting emotional fantasies blind them to reality. Catherine Morland of *Northanger Abbey* lets her romantic ideas, fed by the Gothic novels she loves, run away with her, yet she cannot see how her supposed friend Isabel lies and manipulates people. Mrs. de Winter spends a great deal of time imagining things, even while having dinner with her husband:

> "Do you know you were going through the most extraordinary antics instead of eating your fish?" said Maxim. "First you listened, as though you heard the telephone, and then your lips moved, and you threw half a glance at me. And you shook your

head, and smiled, and shrugged your shoulders. All in about a
second. Are you practising your appearance for the fancy dress
ball?" He looked across at me, laughing, and I wondered what
he would say if he really knew my thoughts, my heart, and my
mind. . . . "You look like a little criminal," he said.

As long as she lives in her fantasy world, Maxim's young wife
misses all the clues about her husband. Like Elizabeth's and Catherine's, her awakening to reality is painful but necessary in order
for her to grow up and learn to see the world as it is. As long as
she sees incorrectly, deluded by her owns hopes and fears, she
is under the power of her own misapprehensions; once she sees
clearly, she can make the right decisions.

The Magic Helper

In many folk and fairy tales, the impossible sorting task is accomplished—often while the heroine sleeps—by a magic helper. Psyche sorts the seeds Venus mixes for her with the help of a talking
ant, and other spirits aid her in further tests. The three impossible tasks that Baba Yaga sets for Vasilisa are carried out by a doll
that her mother gave her. In the Grimm Brothers' version of the
Cinderella story, Cinderella calls upon birds to come accomplish
her impossible task. In several variations on the Rumpelstiltskin
story, three misshapen old women do the spinning that the girl
cannot. None of these magic helpers demand any return, except
to be kept close by (in the case of the doll) or acknowledged publicly (in the case of the three spinners).

These magic helpers represent the nonrational way of solving
a problem. It is "magic" because it is not logical and cannot be
explained in words. To sort out which seeds are edible or spin

flax into usable form requires both a physical (sensory) effort and an intuitive understanding of the process. The magic helper represents this capacity.

It is significant that the heroine often goes to sleep while the magical helper does the task. The rational, "awake" consciousness has nothing to do with the process. One of the criticisms leveled at traditional "women's work" is that it can be accomplished without thinking. But the "thinking" is happening at a deeper level than the rational mind—and meanwhile, the necessary work gets done! All the nonrational psyche asks in return is that we not deny its reality.

The doll and the witch are both necessary. The doll represents the capacity for embodied discrimination unconsciously inherited from the mother, the girl's first role model of feminine wisdom. Yet without the impetus of the demanding teacher, the girl may never learn to use this capacity consciously. Only after the witch presents her with an impossible task does Vasilisa take the doll out of her pocket. When Vasilisa asks the doll—her unconscious—for help, the transcendent function takes over and solves the problem that Vasilisa could not handle using only her conscious mind.

The Secret Chamber: Cleaning Up

Once she has learned how to see clearly, the heroine can help others to see clearly as well. She uncovers secrets that have festered and done harm to her family or community. Like an abscess, these secrets must be opened before they can be healed. Once again, she does this by entering into a secret or forbidden place. "Whenever the door to the forbidden chamber is opened, in fact as well as fiction, someone or something dies," says Joan Gould.[12] But it is something that *needs* to die. We have to lay bare our secrets, our shame, our wounds, for only then can transformation occur.

When Rochester finally brings Jane to the secret attic room where he has kept Bertha, Jane learns the truth Rochester has so desperately tried to hide from everyone. The result is the death of their relationship as it has been. But it was never a true relationship; it was a fantasy that ignored reality. Once the fantasy dies, Rochester is freed from the need to keep up the pretense, and Jane is freed to make a real choice.

Maxim de Winter wants to keep the truth about Rebecca's death a secret. When his new wife comes too close, he warns her off:

> "Listen, my sweet. When you were a little girl, were you ever forbidden to read certain books, and did your father ever put them under lock and key?"
>
> "Yes," I said.
>
> "Well then. A husband is not so very different from a father after all. There's a certain sort of knowledge I prefer you not to have."

But eventually he confesses to her that he killed Rebecca. Only then can Maxim and his wife enter into a real marriage, where no pretense is necessary, and become true partners.

In *Persuasion*, Anne Elliot's father does not want her to visit Mrs. Smith's rooms in a poor part of the town. Anne goes anyway and learns the truth about the heir to her father's estate—he turns out to be a thief, a liar, and a sexual libertine—which puts an end to both men's plans for Anne or her sister to marry the heir. And when Dorothea is finally permitted into her husband's library in *Middlemarch*, she learns that his "great work" is trivial and pointless—knowledge her husband has been desperate to keep not just from her but from himself.

Perhaps this desire to know the truth is the aspect of feminine power that terrifies society the most. When women learn to see the world as it truly is, without prejudice, and apply their skills of "women's work" to cleaning up the mess and choosing what will live and what will die, they manifest the Great Goddess in both her destructive and her nurturing aspects. No one who comes face to face with the totality of her power leaves unscathed. Such power threatens any society, but its capacity to cause upheaval surely is greatest in a society founded not just upon the repression of women, but upon the keeping of secrets.

Stirring the Pot: Alchemical Transformation

Baba Yaga also insists that Vasilisa cook for her. Estés focuses on the fire that must be laid before anything can be cooked, which she sees as a metaphor for eros, creative passion: "A woman must be willing to burn hot, burn with passion . . . with desire for whatever it is she truly loves."[13] The fire that fuels her work must be constantly fed.

Cooking is also an alchemical process by which things are changed into something new, something better. Often it involves taking disparate items—different vegetables, meat, and herbs, for instance—and, with the aid of fire, transforming them into something new, something nourishing, perhaps even something unexpected—a delicious stew, perhaps, made even more delectable by the addition of an unusual spice. Cooking requires artistry as well as chemistry. It is also a magic trick. In *Disturbances in the Field* by Lynne Sharon Schwartz, Lydia is thrown into the Underworld by the deaths of two of her children. She cooks her way out of her grief; when she cannot sleep, when her thoughts will not let her alone, she goes into the kitchen and cooks amazing gourmet meals. Eventually, she finds her way back above ground and is able to go on. Tita, the protagonist of *Like Water for Chocolat* by Laura Esquival, pours all her emotions into her cooking, to the point that everyone who eats her food feels what she feels. Vianne, the heroine of Joanne Harris's *Chocolat*, transforms an entire town through the alchemy of her magic confections; Babette does the same thing in a single night with one single, sublime meal in Isak Dinesan's *Babette's Feast*. Tilo in Chitra Banerjee Divakaruni's *The Mistress of Spices* can change a life by adding a single spice. Cooking, in these stories, is an alchemical process that allows people to move forward, out of their past history, their past selves, into a new life.

In the last two chapters of this book, I discuss other ways that women use their creativity to transform the world. But the process begins here, with the witch and her lessons. As Estés puts it, the witch's tasks "offer ways to think about, to measure, feed, nourish, straighten, cleanse the soul-life. In all these things Vasilisa is initiated."[14] Like Vasilisa, the woman who undertakes to learn from the witch comes away with a clearer sense of what is essential, what is true, and what will make a difference.

IDYLL

Flora Poste's Journey

FLORA POSTE *of Sheila Gibbons's* Cold Comfort Farm *is a most determined young lady. She tells her friends that when she reaches the age of fifty, she intends to write a novel as good as* Persuasion. *Until then, she intends to "live life." Flora has never really known her parents. When they are killed in an accident when she is twenty, she finds herself cast adrift in the world with only one hundred pounds a year to live on. Flora is taken in by her cousins, the Starkadders of Cold Comfort Farm, where nothing has gone right in decades.*

Flora immediately sets to work. She never forces her will on anyone. Instead, she listens, suggests, cajoles, hints, and tricks people into considering a new way of doing things. She also connects them with others. First, she takes her fey cousin, Elphine, to London and transforms her into a smart, modern girl, the perfect wife for the son of the local squire. She talks her fire-and-brimstone preacher cousin, Amos, into taking his message out into the world and leaving the farm in the care of his oldest son, Reuben, the only one who really cares about the farm. Then she brings a film producer to the farm to meet and take muscle-bound, movie-mad cousin Seth away to Hollywood. Finally, she introduces her melancholic aunt Judith to a Freud-like analyst.

By the end of Flora's stay, everyone at Cold Comfort Farm has found their true calling or their true love, the farm is cleaned up and running smoothly, and even old Aunt Ada Doom, who has up until now ruled the farm and everyone on it with a deadly grip, is on her way to Paris to enjoy herself for the first time in her life. Flora has already met her own true love, Charles, who recognized Flora's worth at first sight. He has waited patiently for her to accomplish her goals, aiding and abetting her at times, and shows up when she is ready to move on. They fly away in Charles's plane, leaving behind a transformed community that will be forever grateful to Flora.

CHAPTER 12

On Her Own Terms

When we women offer our experience as our truth, as human truth, all the maps change.

—Ursula K. Le Guin

THE ALETIS WENT APART, not just physically but emotionally and mentally, from the society that would not let her be herself. She found her way through the pathless forest to meet the witch, learn from her, and pass her tests. The next step is for her to return from the forest and create the life she wants to live. She will face more challenges, but she is now equipped for them.

Just as she crossed over a threshold and divested herself of the accoutrements of her old life when she entered the liminal space, now the Aletis must cross the threshold on the other side. In traditional rituals, initiates who are accepted into the order are invested with new clothing and other symbols of their new status. The soldier receives insignia of rank, a weapon, a posting to a new place; the college graduate puts on a suit and is granted a job. But the Aletis chooses for herself what the symbols of her new life shall be and where she shall dwell.

The Odd Woman

The first challenge the Aletis faces is, of course, that the society she once fled still clings to the same attitudes that forced her out before. But now the shoe is on the other foot. Now it is other people who have to learn how to accommodate themselves to *her*. For a while—and in some cases, forever—they may label her as an odd duck, an eccentric. It will take some time for others to learn how to value her.

Women love stories about odd women who go against society's expectations and create unique, unexpected lives for themselves. Pratt gives as examples books by Edna Ferber and Charlotte Perkins Gilman, as well as E. D. E. N. Southworth, who wrote dozens of books in the late nineteenth century about abandoned wives who achieve financial independence and success.[1] Anne Elliot of Austen's *Persuasion* is considered by her family and most of her friends as too "faded" at twenty-seven to be of any interest to potential husbands and, therefore, not an interesting person herself. But Austen's readers adore Anne.

Isolation has allowed the Aletis a space where she can be herself. In many Aletis stories, the returned heroine does all she can to keep that space in her life. Often, she finds a place to dwell where she can remain close to the wilderness. Just as she went into the forest as a young woman to recapture the freedom of childhood, she returns from time to time as a mature adult. Like a pioneer in a new land, she may clear out a place where she can live.

The lessons of the witch are useful here. Women reinventing their lives, both in fiction and in real life, must walk through archetypal landscapes, sort out what is of value, and tear down

old restrictive structures before they can nurture their wildness—their untamed, true selves—within their inner landscapes.

The Loose Woman

Such a reclamation project often involves a period of asexuality,
celibacy, and nonrelatedness. Before the Aletis can figure out how
she can relate to others on her own terms, she needs a time out
from relationships, especially sexual relationships. This aspect of
the heroine's journey seems to parallel the heroic quest, for the
hero is usually celibate until the quest is fulfilled. But it is much
harder for women who want time to explore their inner world
to be left alone. The idea that women have a relational and sexual obligation to men is still very much alive in our society. Any
woman who refuses this obligation may be seen not only as odd
but as a threat to the assumption that has been with us for millen-
nia that women cannot "belong" to themselves only.

Janice Raymond puts it this way: "The independence and
wildness of the loose woman—the virgin, the lesbian, the old
woman—conjures up the vision that women not only will take
power from men but *will take women from men, too*" (emphasis mine).[2] Here Raymond plays with the old epithet of "loose
woman." A loose woman, traditionally, is one who has question-
able morals and may be sexually available to anyone, so that no
man may claim her (or her children) as his alone. But as Raymond uses the term, it means a woman who is running loose,
going her own way, refusing to comply with the rules others think
she ought to follow. She is off the chain. She does not even choose
the socially sanctioned path of celibacy by becoming a nun, a

woman who devotes her physical being to God. Instead, this kind of "loose woman" may choose to deny herself to *everyone*.

In *Jane Eyre*, St. John Rivers believes that he, as a man, has the right to dictate what Jane Eyre's life will be. Moreover, he, as a minister, knows God's will for her better than she does. "God and nature intended you for a missionary's wife.... A missionary's wife you must—shall be. You shall be mine." When Jane tries to set the condition that she will go to India with Rivers only if she can go as a single woman, he replies, "Refuse to be my wife, and you limit yourself forever to a track of selfish ease and barren obscurity." He sees her desire for independence as both selfish and pointless, for he can't imagine a woman achieving anything outside of her role as wife and mother. Provoked beyond endurance, Jane blurts out that to marry him will kill her. St. John turns white with fury and tells her such language is "violent, unfeminine, and untrue." Her refusal to do what he sees as her duty to God and men—and thus himself as the representative of both—offends him deeply. But what really infuriates him is his powerlessness. He cannot force her to do what he wants. He is impotent in the face of her refusal.

The woman who claims the right to refuse her service to others is still seen as selfish by many today, including some surprising groups. There are Jungians still who agree with Jung's contention in his essay on "Women in Europe" that a woman who goes her own way "is doing something not wholly in accord with, if not directly injurious to, her feminine nature.... I do not mean merely physiological injury but above all psychic injury." A woman who puts her own interests first over love for children and men, says Jung, is violating her own deepest nature.[3]

Those who agree with Jung see a woman who goes apart as having fallen under the power of the internalized negative masculine, a condition most Jungians call "animus-possessed." However, many today are not convinced that the animus is a valid concept. For instance, therapist Ann Bedford Ulanov argues instead for the idea that all of us can be taken over by our emotions about the opposite sex from time to time; this "emotional possession" has nothing to do with anima or animus.[4] It makes sense to me that, in a polarized society, both women and men will have complexes about the opposite sex. I think these complexes are not innate or natural to the psyche but learned reactions. As such, we can become aware of them and choose to override them.

Marie-Louise von Franz, on the other hand, believes firmly in the danger of animus possession. She repeatedly warns women in *The Feminine in Fairy Tales* against being overpowered by their animus and thus becoming aggressive and unpleasant to be around, stating that "the source of evil and of things going wrong in women's lives is often a failure to deal with and to get over hurt feelings."[5]

By "things going wrong," von Franz means that a woman who speaks up may ruin her marriage. Men don't like being rebuked for hurting women's feelings, she says, so a good wife should protect her husband from the truth of her own feelings.[6] Because marriage is the ultimate goal for a woman, von Franz goes on, "many young girls refrain from studying or developing their minds, because they rightly feel that if they did they would fall into animus possession and that would prevent them from marrying."[7] Worse than that, developing their minds may take these girls out of relationship with others and put them into communion with *themselves*, "thinking about and discussing things that one cannot tell other people . . . in conversation with an inner spiritual process."[8]

Evidently, von Franz fears that some women may end up pre-
ferring the "conversation with an inner spiritual process" to conversation with others. And indeed, in *Journal of a Solitude* May
Sarton says:

> I live alone, perhaps for no good reason, for the reason that I
> am an impossible creature, set apart . . . thrown off by a word,
> a glance, a rainy day. . . . I often feel exhausted, but it is not the
> work that tires (work is a rest); it is the effort of pushing away
> the lives and needs of others.[9]

Both von Franz and Sarton agree that relationships can demand
so much from a woman that they leave her no time for herself. Sarton chose to make her work more of a priority. It might seem that
von Franz is being hypocritical here, as she never married and,
like Sarton, lived a life of the mind. But von Franz was devoted
to Jung and obeyed his dictates about what work she should do,

---

ECHOES OF PURITANISM?

American society, like the Swiss culture that produced Jung and von Franz,
is heavily influenced by Calvinism. Calvinist Protestants, including the Puri-
tans, believe that all people are inherently sinful and therefore must struggle
against sin in every aspect of life. Duty to God—and, for women, duty to their
husbands and children—comes before all other considerations.

A recent study of American values by Erik Uhlmann found that even those
who consciously reject gender stereotypes still link "male" with "career" and
"female" with "family." The study concluded that "Americans have intuitive
gut feelings about sex that are more in line with their religious heritage than
are their deliberative judgments," particularly when it comes to women's
behavior. This is true even of atheists and agnostics.[10] It is not current religious belief but our Puritan heritage that leads Americans to condemn "loose
women" of any sort.

where she should live, and even what friends to cultivate. She did not follow her own inclinations; she lived her life in service to another—to a man. It is true that once a woman steps away from always trying to be in relationship with others without demanding anything in return, always trying to be nice so that others will like her, she is likely to come face to face with her own resentment against the way she has been treated and the expectations put on her. That resentment *can* open the door to bitterness. But how can she ever get out of the trap if she does not learn to see it for what it is? Once she sees how insidious the chains that bound her are, it is natural that, for a while at least, she will be angry. But that does not mean she will never choose to engage in relationships again.

Resentment is a very different thing from active rebellion. Resentment comes from feeling like a victim; rebellion is a powerful act. Rebellion helps the woman step away into that place where she does not have to be nice: the hut of the witch. Only there can she have that conversation with her inner spiritual self that will allow her to grow. If she does not leave her old life, like Ereshkigal she can become trapped in a never-ending cycle of resentment toward others and see herself as a victim forever.

Many of the unhappy women in stories are Ereshkigals. These discontented mothers and evil stepmothers, bitter aunts and jilted brides live as Ereshkigal lived, relegated to a dark, confined domain that was never their choice. This is also the fate of the wife who is the mother to a "father's daughter," constantly aware that her husband prefers another woman to her but forced to swallow her jealousy because it is her own daughter who is the favorite.

Women who choose to step away from relationships for a while (or forever, for that matter) are not necessarily possessed by a negative aspect of the psyche. Indeed, the bitterest women are those who remain firmly ensconced within the chains of the family and masculine culture. Miss Havisham of Charles Dickens's *Great Expectations* comes to mind, forever stuck at the moment when she was jilted at the altar, devoting her life to taking revenge on all men for it. She is wealthy and has power, but she is the queen of a domain that no one else wants. Yet Miss Havisham could have chosen another life. She and others who let resentment take them over are choosing to stay in Ereshkigal's cave. They are always looking back, holding grudges, and blaming others for their own meaningless lives. Some resolutely refuse to question the very persons who keep them in thrall and, like the mean girls, instead serve as their acolytes and enforcers. Those who rebel and leave are the ones who find a new road. Those who take time out on that road to be alone with the disavowed feminine find their own inner power.

The idea that women must always take care of others first has been promulgated by some modern feminists as well. They have criticized both fictional heroines and real women who pursue their own goals instead of serving society. Even Gloria Steinem, an icon of American feminist thought, drew fire from other feminists for her book *Revolution from Within*, in which she proposed that women often need a time of self-reflection to deal with issues of low self-esteem.[11]

Steinem's book was part of a movement within feminism that believed that "the personal is political" and that self-empowerment is a necessary step to effective action.[12] But this belief is abhorrent to those who believe that taking time for the personal means *sacrificing* the political. Those who share this attitude think that women should not take time apart from the world for any reason, for the only thing such navel gazing accomplishes is to deprive the world of those women's much-needed service. In other words, it is selfish.

Those who argue that women must be political first and foremost are still telling women what they "should" be like instead of allowing them the freedom to decide how to run their own lives. When such critics are angered by someone who refuses to live a life of service to others, they are no different from St. John Rivers. The line between those who think women are just there to be used and those who think women must always be "useful" is a hair's thickness wide.

Also, the premise itself—that women who take time out for themselves will not be useful to society ever again—is a false one. People who pursue their deepest dreams, the urging of that inner voice that James Hillman calls one's daimon or soul calling,[13] are in fact living life in service to an ideal, often an ideal that requires great sacrifice and effort. And those who go apart to find their own inner sources of strength are far more likely to return with the ability to act with power in the world.

Stepping Up

People usually make changes one step at a time, not huge leaps that skip over stages. When it comes to being heroic, men and women start from different places. Men are, for the most part, expected to be in charge of their own lives. Even the orphan boy in hero stories has to manage his own life. He has some power of his own already. So when the boy steps up into being a hero, to being more powerful, he has *some* experience in handling power. But as I have been arguing throughout this book, women have rarely had power, rarely been in charge of their own lives. They have been

MY TRUE CALLING

At age ten, I knew my calling. I was going to be a writer. But everyone around me said that an English degree would be a self-indulgent waste of time and I would end up working as a waitress. Instead, I was urged to get a degree in a field that would allow me to "help others." When I was a girl, this meant becoming a teacher or a nurse.

I grasped at what seemed like a better option and decided to go into medical social work.

But then fate intervened. I took a job at a medical center where I quickly found myself helping doctors write their papers and patient education handouts. This work led to other writing jobs and eventually allowed me to strike out on my own as a freelance writer. My daimon would not be denied.

subject to the rule of their fathers or their husbands; their priests, if they are nuns; or, in the case of career women, their bosses. Their options are determined by their role—as daughters, wives, mothers, or loyal disciples to someone else who holds power over them. For such a woman to "step up," she must first learn how to handle power enough to be in charge of her own life. Once that is accomplished, she may be able to "step up" again and become more powerful: become heroic. But to make the leap from a submissive role to heroine may be too much to do all at once.

In World War II, women were called on to step up into the role of heroine without having first achieved the independent stage. This was possible because society decided that it needed women to take on these roles. They were recruited by the military and businesses; they did not have to fight their way in. The power still lay with others, with the people who decided to "let" women do these tasks. And so thousands of women went to work in the factories, drove ambulances, flew planes—in other words, did men's work. Yet when the war was over and the returning soldiers needed jobs, these women were told by the same powers to go home and be housewives again. Most of them were obedient and complied. (We must wonder, however, how much their simmering resentment over this treatment fueled the Women's Liberation Movement that burst into flame fifteen years later.)

Thus the protagonists of many women's narratives go apart for a while, by choice or by circumstance, and learn how to free themselves from expected roles. They learn how to become loose women and then take power over their lives one step at a time. Once they are free—once they learn how to be powerful—they rarely seek to remain apart from society or from relationships forever.

Going apart may have another benefit. Once freed from the demands of others, the scope of the heroine's vision can widen beyond relationships and social constructs and become more objective. She does not abandon life for a set of abstract ideals divorced from experience, however. Like the witch, she is able to see clearly, neither entirely removed from what she sees nor unduly swayed by emotion. She sees what needs to be done. And then she can step up and take on the power necessary for being a true heroine.

Elizabeth Gilbert, the author of *Eat Pray Love*, took several months away from her work and a string of failed relationships to sit in meditation in an ashram in India, where she had an epiphanic vision. "Simply put, I got pulled through the wormhole of the Absolute, and in that rush I suddenly understood the workings of the universe completely," she wrote.[14] Her former problems shrank to insignificance in the light of this experience. At the same time, she took a good look at how she had been thinking of herself as a victim instead of taking on the responsibility (power) for her own life. She left the ashram soon after and went on to write and love and marry again—and mount a crusade against unreasonable immigration laws in the United States.

Women who gain this objectivity, this wider view, says Annis Pratt, "are escaping from the moil and toil of female roles and duties but not from the stream of life itself: they participate in an organic mode of mysticism shared with the single women, widows, and women wise in herbs."[15] Women apart may well be engaging even more with life than they did when they spent all their energy living up to the expectations and demands of others.

Once a woman sees the world with a wider vision, she can return to society and relationships on her own terms. A time of reflection allows people to find or create their own philosophy about life, a philosophy that will allow them to act out of heartfelt conviction and love instead of either ego-needs or a barren sense of duty. Once they have such a philosophy, they will be able to stay the course in any situation. More importantly, once a person stops seeing herself (or himself) as powerless, as a victim, she can step up and make a difference.

Speaking Up

A necessary part of taking on one's power is to speak up. For a woman, this often starts by publicly asserting her right to her own opinions and to life on her own terms. One famous literary instance is Elizabeth Bennet's response when Lady Catherine tries to force, by threats and insults, a promise from Elizabeth *not* to accept any proposal from Mr. Darcy. Elizabeth replies,

"I am not to be intimidated into anything so wholly unreason-able. . . . You have widely mistaken my character, if you think I can be worked on by such persuasions as these." Lady Cather-ine's attempt to control the situation doubly backfires, for not only does she force Elizabeth to say what she really thinks, but her report of Elizabeth's words to her nephew gives him the cour-age to propose to Elizabeth again—exactly what Lady Catherine wanted to prevent.

Jane Eyre speaks up again and again. As a child she confronts her aunt for that lady's cruelty to her. Her aunt sends her away to school soon after, but Jane's words haunt her aunt for the rest of her life; and as she lies dying, she sends for Jane and confesses that Jane was right. Jane also asserts her right to live as she will to St. John Rivers, as discussed above. But the most important speech she makes is when she claims equal partnership with Edward Rochester:

> Do you think, because I am poor, obscure, plain, and little, I am soulless and heartless? You think wrong!—I have as much soul as you,—and full as much heart! . . . it is my spirit that addresses your spirit, just as if both had passed through the grave, and we stood at God's feet, equal,—as we are!

Rochester has deliberately provoked this speech. Unlike St. John Rivers, he wants to hear what Jane really thinks. He wants her to speak up; he wants her to claim her rights, including her right to love. Most of all, he wants her to claim him as her equal and her lover.

Middlemarch's Dorothea is not freed by the death of her con-trolling husband. Eliot refuses to stoop to such a simple solu-tion, for she wants to make it clear to the reader that her heroine cannot move on until she finally finds the courage to stand up to her husband's spirit. Casaubon has left instructions for Dorothea to carry on his work in a paper titled, "The Synoptical Tabulation for the use of Mrs. Casaubon." What she wanted from him that he was not willing to give her in life—intellectual partnership—he uses to try to chain her in death. This is too much even for dutiful Dorothea, and she is finally inspired to revolt:

> *The Synoptical Tabulation for the use of Mrs. Casaubon* she carefully enclosed and sealed, writing within the envelope, *"I could not use it. Do you not see now that I could not submit my soul to yours, by working hopelessly at what I have no belief in?"*

For Dorothea, this is a tremendous act of rebellion that frees her to take a new path in life. When she rejects her husband's wishes, she silences the voice in her own head that has been telling her that she has no right to go her own way.

Celie of *The Color Purple* is silent until she falls in love with Shug, a woman who says whatever she feels like to anyone. "Her mouth just pack with claws," Celie marvels. Fiery Shug is an example of a woman who, Perera says, "can be obnoxious, but she speaks her own word, and looks deep inside to find it."[16] The influence of such a woman in her life inspires Celie to find the courage to speak up for herself and defy her abusive husband at last. "I give it to him straight, just like it come to me. And it seem to come to me from the trees."

Celie's words come straight from the forest within, the wild space Shug has helped her to find. After this outburst, Celie leaves with Shug and starts her own business as a clothing designer and seamstress. She does not know it yet, but her truthful words will have a lasting impact and change her husband, too. Once "Mister" stops trying to control Celie and learns to see her as an individual, he too is freed. Those who fear the loss of power are as much slaves to the power structure as those who are dominated by it. They must be forever vigilant for any sign of rebellion. "Mister" finds out that life is a lot easier when he doesn't try to control others, and in time he becomes relaxed, philosophic, useful, and kind.

Teaching

Speaking up often means teaching others. Jill Ker Conway claimed a different kind of house for herself when she accepted the position of president of Smith College, although it meant leaving Toronto, a city she loved. "I'd been pushed out of Australia by family circumstance, the experience of discrimination, frustration with the culture I was born in," she says in *True North*, the second volume of her autobiography; but "nothing was pushing me out of this wonderful setting except a cause, and the hope to serve it."[17] The cause was better education for women. The house was the largest women's college in the United States, which had never before been governed by a woman. In the earliest days of her marriage, Conway had realized that domesticity did not feed her soul and that she "needed the faces of eager students."[18] Her calling was teaching; her true home, a school.

The Prime of Miss Jean Brodie by Muriel Sparks is a novel about a woman whose true calling, one that trumps her own romantic dreams, is teaching girls to become unique and unconventional women. Jean Brodie is herself eccentric and sometimes misled by her own fantasies, but there is no denying that she has a lasting impact on the students she calls "my girls." Miss Brodie's philosophy of teaching is succinct: "The word 'education' comes from the root *e* from *ex*, out, and *duco*, I lead. It means a leading out. To me education is a leading out of what is already there in the pupil's soul." Miss Brodie would agree with James Hillman that each person has a personal *daimon* or soul-purpose that needs encouraging. Her calling was to encourage others to follow their own calling, not to tell them what to think or be, as she saw most teachers doing.

Heroine-teachers like Jean Brodie usually go against the rules to champion their students. Bel Kaufman's Sylvia Barrett of *Up the Down Staircase* is a semi-autobiographical portrait of a dedicated teacher in an inner-city high school. Sylvia often has to bend the rigid rules of the school (such as the one that forbids students to walk up the "down" staircase) to get through to the students. Charlotte Brontë's *Villette* is a fictionalized account of her own days at a school for girls in Brussels. Charlotte eventually returned to the family home, but her heroine prospers as a teacher and starts her own school. In all these novels, a leading theme is the heroine's desire and ability to change the lives of her students for the better through teaching.

The Lute-Playing Queen's Journey

THE RUSSIAN FOLK TALE of "The Lute Player" is, says Allan Chinen, a metaphor for how a married couple might navigate the midlife crisis and reimagine their relationship for their remaining years together.[1]

Once upon a time, there was a kingdom ruled, as kingdoms usually are, by a king. He had a queen, too, but she was given little to do as far as ruling went. Their children were grown and gone, and the kingdom was prospering, but the king was bored. He convinced himself that he had a duty to wage war against a despot he'd heard of who lived far away, so he took his army and off he went! But the despot proved to be a canny general who defeated the king's army and took the king prisoner. The king was forced to labor every day and was treated like the most worthless of slaves.

Eventually, the king managed to get a message to the queen, ordering her to send all the royal treasure to the despot as ransom for the king's freedom. The queen, however, saw many problems with this plan. To send all the treasure would impoverish the kingdom; she knew of no one she could trust to take it other than herself; and yet, if she went herself, she would undoubtedly be captured and forced to become the despot's concubine—or worse.

So she came up with a different plan. She cut off her hair, put on the clothing of one of her pages, took her lute, and sneaked out of the castle through a secret gate, telling no one where she was going. The queen was an accomplished musician (she'd had, after all, a lot of time to practice her music), and so she was able to earn her way to the despot's empire and eventually into his court. The despot was so taken with the music of this young man (as he thought) that he granted the lute player a boon of anything he desired. The disguised queen thanked him and said, "I must return to my own land soon. The boon I wish is to be allowed to choose a companion for my journey from one of your slaves." The despot granted this wish, and, of course, the queen chose her own husband.

But the king did not recognize his wife in her disguise. They traveled for weeks together, and never once did he look closely at the lute player. He saw only what he expected to see; when she spoke, he heard only a boy's voice, not his wife's. Finally they reached their own land and came to the castle. The king entered to much rejoicing from his people. But when he looked for the lute player, the young man had disappeared! In the tumult, the queen had run around to the secret gate, from which she made her way up to her rooms, took off her man's clothes, and put on her royal garments. Then she went down to the court to greet her husband.

When he saw her, the king flew into a rage. "Why did you not send the money to ransom me?" he demanded. Then the courtiers—all quick to join the king in his anger—told him that the queen had mysteriously vanished months ago and not been seen again until this day. At hearing this, the king's rage became volcanic and he accused the queen of faithlessness. Before the guards could seize her, the queen quickly ran back to her own rooms, changed into her disguise, took her lute, and found her way back through the secret gate to the outside of the castle.

There, she sat and played. The rumor of this wonderful new musician soon reached the king's ears, and he realized that his companion was still with him. He ran out to the lute player, took him by the hand, and promised him a permanent place at the court and anything else he might desire as a reward for rescuing the king.

At these words, the queen looked him straight in the eyes and said, "All I have ever desired is you, my husband." The blindness fell from the king's eyes and he realized that his wife had been the one to save him while keeping the fortunes of the realm intact. From then on, the king relied on his wife's wisdom every day in the shared rule of their land.

CHAPTER 13

A New Life

We never know how high we are
Till we are called to rise;
And then, if we are true to plan,
Our statures touch the skies.

—Emily Dickinson

ONCE THE ALETIS has learned who she is and what she can do, she can start to create a life on her own terms. Finally she can stop moving on and settle down in a home that suits her needs. As well, now she is able to create relationships that work.

The Home of One's Own

When Jane Eyre inherits money and reunites with Rochester, almost the first thought in her head is about where they will live. After a life spent moving from place to place, always living in someone else's demesne, she is finally ready to create her own home. Tenar, heroine of the *Earthsea* series, does not want to live with either of her grown children, because she foresees that to do so would leave her forever stuck in the role of mother/grandmother. But she has no other options until her old teacher, Ogion, dies and leaves her a cottage. The fourth book of the series, *Tehanu*, ends as Tenar contemplates the future with her lover Ged:

"Shall we live there?...I have money," she said, "enough to buy a herd of goats."...They would have to replant Ogion's garden right away if they wanted any vegetables of their own this summer. She thought of the rows of beans and the scent of the bean flowers. She thought of the small window that looked west. "I think we can live there," she said.

Building or claiming a home of one's own is the final step in the heroine's journey toward finding a place where she can be herself all the time, in her full power. Tenar moves from housewife to head of the household, while Jane Eyre Rochester shifts from governess to the governing personality in the home.

Beatrix Potter claimed her own home when she moved away from her parents' home in London to Hill Top Farm in the Lake District of England, a farm she bought with money she earned from her books. There she created a life to her own liking where she could pursue both her artistic and scientific interests while living close to nature and animals. When she eventually married, her husband moved into Hill Top Farm; there was no question of Beatrix's leaving her chosen home.

The True Lover

Once the heroine has stepped into her power and asserted her individuality, the right mate for her appears, often seemingly out of the blue. There is no magic at work here. The heroine has become both clear-sighted and choosy. She is able to recognize a good partner, and, when she finally chooses, she chooses well.

When the Aletis turned away from relationships earlier, it was not just a refusal to accept a lesser love than she deserved, but a time out during which she identified and rejected what she did not want. I mentioned earlier the technique in which the artist, instead of drawing the thing itself, traces the contours of the shapes and shadows around the thing until everything else is filled in, leaving a "negative" image. The clearer a woman becomes about what she will not accept, the more an image builds in her mind of what it is she *does* want. When it appears before her, she recognizes it.

The true lover also recognizes the quality of the heroine's soul and the value of what she does in the world. Reading *Persuasion*, we know that Frederick Wentworth is the right mate for Anne Elliot because he sees Anne Elliot's worth. When Louisa Musgrove is injured in a fall while on a visit to Lyme and Wentworth discusses with Louisa's brother who should nurse the comatose girl, he says with feeling, "If Anne will stay, no one so proper, so capable as Anne!" Having said this out loud, Frederick admits to himself that Anne is the only woman he could ever marry and sets out to win her heart, culminating in the famous letter in which he declares to her, "You pierce my soul." It is not her beauty that pierces him to the quick, but her entire self.

The hero *has* to recognize the heroine's worth, or she won't have him. Elizabeth Bennet turns down Mr. Collins because he believes the value is all on his side. Mr. Darcy, who outranks Mr. Collins by every possible measure, knows better. He tells Elizabeth how much he values her opinion, without which he would have gone on being an arrogant and selfish being all his life:

> But for you, dearest, loveliest Elizabeth! What do I not owe you? You taught me a lesson, hard indeed at first, but most advantageous. By you I was properly humbled. I came to you without a doubt of my reception. You showed me how insufficient were all my pretensions to please a woman worthy of being pleased.

Elizabeth's belief in her own value as a person, despite being poorer and of a lower social status, challenges Darcy to look at himself and the precepts by which he has been living. He becomes a wiser man. As he learns how to see himself as he truly is, he also learns to see Elizabeth as she truly is: a woman of great worth.

Relationship as Opportunity

Darcy and Elizabeth both grow as individuals as a result of knowing each other. In many women's narratives, a love relationship transcends the fairy-tale idea of "happily ever after" to become a vehicle for enhanced self-knowledge. Pratt points to Dorothy Richardson (*Pilgrimage*), Gail Godwin (*The Odd Woman*), and May Sarton (*Journal of a Solitude*) as examples of women who learn to see personal relationships "as a step towards the ultimate goal of selfhood."[1]

Elizabeth Gilbert learned the same lesson during her year apart that she chronicles in *Eat Pray Love*. These women come to see that a relationship with another, no matter how happy, is not the ultimate goal; what matters is a good relationship to one's self. But at the same time, a relationship with another person whom one values can be a most effective tool for gaining self-knowledge, as Mr. Darcy would no doubt agree.

This attitude may free a woman to have relationships without ever feeling the need to marry. Actress Katherine Hepburn married once, early on, but realized that she was, essentially, too self-involved to be a wife (as that role was defined at the time). She took a series of lovers instead. When one lover broke off their affair to get married, she was upset, but realized it was her own fault for refusing to marry him. "I was not in the business of capturing anyone into a marriage. I just did not want to marry anyone. I liked the idea of being my own single self."[2] Hepburn later fell in love with Spencer Tracy, and their affair lasted twenty-seven years until his death, but marriage was never on the table.

Jill Ker Conway had a similar attitude toward marriage:

> I wasn't interested in 1950s-style romance. I had long since concluded that marriage was not for me. . . . I seemed to do better navigating under my own steam. I wasn't afraid of being classified an old maid. I'd had deeply fulfilling relationships with lovers who had mattered a great deal to me . . . not wanting to be married didn't preclude close relationships with men.[3]

When she met John Conway, however, she found someone to whom she could reveal the "secret side of my apparently calm self."[4] She accepted his proposal because "it felt *right* to be planning life with this man. . . . The certainty came, not from romantic love, but from the deeper bond between two adults who recognize a true affinity."[5] She married because she believed that she could remain herself with such a husband. The marriage was a happy and mutually supportive one that lasted until John's death thirty-three years later.

Children

One might expect that women writers of fiction would dwell at length on the experiences of pregnancy, giving birth, and raising children. But in fact, while children figure in most women's narratives, they are usually incidental to the plot. Many women writers mention children only as part of the backdrop. Through the nineteenth century, women's narratives often end before the her-oine has a chance to become a mother. We are told at the end of *Jane Eyre* that Jane has children with Rochester and at the end of *Middlemarch* that Dorothea has at least one child with Will Ladi-slaw, but that is all we ever hear of them as mothers.

This apparent omission may reflect women's pragmatic atti-tude toward children. Until the advent of effective birth control in the mid-twentieth century, children were simply a fact of life for most women. Children take a lot of work; women know this. In *Tehanu*, Tenar adopts an abandoned, abused child and has to remind her lover Ged constantly of the simple realities of child-care. His obliviousness causes her to ponder "the indifference of a man towards the exigencies that ruled a woman: that someone must be not far from a sleeping child." Later she snaps at Ged, "Why do you think only of yourself? Always of yourself?" To think only of herself is a luxury a mother never has.

But just as the heroine does not define herself by her relation-ship to a man, neither does she define herself by her relationship to her children. She may be a devoted mother who puts her chil-dren first most of the time, but, in her thoughts, that is simply a fact of life—another reality, like the necessity for food. She takes care of what must be taken care of, but that does not define who she is in her deepest self.

In twentieth-century novels, women often marry and have children in an unconscious state because it is expected of them. When they wake up and leave the marriage, they usually take the children with them because there is no other option. They will not trust the indifferent man with the care of a child. If there is someone else who *can* be trusted, the woman may fly away on her own, as Edna of *The Awakening* does. She loves her children, but she leaves them at her mother-in-law's, where she knows they will be cared for.

In fact, heroines of the women's narratives covered in this book rarely find their true purpose in life through being a mother. Lydia, a happy mother of four in Lynne Sharon Schwartz's *Disturbances in the Field*, spends far more time thinking about her work than she does her children. She takes care of their needs as a matter of course, enjoys their individual characters, and is devastated when two of them are killed in an accident. But her inner life, her soul purpose, is taken up with music.

That does not mean that one cannot be a parent and also follow one's daimon. The fact that many women feel a conflict between the two, but men usually do not, reflects something deeply wrong in society. More than that, the single-minded insistence that all women ought to become mothers may also be detrimental to those women whose inner calling *is* motherhood. What would society be like if only those women and men who deeply desire to be parents actually had children? What if those people were celebrated in the same way that we celebrate excellence in other fields?

Instead, many women become mothers unconsciously, as it were, without ever really thinking about or making any effort to learn what good mothering entails. If they had good role models in their own mothers, this may not be a problem. Nor is it a problem if a new mother is conscious of the need to learn from others how to parent well. But in too many families, poor parenting is passed down like any other familial trait. Abuse runs in families just as alcoholism does.

Fortunately, our society seems to be in the process of recreating and reimagining the archetypes of the Good Mother and the

Good Father. I'm intrigued by how many movies are coming out these days that feature a man whose first priority is being a good father: *The Pursuit of Happyness, Boyz N the Hood, Finding Nemo,* and *Up* are some examples. Tough guys Arnold Schwarzenegger and Duane "The Rock" Johnson have played a kindergarten teacher and a tooth fairy, respectively, in films that show a man learning how to nurture children. Actors who built their careers playing comedic ne'er-do-wells are now taking roles that show a formerly irresponsible man stepping up into the role of husband and father.

I believe that the baby boomer generation consciously took on the tasks, not just of gaining rights for women and people of color, but of bringing light to bear on many of the shadowy aspects of family life. They spoke up about alcoholism, once the "elephant in the room" and a forbidden topic for many families. They spoke up about abuse and incest at home and in the church. Their children have taken this challenge further, addressing other shadow issues such as oppression of gays, lesbians, and transgender people; lack of awareness about the needs of the "differently abled"; and bullying in schools. As we become more aware about the many ways that children have been and still are mistreated, we participate collectively in creating a new archetype: that of the Good Parent.

IDYLL

Ista dy Chalion's Journey

ISTA DY CHALION, *the dowager royina (queen) of Chalion, a mythical land in Lois McMaster Bujold's books* Curse of Chalion *and* Paladin of Souls, *marries into the royal family without knowing that the marriage will bring her under a curse laid upon the entire family. Ista is touched by the gods with the ability to see the curse as a shadow following everyone in the family, as well as the ghosts haunting the castle. But when she tries to tell others about what she sees and what must be done about it, they think her insane. After the death of her husband, she is sent back to live under the care of her mother, essentially imprisoned by well-intentioned people. Eventually the curse also causes the death of her son, despite all her efforts to protect him.*

Even after the curse is lifted and Ista loses her second sight, most of the people around her think of her as "mad Ista." However, the man who has lifted the curse, now Chancellor of Chalion to Ista's daughter, the new royina Iselle, knows that Ista is and always has been sane and only ever spoke the truth. Determined to escape her prison, Ista appeals to the Chancellor and to her daughter to be allowed to make a holy pilgrimage—an excuse to get away and go somewhere, anywhere, else. These allies aid Ista in her desire to flee by sending her new companions who do not think of her as mad or unstable.

Ista revels in her new freedom for a couple of weeks. But then her second sight returns. Ista learns that there is another problem afflicting Chalion—a dangerous influx of demons who possess people and turn them to evil—and that the gods have chosen her as their agent to address this problem. Only too mindful of her prior failure, Ista fights and protests her destiny for a while, but finally accepts the mantle and the gifts that allow her to lift the demons from others' souls. When she does this, her own soul, so long tormented by the past, is healed. Ista never returns to her old home. She finds love and goes on to do useful work in the world.

CHAPTER 14

Creativity

The process of thinking for oneself, finding one's voice, creating authentic work, is usually a complicated one for women.

—Patricia Reis

MANY A HEROINE of women's narratives finds her true life work and creativity after she frees herself from the claims of others or the expectations of society. This freedom means her imagination can now soar. And often, her creative urge turns out to be exactly what society needs.

In the last chapter, I talked about how teaching is one way that women transform the world. As more and more areas of endeavor are opened to women, we are seeing women put their unique stamp on other careers. It's been an uphill battle all the way. Women have traditionally had too many other calls on their time and have not been provided with the sort of support that creative men can expect to rely on. Women who do manage a creative life usually either have very supportive spouses or choose to live alone and not have children so that they can devote themselves to their work.

Many studies have been done and essays written on the issue of whether women are as capable as men in the professions or creative fields like art and music. As I read these arguments, one finding leapt out at me: people will work harder if they believe their work will be recognized and valued. Until recently this has simply not been the case for women in most fields of endeavor, just as it has not been the case for minorities. The knowledge that no recognition may be forthcoming no matter how good one's work is can be enough to prevent a person from even trying. For one thing, most of us cannot afford it. Why spend the years and money required to become good at something if you'll never be rewarded for doing it?

The woman whose sense of an inner calling is so strong that it pushes her to keep working toward achieving her dreams despite lack of support and recognition is still a rare bird. One has to wonder just how history would be different if more talented women had been encouraged to develop their gifts. Here again, women authors have been ahead of the curve of social trends in imagining how a woman might include creativity in her life.

The Handless Maiden

The story of the girl without hands is found in many cultures. How the girl comes to lose her hands varies. In some versions, she cuts them off herself to make herself repellent to her father or her brothers and thus avoid their unwanted sexual advances. In other versions, her father has made a bargain with the devil whereby he will be made rich in exchange for his daughter. But the girl is so pure that the devil can't come near her. To prevent her from cleaning herself, the father chops off her hands (in some stories, of his own volition; in others, the devil makes him do it). But her tears wash her clean and the devil is still unable to take her. After this terrible event she wanders out into the forest by herself, where she meets a king who falls in love with her and makes silver hands for her to wear. More complications follow, but eventually either her hands regrow on their own or the silver hands turn into real ones.

Robert Johnson, a Jungian psychologist who writes beautifully clear books about the psychology of men and women, wrote extensively about the story of the Handless Maiden in *The Fisher King and the Handless Maiden*. He sees the story as a metaphor for how both men and women can get cut off from their own true feelings.[1] Clarissa Pinkola Estés devotes an entire section of her book to the story. She finds many layers of meanings in it, including how women can be severed from their own wisdom and power.[2]

I have a different take on the story. For many years, I made my living as a science writer. This career required me to be very much in my left brain most of the time. Shortly before I quit this work to go back to school for my doctorate, I had a dream that terrified me. In the dream, I was walking down a trail when I came across what at first appeared to be a sculpture of three hands, severed at the wrists and with blood coming from the stumps. But then the hands moved, walking on their fingers, and I realized in the dream that they were still alive. "Who has done this awful thing?" I cried out, and woke, but I could not shake the image of the bleeding, severed hands. I took the dream to a Jungian analyst, but she refused to interpret it for me. "It's too personal," she said. "You have to figure out what it means for yourself."

In my first quarter at school, I took a class on dream interpretation where we read James Hillman's *The Dream and the Underworld*. Hillman is not a proponent of "interpreting" dreams;

instead, he suggests that one simply sit with the image exactly as it appeared in the dream.[3] (Hillman once famously gave a lecture on dream interpretation in which he said only, "If you dream about a dog, stay with the dog," and sat down again.) In my class, we were assigned to pick a dream image of ours and work with it in any way that seemed right to us. I thought of the severed hands, and the idea came to me to make a sculpture of the image. The terror I had felt whenever I thought of the image immediately dissipated. Instead, the time that I spent working on this sculpture was filled with joy.

The sculpture took a month to complete. About halfway through, I felt compelled to stop working on it and take time to make beaded bracelets for everyone in the class. When I finally finished the sculpture, I realized what the dream meant. I had become cut off from my creativity, from work done with the hands. Even the writing I did was directed by other people. The bracelets I had made—which go around the wrists—were my way of reconnecting the hands. Once I "connected" the images with what was going on in my life, I could write what *I* wanted to say.

As the preceding idyll relates, Ista, the heroine of Lois McMaster Bujold's *Paladin of Souls*, has been powerless for years because of a curse that she walked into, all unknowing, as an innocent young maiden. But at midlife she rediscovers her own spiritual gifts, which she uses by touching others with her "spirit hands"— hands that no one else can see but that have great power to heal.

The recent animated film *Frozen*, a retelling of the Hans Christian Anderson story "The Snow Queen," features a princess who has a strange power: she can create snow and frost through her hands. Her younger sister loves this power and encourages the princess to use it, but her parents are terrified that she will only cause harm. They lock her away from others, including her sister, and teach her to fear her own power. They make her wear gloves all the time, turning her into a Handless Maiden.

When the king and queen are drowned on a voyage, the ice princess becomes queen. At her coronation, she must take off the gloves. As she fears, her power immediately manifests. Because she has never learned how to embrace and manage this power, she is helpless to stop herself and brings eternal winter down on the kingdom. It is only after she learns from her innocent, non-judgmental sister how to wield her power with love instead of fear that she can harness it and put it to good use.

How many people (women and men alike) are Handless Maidens, cut off from their creative power by fear? In the Aletis story, the heroine learns to reconnect her hands and be the creative person she is meant to be.

Weaving

One common motif in folk tales is the woman as a weaver or seamstress. The old weaver woman shows up in Native American stories about Spider Woman, the Creator. We see her in the Egyptian goddess Neith, goddess of war and weaving, and her Greek counterpart, Athena. The Greeks also tell of the Three Fates, three old women who spin the lives of humans. In Mayan mythology, the goddess Ixchel, whose domains include birth and healing, is depicted with weaving instruments in her headdress. All these goddesses wield the power of making and unmaking, of birth and death.

Vasilisa, returned from the forest and free of the restraints put on her by her stepmother and stepsisters, moves in with a kind old woman in the town and begins spinning and weaving the finest linen cloth ever seen. The old woman brings the wondrous cloth to the attention of the tsar, who recognizes its uniqueness at once. Primed to see clearly by the cloth, when he meets Vasilisa, he immediately sees her worth (as a real prince would) and makes her his tsarina.

Celie finds her true calling through sewing as well. "I sit in the dining room making pants after pants. I got pants now in every color and size under the sun. I ain't been able to stop." Pants are unisex clothes. For Celie, they represent her shift from life as a drudge wearing a "house dress" to a free woman who steps with confidence in the world. She wants to share that freedom with everyone—women, men, children. Each pair of pants she makes is unique and exactly right for the individual who wears them. Her passion grows into a successful business, and Celie becomes the center of a thriving and happy family.

Weaving, spinning, and sewing are powerful metaphors in women's narratives. Such activities are not just creative. Instead, they "refine and shape what is considered crude, unaesthetic, and unserviceable. As such, they may also be viewed as transformation rituals," says Bettina Knapp in *Women in Myth*.[4] The heroine learns from the witch how to sort out the materials available to her, but it is her own creativity she uses when she takes those materials and makes them into something meaningful.

The unnamed sister in the fairy tale "The Six Swans" spends six years sewing shirts that magically restore her brothers—turned into swans by their stepmother—to human form. In folk tales, Maria Tatar notes, "spinning, weaving, and sewing . . . appear to have the power to turn animals into men and to domesticate the ferocious beasts."[5] Sometimes men themselves are the beasts women domesticate. For example, Celie manages to weave her husband back into her life as a friend who respects and understands her and as a creative partner who designs and sews shirts to go with her marvelous pants. Her power to transform another person is reflected in a conversation she holds with "Mister" near the end of the book. "Mister" begins:

> If you ast yourself why you black or a man or a woman or a bush it don't mean nothing if you don't ast why you here, period.
>   So what you think? I ast.
>   I think us here to wonder, myself. To wonder. To ast. And that in wondering bout the big things and asting bout the big things, you learn about the little ones, almost by accident. . . . The more I wonder, he say, the more I love.
>   And people start to love you back, I bet, I say.

"Mister," by working in partnership with Celie instead of trying to dominate her, learns from her not just how to be creative but how to take a wider, less personal view of the world.

Art

Art historian Griselda Pollock, coauthor of *Old Mistresses: Women, Art, and Ideology*, laments that when it comes to artists, "The image in the West [is] of a lonely, tortured white man. I could run rings around you with great women artists but there isn't space in the cultural imagination."[6] This lack of space in the imagination cannot be due to a lack of images provided for us in women's stories, however. For instance, in *To the Lighthouse*, Virginia Woolf gives us a portrait of her sister Vanessa Bell, an artist, in the character of Lily Briscoe. Lily is devoted to painting but has to struggle against criticism from both men and women who do not take her seriously.

Although she teaches for a living, at heart Jane Eyre is an artist. She is frustrated with her inability to put the visions of her "spiritual eye" down on paper and considers the results "but a pale portrait of the thing I had conceived." But Rochester sees past her lack of training, understands what she is trying to convey, and is impressed. He asks Jane if she was happy when she painted the pictures and if she was caught up in her painting so much that she sat for a long time at each—a precise description of the experience psychologist Mihaly Csikszentmihalyi calls "flow." In an interview by John Gierland for *Wired* magazine, Csikszentmihalyi described "flow" more fully as:

> . . . being completely involved in an activity for its own sake. The ego falls away. Time flies. Every action, movement, and thought follows inevitably from the previous one, like playing jazz. Your whole being is involved, and you're using your skills to the utmost.[7]

Rochester calls this state of flow the "artist's dream." He doesn't just understand what it means to be an artist; he sees that Jane has the potential to be one. We know he is the right mate for her, as the tsar is for Vasilisa, because he sees value in her work.

Helen of *The Tenant of Wildfell Hall* is also an artist. Before she marries, Helen creates a painting that conveys the inner wilderness of a girl who has not yet been disillusioned by life:

> By the bright azure of the sky, and by the warm and brilliant lights, and deep, long shadows, I had endeavoured to convey the idea of a sunny morning. I had ventured to give more of the bright verdure of spring or early summer to the grass and

foliage, than is commonly attempted in painting. The scene represented was an open glade in a wood . . . in the foreground, were part of the gnarled trunk and of the spreading boughs of a large forest tree . . . beneath it, a young girl was kneeling on the daisy-spangled turf, with head thrown back and masses of fair hair falling on her shoulders, her hands clasped, lips parted, and eye intently gazing upward . . .

Helen considers this piece "my masterpiece." After she succeeds in escaping from her abusive husband, Helen's ability to paint beautiful landscapes enables her to earn a living. Her gift also impresses Gilbert Markham, who eventually proves himself worthy of her heart, in part because he both admires her work and plays with her child while she works, taking on the role of parent so she can take on the role of artist.

Writing

As I explored the themes of creativity in women's fiction, I was struck by how few women writers create heroines who are writers, too. For instance, Mary Stewart, who made a specialty of thrillers starring heroines before writing the award-winning *Crystal Cave* series about Merlin, gives every one of her protagonists a different profession, from actress to veterinarian—but only one of them writes. However, two of them fall in love with men who write, and Stewart tells us through *those* characters something about the writing process. In Ursula Le Guin's novels, she imagines women characters who are farmers, doctors, diplomats, electricians—even dragons—but again, no writers. Anna Wulf in *The Golden Notebook* publishes one successful novel but comes to despise her own work. She determines that she is not, in fact, capable of writing the kind of novel she herself would want to read, and she never writes another.

Women have no trouble talking about life as a writer in non-fiction works; I have a shelf full of works by women authors on the writing process. But most of them caution that one must edit out the thing you love. Perhaps women who have succeeded at making a life as writers love writing too much to write about it in fiction. It may lie too close to the heart for them to expose it to just anyone.

Or perhaps, women writers are more concerned with saying what it's like to be a woman, or to be a particular kind of woman. For instance, Octavia Butler, author of many award-winning science fiction novels, said when interviewed by the *New York Times*:

> When I began writing science fiction, when I began reading, heck, I wasn't in any of this stuff I read. I certainly wasn't in the science fiction. The only black people you found were occasional characters or characters who were so feeble-witted they couldn't manage anything anyway. I wrote myself in, since I'm me and I'm here and I'm writing. I can write my own stories and I can write myself in.[8]

The heroine of Butler's *The Parable of the Sower* is a young black woman. Butler couldn't find a heroine she could relate to in the science fiction she loved, so she wrote one. By this act she not only created a role model for other young black women but also got to say to her readers, "*This* is what a black woman is like." Like Lady Wroth had done four hundred years before, she broke new ground when she wrote a character like herself.

Writing a character like oneself raises the risk of the "Mary Sue" problem. A Mary Sue is a heroine who is an idealized portrait of the author herself. The term came out of fan fiction—fiction written by fans of shows or books where they imagine new adventures for the characters invented by the original authors. Many of these secondary authors inserted themselves into the stories as characters who either become love objects for the original characters or are accepted as part of the team after they perform a heroic deed or demonstrate amazing powers. Thus, most Mary Sue characters represent a kind of wish fulfillment figure that good writers try to avoid. (Few people seem concerned about whether men write wish-fulfillment characters, too; Tom Robbins, for one, wrote himself into *Even Cowgirls Get the Blues* as a "Dr. Robbins" who has sex with some of the characters.)

Dorothy Sayers, who wrote murder mysteries starring the noble and eccentric Lord Peter Wimsey as a brilliant amateur detective, inserted someone very much like herself into her stories in the figure of Harriet Vane. Harriet resembles Dorothy physically; she attended Oxford University where she sang contralto in the Bach choir just as Dorothy had; she had an affair out of wedlock as Dorothy had; and she writes murder mysteries like her creator did. Lord Peter, until then a man-about-town with a penchant for Italian sopranos, falls in love with Harriet at first sight, pursues her for three books, and marries her in the fourth.

Elizabeth Trembley argues that both Dorothy and Harriet are "father's daughters" who struggled with feeling androgynous in a society that requires people to be either all male or all female. (Harriet's father has the same name and the same profession as Dorothy's.) She believes that Sayers wrote the Harriet Vane books as an attempt to resolve her own sense of being a fish out of water in her own culture.[9]

Perhaps Sayers, having invented the man in the first place,

could not imagine a better partner for Lord Peter than herself. But I suspect that what she was really after was trying to imagine a marriage that would allow her both romantic fulfillment and the opportunity to keep her identity as a writer. What better spouse for a murder mystery author than a detective? Also, Harriet is not idealized; she has many faults, including pride and a tendency to project hidden motives to others' actions. Thus, Harriet is more than a Mary Sue—she is the means by which Sayers takes a critical look at her own life. To write such a character requires tremendous honesty and the courage to reveal a great deal about oneself.

This is also the case with Sybylla, the semi-autobiographical lead character of Miles Franklin's *My Brilliant Career*, written when Franklin was in her late teens. Two themes dominate the book: Sybylla's anger at her life that prevents her from following her own passion and her determination to write, nonetheless. But she also wonders, "Why do I write? For what does anyone write? Shall I get a hearing? If so—what then?" In fact, Franklin was supported in her aims by two mentors, a sympathetic teacher and the editor of the local paper who thought her writing held great promise. But what Franklin gives us in this first early novel is a portrait of an emotional adolescent who can only see the obstacles in her path and has not yet learned patience and perspective.

The Aletis story is not, after all, a story about what it means to be a creative person in a particular medium, although we may find out about that through the character. In the end, the Aletis story is about how a woman gets in touch with her true, creative self and learns to express that self in the world.

Merida's Journey

BRENDA CHAPMAN'S 2012 *animated movie* Brave *provides a perfect example both of the Aletis story and of the transformative power of the queen. The young princess Merida hates the restrictions put on her by her community, which expects her to do nothing more than look pretty and be married off as a prize to the most deserving of the clans' scions. Merida escapes into the forest every chance she gets, where she practices shooting arrows as she races through the trees on a horse. When the time comes for her to be "won," she stipulates that the competition be an archery contest, stands up to compete for her own hand, and wins.*

But instead of winning Merida the right to self-determination, her actions bring the kingdom to the brink of war. Her community has no framework through which it can understand the idea of a princess who wants to go her own way. As the men square off against each other in the castle hall, a desperate Merida flees into the woods. There she meets a witch who promises her a potion that will "change" her mother, the queen—the person Merida blames most for her problems.

Merida returns to the castle and tricks her mother into eating a cake made with the potion. The potion does change the queen, but it changes her body, not her mind. Merida's mother becomes a bear. To protect her mother from being killed, Merida runs away with her into the forest once again. There, in that wild place, her mother comes to see Merida's unique qualities, while Merida learns to appreciate her mother's strength and wisdom. She remembers that, while her mother rarely intervened in affairs at court, on the few occasions when the queen did stand up and walk slowly and calmly into the center of the hall, all the men would fall silent and listen to her. Merida realizes that her mother does have power of a very different kind than that of the loud, posturing males at court.

Following her mother's example, Merida returns to the castle and, her head held high, marches into the midst of the arguing clans. They fall silent at the sight of her. Now that she has their attention, she makes her case for the right to choose when and whom she will marry. Although she is arguing with the clan lairds, it is their sons—those of her own generation who also chafe under the old rules—who hear and agree with her and then appeal to their fathers for a new way of doing things. The lairds give in and war is averted. Merida has learned how to call upon the power of the queen and use it to transform her community.

CHAPTER 15

Transforming the World

You change the world by being yourself.
—Yoko Ono

IN CHAPTER 3, I touched on how women who have found their power act in the world: neither passively observing nor aggressively trying to enforce change but, instead, acting in a way that honors the process and enables transformation at the right and perfect moment. In this chapter, I expand on the specific ways that heroines of women's stories act to transform the world.

Sovereignty

Earlier I said that I wanted a fourth archetypal image to add to the Maiden, the Mother, and the Crone. We need an image that represents a woman in the full flower of life and her Self. Just as the heroine's story has always been before us, so has the image of a woman as her sovereign self not in relationship to others—the queen.

Ultimately, many heroines of women's narratives become queens or rule in other ways. This is not fantasy; we have only to look at history for the stories of queens Elizabeth I and II, Catherine the Great, Indira Gandhi, Margaret Thatcher, or Hillary Clinton, to name just a few women who have wielded great power. Knowing about them, we have no trouble believing that the tsarina Vasilisa or Mrs. Elizabeth Darcy, mistress of Pemberley, were fair and wise rulers of their domains.

The queen is a woman who has sovereignty, the right of self-governance. A heroine may also grant sovereignty to her mate so that he becomes a better and wiser man. In the Celtic

---

GAWAIN AND RAGNALL

Once upon a time, King Arthur found himself in a quandary: unless he could answer the question "what do women want?" he would have to let a fearsome giant chop off his head. Arthur had no idea how to answer this question, and neither did the men in his court. Gawain, first and best of the knights, suggested that Arthur ask the old wise women of the villages for the answer.

After many months, Arthur came across Ragnall, the ugliest woman he'd ever seen. "I know the answer," she told the king. "But my price is this: you must marry me to Gawain."

Desperate, Arthur agreed. "Women want sovereignty," Ragnall told him. "They want to determine their own lives." This was the right answer, and the giant let Arthur live.

Arthur returned to Camelot with the hideous woman. The court was horrified, but Gawain said that the king's promise must be honored and married her. In their bedroom, Ragnall told Gawain to kiss her. He did, and she turned into a beautiful maiden! "Now you must choose," she said. "I can be lovely at night when we are alone, or by day when others can see me."

"I can't decide that," replied Gawain. "It must be your choice." Ragnall smiled and said, "Because you gave me sovereignty, I will be beautiful both day and night." Gawain, the Knight of the Goddess, understands that all women require sovereignty.

and Russian traditions, the goddess *was* the land, and only a man who respected and honored her would be chosen as her mate and thereby become the king. The term *sovereignty* in Celtic tradition referred both to the queen or goddess of the land *and* to the rule over the land that the king gained after he wed that queen.

The queen is the model for the yang woman discussed in chapter 3. But what about the *yin* woman, the woman who does not wish for a leading role and prefers to work like the yin man does, as the power behind the throne? Dorothea of *Middlemarch* inspires a man—Will Ladislaw, who until he met Dorothea had drifted through life with little sense of purpose—to do the good in the world she herself is not allowed to accomplish. Eliot cannot imagine a different life for her heroine, "for there is no creature whose inward being is so strong that it is not greatly determined by what lies outside it." The constraints of Victorian England are too much for gentle, well-intentioned Dorothea. Still, Eliot suggests in the final sentence of the book "that things are not so ill with you and me as they might have been, is half owing to the number who lived faithfully a hidden life, and rest in unvisited tombs." Without Dorothea, Will would not have turned his life to good account and helped others.

Eliot invites us to imagine how many other great men have had a great wife or mother or sister standing in the shadows behind them. We already have names for this type of yin woman. Some call her the muse; some, a "helpmeet"; Jungians often refer to her as an "anima woman" who facilitates a man's connection to his own *anima* (which, after all, means "soul").

Toni Wolff, Jung's long-time lover and associate who inspired Jung's ideas of personality types, presents her own ideas of female archetypes in her essay, "Structural Forms of the Female Psyche."

She posits that women's personalities fall into four major categories: *the Mother* and *the Hetaira,* whose primary focus is relationship to others; and *the Amazon* and *the Medial Woman,* who seek power in their own right.[1] (The Amazon competes directly with men in the professional world; the Medial Woman offers spiritual guidance.) The Mother and the Hetaira are yin types who either serve others or inspire them, respectively. We see the Amazon in the many powerful women in politics or business today and the Medial Woman in figures like Mother Teresa and Ammaji, the "hugging saint" of India.

Like Gawain, the First Knight who is the king's right arm and best and wisest counselor, we also have the model of the First Lady, wife of the President, who provides a role model of grace, wisdom, and compassion while inspiring others to do their best. She too is a sovereign, and the power she wields, even if not always obvious, can be considerable.

Yet the ultimate outcome, I hope, will be that we move past all labels. Instead of trying to put people in boxes, we will get to the point where each person is free to be the unique person they are meant to be, with sovereignty over their own lives. When we try to describe such people, a single label will not suffice for the scope and breadth of their abilities, knowledge, and accomplishments.

Transforming Communities

The power of women to transform others and, through them, society is gaining new recognition today as people look at the ramifications of the late-twentieth-century influx of women into the workplace. For example, Cristian Dezso and David Gaddis Ross recently conducted a study finding that companies who had women in top management roles out-performed companies that did not.[2] In their 2013 book *The Athena Doctrine,* John Gerzema and Michael D'Antonio report on their survey of over sixty-four thousand business people around the world; they found that the feminine traits of "collaboration, transparency, inclusion, mentoring, and innovation" are the traits most valued these days by business leaders.[3] These are the weapons of the transformers.

One example of such a transformative woman at work is social activist Lynne Twist, author of *The Soul of Money.* After years spent trying to eradicate hunger in Third World countries, Twist realized that simply throwing money at the problem did nothing to change it; in fact, it tended to create feelings of dependency and helplessness in the people being "helped." Instead, she asked people living in hardship conditions to imagine what *they* could do to change things if they had everything they needed. The results were astounding: people came up with innovative ideas that required very little in the way of equipment or startup monies and were self-sustaining. But more than that, because they were solving the problem themselves, the people gained self-confidence and felt far more positive about the future. Communities pulled together and came up with even more ideas—and reached out to other communities to teach them how to create positive visions for the future and act upon them.[4] Twist's example gives credence to Estés's claim that "a single creative act has the potential to feed a continent."[5]

Charles Dickens created a beautiful example of an Aletis in the character of Lizzie Hexam in *Our Mutual Friend.* At first glance Lizzie seems like a typical Dickensian heroine: beautiful and submissive to others, with never a thought for herself. But then the refusals begin. First, Lizzie enables her brother Charlie to escape from their father's iron grip so that Charlie can follow his destiny of becoming a teacher—something he can never do while living at home, as their father is strongly opposed to education or seeking to better oneself. After the father dies, Lizzie upsets both the local community and Charlie by choosing to live with a crippled girl, Jenny Wren, who sews clothes for dolls, instead of accepting the helping hand held out to her by the reigning matriarch of the neighborhood. Lizzie then refuses to marry her brother's mentor, Bradley Headstone, despite Charlie's threat that he will shun her in the future if she does not. She is devastated when Charlie makes good on his threat, but she will not marry to please him.

Lizzie has a secret. She has fallen in love with a man from a higher level of society, Eugene Wrayburn, a charming ne'er-do-well. But she also defies Eugene. She knows that he does not intend to marry her; like Jane Eyre, she refuses to sink to becoming someone's mistress. She also fears that Bradley Headstone suspects her secret and may harm Eugene to remove his rival. Like Jane, she flees into the country. But both men follow her. Eugene finds her first and presses his suit, not knowing that Bradley lurks close by and hears all they say. A desperate Lizzie makes the situation clear to him:

> You will drive me away. I live here peacefully and respected, and I am well employed here. You will force me to quit this place as I quitted London, and—by following me again—will force me to quit the next place in which I may find refuge, as I quitted this.

The unrepentant Eugene forces her to admit she loves him but eventually promises to try to leave her alone. He wanders along the river as the sun sets and for the first time examines his own soul. Then Bradley appears and in a jealous rage beats Eugene nearly to death. Lizzie hears the splash when Bradley throws Eugene's body into the river. She rescues Eugene and sits by his bedside as his friends gather in what they think is a deathbed vigil.

Buoyed by Lizzie's love, Eugene surprises them all and recovers. He vows to become a better man. He defies society in his turn to marry Lizzie and becomes a dedicated lawyer and advocate. His best friend, Mortimer, follows his example and also becomes a worthy man. Lizzie's crippled friend, Jenny, finds a husband of her own—a man who ignores her disability and sees her inner beauty and appreciates her artistry (the first thing he does for her is make her a cabinet to hold her supplies). Lizzie's example also inspires the selfish and avaricious Bella Wilfer to soften and let herself love the social nobody—the "mutual friend"—who loves her. (In typical Dickens fashion, her frog turns out to be a wealthy prince of a man.) Thus, all the people around Lizzie are transformed by her courage and refusal to be anyone other than herself.

Leaving a Legacy

The heroine finds her true work, presents herself to society again through this work, and often transforms that society. When she dies, she leaves behind a legacy.

Beatrix Potter is famous primarily for her illustrated books, but her real passion in life was science. Once she was free to follow that passion, she became interested in breeding sheep and worked hard to preserve and improve the stock of the native Hardwick sheep of the Lake District. Through this work she earned the respect of the other breeders in the area. Eventually, the role of advocacy fell to her; as she said, "I am the only person who could have written about the sheep, for I know them and the fell like a shepherd; but the Hardwick men are not articulate."[6] In 1942, she became the first woman president-elect of the local breeders' association (sadly, she died before she could take office). She left four thousand acres of land in the Lake District to the National Trust for preservation. Hardwick sheep still graze those hills.

In Miles Franklin's case, the answer to the "what then?" she asked at the end of *My Brilliant Career* far exceeded her hopes. Although she had to work as a nurse, a housemaid, and a secretary for many years to make a living, she continued to write and be published and eventually became able to support herself through writing. Her 1936 novel, *All That Swagger*, is considered her masterpiece; she was nominated for the Order of the British Empire the next year but declined the honor. Franklin helped shape the emerging field of Australian literature by mentoring young authors. In her will, she established an annual prize for Australian authors. The Canberra suburb of Franklin is named after her.

Anthropologist Margaret Mead had a lasting effect not just on her field but on Western society. Her reports on attitudes toward sex in the South Pacific are credited with helping spur the sexual revolution of the 1960s in North America and Europe. After her death, President Jimmy Carter awarded her with the Presidential Medal of Freedom; the citation presented to her daughters with the medal reads in part:

Margaret Mead was both a student of civilization and an exemplar of it. To a public of millions, she brought the central insight of cultural anthropology: that varying cultural patterns express an underlying human unity. She mastered her discipline, but she also transcended it. Intrepid, independent, plain spoken, fearless, she remains a model for the young and a teacher from whom all may learn.[7]

Mead also left us with this thought: "Never doubt that a small group of committed people can change the world. Indeed, it is the only thing that ever has."[8]

→ ←

This book is already out of date. The works I focus on were written in the twentieth century or before. We are living in different times now, and new stories are already being told. So what's next?

Transforming Gender Identities

I believe we are in the middle of a major transformation in our cultural definitions of masculine and feminine. These definitions have proved to be too rigid and limiting, not just for women but for men as well. These ideas came into being over centuries, and it will take centuries for them to change, but the process is already well on its way. While women have been making progress toward sovereignty for the last century, men have also been rethinking their roles. In books, movies, and television, we can see many examples of yin males breaking free of their former "sidekick" status and stealing the show away from the hero.

This book focuses on the journey that many women take and

write about; it was beyond the scope of this work to look also at how many men might follow a similar journey, and I also feel that a man should do that work. However, as I thought about it, I realized that many of the male partners of the heroines in the books I read do, in fact, follow a similar story arc. They, too, have difficult parents or no parents; they often must defy those difficult parents and go out into the world to find their own way; and, at the end, they often find a new home and a new career. Edward Rochester, Edward Ferrars, Eugene Wrayburn, Will Ladislaw, Frederick Wentworth, Faramir, and Ged are all examples of heroes who do not "return home" in the end but go on to new lives at the side of the Aletis.

There are clues that the heroic quest story is morphing in this direction. George Lucas, the writer and director of the *Star Wars* movies, deliberately based the first three films on the motifs of the heroic quest outlined by Campbell. Yet the young hero Luke Skywalker does not in fact follow the pattern to the end. Like the Aletis, he never returns home; he claims no throne and does not marry the princess (a good thing, as she turns out to be his sister). Instead, he wanders from planet to planet before he finally learns how to be fully himself as a Jedi master. In the recent *Thor: The Dark World* movie, Thor defeats the big bad guy and wins the right to return home and replace his father as king of Asgard. But he rejects the throne, opting instead to follow his heart's desire to Earth so he can be with the woman he loves and do his best to be a "good man." I am curious to see how this trend plays out. Will both the heroic quest and the heroine's journey stories become obsolete, or are they moving toward each other, morphing into a new story in which gender is irrelevant?

Forming New Partnerships

The hero of the Aletis story is a man who recognizes the value of partnership with the right woman; the man who can and wishes to embrace the feminine both within himself and in another person. Perhaps we are spiraling back to the idea that the ultimate goal is marriage with the *other*, the formerly disavowed or unappreciated self; but this time we are coming to it with the goal that both people are able to be fully themselves both in the world and in the relationship. In other words: true partners.

I have watched with great interest the trend, over the last few decades, of pairing a scientific-minded woman with an emotional or intuitive man in TV shows and movies. The iconic example is the partnership of Dana Scully, the skeptical medical examiner, and "I believe in UFOs" researcher Fox Mulder in *The X-Files*. Such a pairing quickly became a television trope and led to similar couples being cast in procedural dramas. In *Bones*, forensic anthropologist Temperance Brennan believes only in that which can be proved by empirical evidence, which often puts her at odds with FBI agent Seeley Booth's openness to concepts like faith and God. In *NCIS*, Special Agent Jethro Gibbs relies primarily on his intuition to solve cases but knows he needs the backing of the hard evidence provided by his forensic specialist, Abby Sciuto.

A variation on this theme is the no-nonsense policewoman who pairs up with an intuitive man. In the series *Castle*, detective Kate Beckett at first pooh-poohs but eventually comes to depend on the insights of novelist Rick Castle, who knows how stories work. Another show, *Perception*, pairs a female FBI agent with a professor of neuropsychiatry who is himself schizophrenic and has hallucinations—which often point out to him the things that both the agent and his own logical, conscious mind have missed.

Recent science fiction shows also like to give us a gentle man who falls in love with a strong, focused warrior woman. In *Farscape*, astronaut John Crichton falls for the fierce Peacekeeper soldier Aeryn Sun; reluctant warrior Lee "Apollo" Adama loves strong-willed Kara "Starbuck" Thrace in *Battlestar Galactica*; and happy-go-lucky starship pilot Hoban "Wash" Washburne marries former rebel soldier Zoe Alleyne in *Firefly*. In each case the woman helps the man become more of a hero, while he teaches her how to be more empathetic and trust her feelings.

Movies also often pair the no-nonsense or scientific woman with an action hero. *The Avengers* series of movies give us not one but three examples: The Hulk and Betty Ross, who in the latest *Hulk* movie is a professor of cell biology; "Iron Man" Tony Stark, who is balanced by his logical and efficient personal assistant-turned-lover Pepper Potts; and the warrior god Thor, who loves Jane Foster, an astrophysicist. In these cases, the heroes are all physically strong men who rely on their strength and tend to act on impulse; the women help curb their initial impulses and get them to *think*.

And the Story Continues

Hopefully, the Aletis story will not need to be told much longer—at least, not in mainstream Western culture. Instead, we will see more and more stories about real heroines: women who have sovereignty over their own lives already and so can step up to be heroic in the full sense of the word, fighting on behalf of others. And as our world becomes more of a global community, we will hear more and more stories about women breaking free from and transforming oppressive cultures.

A revolution is already underway in Hollywood. As Lena Headey, who played Queen Gorgo of Sparta in the *300* movies and Queen Cersei in "Game of Thrones" on HBO, put it in a recent interview:

> Women are now being allowed to be written as interesting characters . . . the TV world is kind of leading it . . . all these great shows with incredibly fascinating female characters who were in positions of strength and leading storylines and holding stories. I feel like people are [realizing that] women are interesting and can be . . . crazy and ugly and mean and all the things that men have been celebrated as being. It's now becoming allowed for us, which is a [expletive] relief, because who wants to be the pretty lady sitting on a sofa?[9]

Popular culture is also reexamining the yin female with shows like "The Good Wife" and "Scandal," in which women who occupy traditional roles as wives or mistresses are, while still remaining in their relationships, exploring their own strength and ways to express themselves in the world.

I am also heartened by the recent trend in books, television shows, and films to reclaim or redeem the darkened feminine. Gregory Maguire's *Wicked* tells the story of the Wicked Witch of the Oz stories from the witch's perspective, and his *Confessions of an Ugly Stepsister* does the same for the stepsister of Cinderella. The Disney animated movie *Frozen* casts a sympathetic eye on Hans Christian Andersen's Snow Queen, while the live-action *Maleficent* tells us what had happened to the witch of the Sleeping Beauty story that made her the way she is. The television series *Once Upon a Time* shows us the backstory of Snow White's stepmother Regina—a woman who longed for the love of her husband but realized in time that his heart was given entirely to his daughter. No Mrs. Bennet, Regina refuses to sink into obscurity and instead seeks out power, which she misuses until her heart is redeemed through her love for Snow White's grandson. All of these works invite us to sympathize with and understand the Ereshkigals around us instead of condemning them for refusing to stay in the shadows any more.

The hero's quest story tells how a boy becomes a mature man. In the final stages of the quest, the hero meets and marries the princess or goddess. She is his reward and the proof that he is ready to step into the role of king and father. She is important because of the role she plays in the hero's life as a metaphor, a symbol of his own neglected feminine aspects. She is not a person in her own right, and we know almost nothing about her. How did she get there? What journey did *she* take to become the partner of the hero?

Yet the heroine's story has always been before our eyes. When we look at the tales women themselves tell, the stories women have always told, her story is there. Her story is convoluted, spiraling in and out of the forest, away from home and on to new households. The story is not linear, nor does it always follow the same series of events. A particular character or motif may appear early in one woman's childhood but not until later life in another's. Because the heroine's main task is to define herself regardless of what attitudes society may hold about women, the challenges she faces are different in every era. There is no one victory, no single achievement, that makes a heroine. Her challenges morph each time she overcomes them and take a new shape to challenge her again. Her biggest test is not courage or physical strength but resolve—the capacity to keep on fighting for the right to be herself: to be a unique and special individual. The woman who can keep on fighting wins the prize, and it is not a husband or a throne. What she wins is not just an unshakeable sense of self, but the capacity—regardless of what others would have her be and do, regardless of the situation in which she finds herself—to live as she wills. She becomes the queen of her own life.

Imagination allows a new idea to emerge. Fiction writers ask "what if?" and then imagine the possibilities into being. For once a thing has been imagined, people can see it as a goal to work toward and make happen. Fiction about heroines may, in fact, be a more effective tool for changing women's lives than nonfiction works that focus on the present reality of women's lives. The visionary women and men who write Aletis stories are showing us our future: a future in which women are no longer seen as objects by others and instead are the subjects of their own lives.

What transformations will become possible—for men as well as women—when people no longer have to fight for the right to be unique? If each person were free to follow their own *daimon*, where would they put their power to work, and what would happen to society as a result? One thing is sure: writers will continue to imagine where our culture is headed long before we get there.

Notes

Introduction

1. Linda Lear, *Beatrix Potter: A Life in Nature* (London: St. Martin's, 2007), ix.
2. James Hillman, *The Dream and the Underworld* (New York: HarperPerennial, 1979), 4.

Chapter 1

1. Glen Slater, "Jungian Psychology" (lecture presented at Pacifica Graduate Institute, Carpinteria, CA, April 2009).
2. Rick Tarnas, "James Hillman and the Return of Soul: A Weekend of Reflections on His Life and Legacy" (lecture presented at Pacifica Graduate Institute, Carpinteria, CA, June 21, 2014).
3. Sigmund Freud, *Three Essays on the Theory of Sexuality*, rev. ed. (Basic Books, 2000), 37.
4. Deborah Lyons, *Gender and Immortality: Heroines in Ancient Greek Myth and Cult* (Princeton: Princeton University Press, 1996), chap. 4, para. 31.

Chapter 2

1. Larry Curtis, "How a Soldier Found Tolkien to Heal His War Wounds," theonering.net (September 13, 2011).
2. Nancy Armstrong, *How Novels Think: The Limits of Individualism from 1719–1900* (New York: Columbia University Press, 2005).
3. John Matthews, *Gawain, Knight of the Goddess: Restoring an Archetype,* (Wellingborough, UK: Aquarian, 1990).
4. Doris Lessing, *The Golden Notebook* (New York: HarperPerennial, 2008), xiv.
5. See Elizabeth Wanning Harries, *Twice upon a Time: Women Writers and the History of the Fairy Tale* (Princeton: Princeton University Press, 2001); Jack David Zipes, *Breaking the Magic Spell: Radical Theories of Folk and Fairy Tales*

(Lexington: University of Kentucky Press, 2002); and Maria Tatar, *The Hard Facts of the Grimms' Fairy Tales* (Princeton: Princeton University Press, 2003).

6. Harries, *Twice upon a Time*, 3.

7. Ibid., 72.

8. Ibid., 26.

9. William Hazlitt, "Standard Novels and Romances," *The Collected Works of William Hazlitt*, ed. A. R. Waller (Whitefish, MT: Kessinger, 2007), 43.

10. Annis Pratt, *Archetypal Patterns in Women's Fiction* (Bloomington, IN: Indiana University Press, 1981), 81.

11. Lessing, *Golden Notebook*, xiii.

12. Benedicte Page, "Research shows male writers still dominate books world," *The Guardian* (February 4, 2011). *http://www.theguardian.com/books/2011/feb/04/research-male-writers-dominate-books-world*.

Chapter 3

1. Joseph Campbell, *The Hero with a Thousand Faces*, Bollingen Series 17 (Princeton, NJ: Princeton University Press, 1949), 17.

2. Lyn Cowan, "Dismantling the Animus," *The Jung Page*, http://www.cgjungpage.org/learn/articles/analytical-psychology/105-dismantling-the-animus (2000), part 2, sec. 3, para. 10.

3. Campbell, *Hero*, 97.

4. Michael Kimmer, quoted in Jennifer Siebel Newsom, director, "The Mask You Live In" (Ross, CA: The Representation Project, 2014).

5. Terrence Real, *I Don't Want to Talk about It* (New York: Fireside, 1997).

6. Genia Pauli Haddon, "The Personal and Cultural Emergence of Yang Femininity," *To Be a Woman: The Birth of the Conscious Feminine*, ed. Connie Zweig (Los Angeles: Jeremy P. Tarcher, 1990).

7. Joseph Campbell, "On the Great Goddess," *Goddesses: Mysteries of the Divine Feminine (Collected Works of Joseph Campbell)*, ed. Saffron Rossi (Novato, CA: New World Library, 2013).

8. Maureen Murdock, *The Heroine's Journey: A Woman's Journey to Wholeness* (Boston and London: Shambhala, 1990), 2.

9. Ibid., 1.

10. Jean Benedict Raffa, *The Bridge to Wholeness: A Feminine Alternative to the Hero Myth* (San Diego: LunaMedia, 1992), 166.

11. Pratt, *Archetypal Patterns*, 141 (see chap. 2, n. 10).

12. Kim Hudson, *The Virgin's Promise: Writing Stories of Feminine Creative, Spiritual, and Sexual Awakening* (Studio City, CA: Michael Wiese, 2009).

13. Clarissa Pinkola Estés, *Women Who Run with the Wolves: Myths and Stories of the Wild Woman Archetype* (New York: Ballantine, 1992), 14.

14. Christine Downing, *The Goddess: Mythological Images of the Feminine* (New York: Author's Choice, 2007), 4.

15. Madonna Kolbenschlag, *Kiss Sleeping Beauty Good-Bye: Breaking the Spell of Feminine Myths and Models* (New York: Bantam, 1979).

16. Karen E. Rowe, "Feminism and Fairy Tales," *Women's Studies: An Inter-Disciplinary Journal* 6.3 (1979), 219.

17. Christine Downing, *The Long Journey Home: Re-Visioning the Myth of Demeter and Persephone for Our Time* (Boston: Shambhala, 1994), 1.

18. Ibid., 3.

19. Sylvia Brinton Perera, *Descent to the Goddess: A Way of Initiation for Women* (Toronto: Inner City, 1981), 14.

20. Betty DeShong Meador, *Uncursing the Dark: Treasures from the Underworld* (Wilmette, IL: Chiron, 1992), xi.

21. Ibid., 132–33.

22. Dara Marks, "Engaging the Feminine Heroic: Beyond the Hero's Journey, the Other Side of the Story" (paper presented at *The Writer's Journey* conference, Pacifica Graduate Institute, Santa Barbara, CA, April 26–28, 2013).

23. Meador, *Uncursing the Dark*, xi.

24. Marion Woodman, *Addiction to Perfection: The Still Unravished Bride* (Toronto: Inner City, 1982), 178.

Chapter 4

Epigraph: Melissa Etheridge, quoted by Mark Kennedy in "Melissa Etheridge Takes a Look Back with 12th Album," *The Huffington Post* (September 5, 2012).

1. Alan Oak, "Women's Hero Journey: An Interview with Lois McMaster Bujold on *Paladin of Souls*," http://www.womenwriters.net/june09/paladin_interview.html.

2. Ibid.

Chapter 5

1. Campbell, *Hero*, 21 (see chap. 3, n. 1).

2. Judy Blunt, *Breaking Clean* (New York: Random, 2002), 145.

3. Patricia Reis, *Daughters of Saturn: From Father's Daughter to Creative Woman* (New Orleans: Spring, 1995), 19.

4. Mary Pipher, *Reviving Ophelia: Saving the Selves of Adolescent Girls* (New York: Ballantine, 1994), 286.

5. James Hillman, *The Soul's Code: In Search of Character and Calling* (New York: Warner, 1996), 63–91.

6. Estés, *Women Who Run*, 77 (see chap. 3, n. 11).

7. Maria Shriver, "Maria Shriver Interviews the Famously Private Poet Mary Oliver," http://www.oprah.com/entertainment/Maria-Shriver-Interviews-Poet-Mary-Oliver/ (March 9, 2011).

8. Lear, *Beatrix Potter*, 22 (see intro., n. 1).

9. Jill Ker Conway, *The Road from Coorain* (New York: Knopf, 1989), 149.

10. Ibid., 175.

11. Ibid., 237.

12. Ibid., 237.

13. Suzanne Fields, *Like Father, Like Daughter: How Father Shapes the Woman His Daughter Becomes* (New York: Little Brown, 1983), 5.

14. Linda Schierse Leonard, *The Wounded Woman: Healing the Father-Daughter Relationship* (Boston: Shambhala, 1982), 11.

15. Ziauddin Yousafzai, "My Daughter Malala," TED talk (March 2014), https://www.ted.com/talks/ziauddin_yousafzai_my_daughter_malala.

16. Shriver, "Maria Shriver Interviews Mary Oliver."

17. Maya Angelou, *I Know Why the Caged Bird Sings* (New York: Ballantine, 2009), 92.

18. Ibid., 100.

19. Ibid., 101.

20. Marion Woodman, *Leaving My Father's House: The Journey to Conscious Femininity* (Boston: Shambala, 1992), 37.

21. Leonard, *Wounded Woman*, 13.

22. Blunt, *Breaking Clean*, 187.

23. Maureen Murdock, *Father's Daughters: Breaking the Ties that Bind* (New Orleans: Spring, 1994), xi.

24. Marion Woodman, *Addiction to Perfection: The Still Unravished Bride* (Toronto: Inner City, 1982), 9.

25. Jean Shinoda Bolen, *Goddesses in Everywoman: Powerful Archetypes in Women's Lives* (San Francisco: Harper and Row, 1984), 82.

26. Leonard, *Wounded Woman*, 17.

27. Woodman, *Addiction to Perfection*, 52.

Chapter 6

1. Janice Raymond, *A Passion for Friends: Toward a Philosophy of Female Affection*, rev. ed. (North Melbourne: Spinifex, 2001), xiii.

2. Pratt, *Archetypal Patterns*, 96 (see chap. 2, n. 10).

3. Lucy Jago, *Regency House Party* (London: Times Warner, 2004).

4. Ana Martínez Alemán, "Understanding and Evaluating Female Friendship's Educative Value," *The Journal of Higher Education* 68.2 (March/April 1997), 119–159.

5. Annabel Robinson, *The Life and Work of Jane Ellen Harrison* (New York: Oxford, 2002), 109.

6. Pipher, *Reviving Ophelia*, 274 (see chap. 5, n. 4).

7. Ibid., 38.

8. Blunt, *Breaking Clean*, 168 (see chap. 5, n. 2).

9. Rosalind Wiseman, *Mean Girls and Wannabes: Helping Your Daughter Survive Cliques, Gossip, Boyfriends, and Other Realities of Adolescence* (New York: Three Rivers, 2009), 79.

10. Ibid., 193.

11. Margaret Mead, *Blackberry Winter: My Earlier Years* (New York: Kodansha, 1995), 101.

12. Shadee Ashtari, "Phyllis Schlafly claims women paid the same as men won't find husbands," *The Huffington Post* (April 15, 2013), http://www.huffingtonpost.com/2014/04/15/phyllis-schlafly-equal-pay_n_5154150.html.

13. David Edwards, "Coulter: Obama's base is 'stupid single women'," *The Raw Story* (August 9, 2012), http://www.rawstory.com/rs/2012/08/09/coulter-obamas-base-is-stupid-single-women/.

14. Libby Copland, "Hail to the housewife: Can Michele Bachmann be the leader of the free world and still obey her husband like a good evangelical?" *Slate* (June 30, 2011), http://www.slate.com/articles/double_x/doublex/2011/06/hail_to_the_housewife.html.

15. Lear, *Beatrix Potter*, 46 (see intro., n. 1).

16. Blunt, *Breaking Clean*, 2.

Chapter 7

1. Estés, *Women Who Run*, 47 (see chap. 3, n. 11).

2. Ibid., 49.

3. Leonard, *Wounded Woman*, 16 (see chap. 5, n. 14).

4. Pratt, *Archetypal Patterns*, 48 (see chap. 2, n. 10).

5. Estés, *Women Who Run*, 48.

6. Blunt, *Breaking Clean*, 202 (see chap. 5, n. 2).

7. Ibid., 3.

8. Ibid., 279.

9. Ibid., 295.

10. Nancy Miller, "Emphasis Added: Plots and Plausibilities in Women's Fiction." *PMLA* 96.1 (Jan. 1981), 41.

11. Ibid., 42.

Chapter 8

Epigraph: Leonard, *Wounded Woman*, 157 (see chap. 5, n. 14).

1. Campbell, *Hero*, 55 (see chap. 3, n. 1).

2. Joan Gould, *Spinning Gold into Straw: What Fairy Tales Reveal about the Transformations in a Woman's Life* (New York: Random House, 2005), 103.

3. Estés, *Women Who Run*, 59 (see chap. 3, n. 11).

4. Lessing, *Golden Notebook*, xxi (see chap. 2, n. 4).

5. Gould, *Spinning Straw into Gold*, 250.

6. John Rignall, ed., *Oxford Reader's Companion to George Eliot* (Oxford: Oxford University Press, 2000), 11.

7. Conway, *Road to Coorain*, 234 (see chap. 5, n. 9).

8. Gould, *Spinning Straw into Gold*, 245.

Chapter 9

1. DeAnne Blanton, "Women Soldiers of the Civil War," *Prologue* 25.1 (Spring 1993).

2. Ursula Le Guin, *The Wave in the Mind: Talks and Essays on the Writer, the Reader, and the Imagination* (Boston: Shambhala, 2004), 111.

3. Ibid., 111.

4. Marie-Louise von Franz, *The Feminine in Fairy Tales*, rev. ed (Boston: Shambhala, 1993), 97.

5. Simone de Beauvoir, *The Second Sex* (New York: Knopf, 1953), 362.

6. Gould, *Spinning Straw into Gold*, 276–9 (see chap. 8, n. 2).

7. Chery Strayed, *Wild: From Lost to Found on the Pacific Crest Trail* (New York: Random, 2012), 207.

8. von Franz, *Feminine in Fairy Tales*, 172.

9. Jill Ker Conway, *True North: A Memoir* (New York: Vintage, 1994), ix.

10. Virginia Woolf, *A Room of One's Own* (Orlando, FL: Harcourt, 1989), 38.

Chapter 10

Epigraph: "Prayer to the Mothers" copyright 1990 by Diane di Prima. Reprinted by permission of City Lights Books.

1. Campbell, *Hero*, 116 (see chap. 3, n. 1).

2. Perera, *Descent to the Goddess*, 30 (see chap. 3, n. 17).

3. Estés, *Women Who Run*, 92 (see chap. 3, n. 11).

4. Cheryl Dahle, "Women's Ways of Mentoring" (Fastcompany.com, August 31, 1998), 1.

5. Gould, *Spinning Straw into Gold*, 225 (see chap. 8, n. 2).

Chapter 11

1. Carl G. Jung, "Psychological Types," *The Collected Works of C. G. Jung*, trans. R. F. C. Hull, vol. 6 (Princeton: Princeton University Press, 1971).

2. Carol Gilligan, *In a Different Voice: Psychological Theory and Women's Development* (Cambridge, MA: Harvard University Press, 1982), 69.

3. Mary Field Belenky, Blythe McVicker Clinchy, Nancy Rule Goldberger, Jill Mattock Terule, *Women's Ways of Knowing: The Development of Voice, Self, and Mind* (New York: BasicBooks, 1986), 24.

4. Ibid., 71.

5. Ibid., 53.

6. Michel Tuam Phan, Joel B. Cohen, John W. Pracejus, and G. David Hughes, "Affect Monitoring and the Primacy of Feelings in Judgment," *Journal of Consumer Research* (September 28, 2001), 167–188. See also Tilmann Betsch, "The Nature of Intuition and Its Neglect in Research on Judgment and Decision-Making," *Intuition in Judgment and Decision-Making*, ed. Henning Plessner (New York: Taylor and Francis, 2008), 3–22.

7. Belenky, et al., *Women's Ways of Knowing*, 92.

8. Ibid., 97.

9. Estés, *Women Who Run*, 59 (see chap. 3, n. 11).

10. Carl G. Jung, "The Transcendent Function," *The Collected Works of C. G. Jung*, trans. R. F. C. Hull, vol. 8 (Princeton: Princeton University Press, 1969), 67–91.

11. Perera, *Descent to the Goddess*, 32 (see chap. 3, n. 17).

12. Gould, *Spinning Straw into Gold*, 272 (see chap. 8, n. 2).

13. Estés, *Women Who Run*, 97.

14. Ibid.

Chapter 12

Epigraph: Ursula Le Guin, "Bryn Mawr Commencement Address," *Dancing at the Edge of the World: Thoughts on Words, Women, Places* (New York: Harper and Row, 1989), 160.

1. Pratt, *Archetypal Patterns*, 114 (see chap. 2, n. 10).

2. Raymond, *A Passion for Friends*, 64 (chap. 6, n. 1).

3. Carl G. Jung, "Women in Europe," *The Collected Works of C. G. Jung*, trans. R. F. C. Hull, vol. 10 (Princeton: Princeton University Press, 1970), 113–133.

4. Ann Bedford Ulanov, *Receiving Woman: Studies in the Psychology and Theology of the Feminine* (Ensidelen: Daimon, 2001), 124.

5. von Franz, *Feminine in Fairy Tales*, 31 (see chap. 9, n. 4).

6. Ibid., 32.

7. Ibid., 94.

8. Ibid., 116.

9. May Sarton, *Journal of a Solitude* (New York: Norton, 1973), 12.

10. Eric Luis Uhlmann, T. Andrew Poehlman, David Tannenbaum, John A. Bargh, "Implicit Puritanism in American Moral Cognition," *Journal of Experimental Social Psychology* 47 (2011), 312–320.

11. Gloria Steinem, *Revolution from Within: A Book of Self-Esteem* (New York: Little Brown, 1992).

12. Celia Kitzinger, "Therapy and how it undermines the practice of radical feminism," *Radically Speaking: Feminism Reclaimed*, eds. Renate Klein and Diane Bell (North Melbourne: Spinifex, 1996), 92–101.

13. Hillman, *The Soul's Code*, 8 (see chap. 5, n. 5).

14. Elizabeth Gilbert, *Eat Pray Love* (New York: Penguin, 2006), 199.

15. Pratt, *Archetypal Patterns*, 131 (see chap. 2, n. 10).

16. Perera, *Descent to the Goddess*, 41 (see chap. 3, n. 17).

17. Conway, *True North*, 250 (see chap. 9, n. 9).

18. Ibid., 91.

Idyll: The Lute-Playing Queen

1. Allan B. Chinen, *Once upon a Midlife: Classic Stories and Mythic Tales to Illuminate the Middle Years* (New York: Jeremy P. Tarcher/Perigee, 1992), 86.

Chapter 13

1. Pratt, *Archetypal Patterns*, 128 (see chap. 2, n. 10).
2. Katharine Hepburn, *Me: Stories of My Life* (New York: Ballantine, 1991), 193.
3. Conway, *True North*, 72 (see chap. 9, n. 9).
4. Ibid., 75.
5. Ibid., 79.

Chapter 14

Epigraph: Reis, *Daughters of Saturn*, 115 (see chap. 5, n. 3).

1. Robert Johnson, *The Fisher King and the Handless Maiden: Understanding the Wounded Feeling Function in Masculine and Feminine Psychology* (New York: Harper One, 1993), 63.
2. Estés, *Women Who Run*, 387–455 (see chap. 3, n. 11).
3. Hillman, *The Dream and the Underworld*, 4 (see intro., n. 2).
4. Bettina Knapp, *Women in Myth* (Albany, NY: SUNY P., 1997), 161.
5. Maria Tatar, *The Hard Facts of the Grimms' Fairy Tales*, 2nd ed. (Princeton: Princeton University Press, 2003), 115.
6. Griselda Pollock, as quoted in Nick Clark, "What's the biggest problem with women artists? None of them can actually paint, says Georg Baselitz," *The Independent* (Feb. 6, 2013).
7. John Geirland, "Go with the Flow," *Wired* 4.09 (September 1996).
8. Gary Settle, "We Tend to Do the Right Thing When We Get Scared," *The New York Times* (Jan. 1, 2000).
9. Elizabeth A. Trembley, "Feminism Reads Dorothy L. Sayers," In *Women Times Three: Writers, Detectives, Readers*, ed. Kathleen Gregory Klein (New York: Popular Press, 1995).

Chapter 15

Epigraph: Nadja Sayej, "We interviewed Yoko Ono on her 80th birthday," *Vice* (Feb. 20, 2013), http://www.vice.com/en_ca/read/we-interviewed-yoko-ono-on-her-80th-birthday.

1. Toni Wolff, "Structural Forms of the Feminine Psyche," trans. Gela Jacobson, *Psychological Perspectives* 31.1 (Spring 1995), 77–90.

2. Cristian Dezso and David Gaddis Ross, "Does Female Representation in Top Management Improve Firm Performance? A Panel Data Investigation," *Social Science Research Network* (Jan. 31, 2008).

3. John Gerzema and Michael D'Antonio, *The Athena Doctrine: How Women (and the Men Who Think Like Them) Will Rule the Future* (San Francisco: Jossey-Bass, 2013), 2.

4. Lynne Twist, *The Soul of Money: Reclaiming the Wealth of Our Inner Resources* (New York: Norton, 2003).

5. Estés, *Women Who Run*, 299 (see chap. 3, n. 11).

6. Lear, *Beatrix Potter*, 354 (see intro., n. 1).

7. Jimmy Carter, Presidential Medal of Freedom Announcement of Award to Margaret Mead (January 19, 1979), http://www.presidency.ucsb.edu/ws/?pid=32524.

8. Margaret Mead, Institute for Cultural Studies, original source unknown.

9. Don Kaye, "Lena Headey on the 300 sequel, wielding a sword and becoming a genre queen," *Blastr*, http://www.blastr.com/2014-3-7/exclusive-lena-headey-300-sequel-wielding-sword-and-becoming-genre-queen, (March 7, 2014).

Works Cited

Angelou, Maya. *I Know Why the Caged Bird Sings*. 1969. New York: Ballantine, 2009.

Austen, Jane. *Emma*. 1815.

_____. *Mansfield Park*. 1814.

_____. *Northanger Abbey*. 1818.

_____. *Persuasion*. 1817.

_____. *Pride and Prejudice*. 1813.

_____. *Sense and Sensibility*. 1811.

Belenky, Mary Field, Nancy Rule Goldberger, Jill Mattuck Tarule, and Blythe McVicker Clinchy. *Women's Ways of Knowing: The Development of Self, Voice, and Mind*. New York: Basic Books, 1986.

Blunt, Judy. *Breaking Clean*. New York: Random House, 2002.

Brontë, Anne. *The Tenant of Wildfell Hall*. 1848.

Brontë, Charlotte. *Jane Eyre*. 1847.

Burney, Fanny. *The Wanderer*. 1814.

Campbell, Joseph. *The Hero with a Thousand Faces*. Bollingen Series 17. Princeton, NJ: Princeton University Press, 1949.

Conway, Jill Ker. *The Road from Coorain*. New York: Knopf, 1989.

_____. *True North*. New York: Vintage, 1994.

Dahle, Cheryl. "Women's Ways of Mentoring." *Fast Company*. http://www.fastcompany.com/34854/womens-ways-mentoring. Accessed August 31, 2013.

Downing, Christine. *The Goddess: Mythological Images of the Feminine*. New York: Author's Choice, 2007.

_____. *The Long Journey Home: Re-visioning the Myth of Demeter and Persephone for Our Time*. Boston: Shambhala, 1994.

Du Maurier, Daphne. *Rebecca*. 1938. New York: Avon, 1971.

Eliot, George. *Middlemarch*. 1871–2.

Estés, Clarissa Pinkola. *Women Who Run with the Wolves*. New York: Ballantine, 1992.

Fields, Suzanne. *Like Father, Like Daughter: How Father Shapes the Woman His Daughter Becomes.* New York: Little, Brown, 1983.

Franklin, Miles. *My Brilliant Career.* 1901.

Gaskell, Elizabeth. *North and South.* 1854–55.

Gilman, Charlotte Perkins. *The Yellow Wallpaper.* 1892.

Harrison, Jane. *Reminiscences of a Student's Life.* 1926.

Geirland, John. "Go with the Flow." *Wired* 4, no. 9 (September 1996).

Gerzema, John, and Michael D'Antonio. *The Athena Doctrine: How Women (and the Men Who Think Like Them) Will Rule the Future.* San Francisco: Jossey-Bass, 2013.

Gilbert, Elizabeth. *Eat Pray Love.* New York: Penguin, 2006.

Gould, Joan. *Spinning Straw into Gold: What Fairy Tales Reveal about the Transformations in a Woman's Life.* New York: Random House, 2005.

Haddon, Genia Pauli. "The Personal and Cultural Emergence of Yang Femininity." *To Be a Woman: The Birth of the Conscious Feminine.* Edited by Connie Zweig. Los Angeles: Jeremy P. Tarcher, 1990.

Hepburn, Katharine. *Me: Stories of My Life.* New York: Ballantine, 1991.

Hillman, James. *The Dream and the Underworld.* New York: HarperPerennial, 1979.

Hudson, Kim. *The Virgin's Promise: Writing Stories of Feminine Creative, Spiritual, and Sexual Awakening.* Studio City: Michael Wiese, 2009.

Jago, Lucy. *Regency House Party.* London: Times Warner, 2004.

Johnson, Robert. *The Fisher King and the Handless Maiden: Understanding the Wounded Feeling Function in Masculine and Feminine Psychology.* New York: Harper One, 1993.

Jung, C. G. "Women in Europe." 1927. *The Collected Works of C. G. Jung.* Vol. 10. Translated by R. F. C. Hull. Princeton, NJ: Princeton University Press, 1970: 113–133.

Kaye, Don. "Lena Headey on the 300 sequel, wielding a sword and becoming a genre queen." *Blastr.* http://www.blastr.com/2014-3-7/exclusive-lena-headey-300-sequel-wielding-sword-and-becoming-genre-queen. Accessed March 7, 2014.

Lear, Linda J. *Beatrix Potter: A Life in Nature.* New York: St. Martin's, 2007.

Le Guin, Ursula. *Tehanu.* 1991. New York: Aladdin, 2001.

_____. "The Wilderness Within." *The Wave in the Mind: Talks and Essays on the Writer, the Reader, and the Imagination.* Boston: Shambhala, 2003.

Leonard, Linda Schierse. *The Wounded Woman: Healing the Father-Daughter Relationship.* Boston: Shambhala, 1982.

Lessing, Doris. *The Golden Notebook.* 1962. New York: HarperPerennial, 2008.

Mead, Margaret. *Blackberry Winter: My Earlier Years.* 1972. New York: Kodansha, 1995.

Meador, Betty DeShong. *Uncursing the Dark: Treasures from the Underworld.* Wilmette, IL: Chiron, 1992.

Miller, Nancy K. "Emphasis Added: Plots and Plausibilities in Women's Fiction." *PMLA* 96.1 (Jan. 1981): 36–48.

_____. *The Heroine's Text: Readings in the French and English Novel, 1722–1782.* New York: Columbia University Press, 1980.

Mitford, Nancy. *The Pursuit of Love.* 1945. New York: Vintage, 2001.

Murdock, Maureen. *The Heroine's Journey.* Boston and London: Shambhala, 1990.

Newsom, Jennifer Siebel. "The Mask You Live In." Documentary. Directed by Jennifer Siebel Newsom. Ross, CA: The Representation Project, 2014.

Oak, Alan. "Women's Hero Journey: An Interview with Lois McMaster Bujold on *Paladin of Souls.*" http://www.womenwriters.net/june09/paladin_interview. html.

Oates, Joyce Carol. *Wonderland.* 1971. New York: Modern Library, 2006.

Page, Benedicte. "Research shows male writers still dominate books world." *The Guardian.* http://www.theguardian.com/books/2011/feb/04/research-male-writers-dominate-books-world. Accessed February 4, 2011.

Parker, Rozsika, and Griselda Pollock. *Old Mistresses: Women, Art and Ideology.* 1981. London: L. B. Tauris, 2013.

Perera, Sylvia Brinton. *Descent to the Goddess: A Way of Initiation for Women.* Toronto: Inner City, 1981.

Pipher, Mary. *Reviving Ophelia: Saving the Selves of Adolescent Girls.* New York: Ballantine, 1994.

Pratt, Annis. *Archetypal Patterns in Women's Fiction.* Bloomington: Indiana University Press, 1981.

Raffa, Jean Benedict. *The Bridge to Wholeness: A Feminine Alternative to the Hero Myth.* San Diego: LunaMedia, 1992.

Raymond, Janice G. *A Passion for Friends: Toward a Philosophy of Female Affection.* 1986. Rev. ed. North Melbourne: Spinifex, 2001.

Real, Terrence. *I Don't Want to Talk About It: Overcoming the Secret Legacy of Male Depression.* New York: Fireside, 1997.

Reis, Patricia. *Daughters of Saturn: From Father's Daughter to Creative Woman.* New Orleans: Spring Publications, 1995.

Rowe, Karen E. "Feminism and Fairy Tales." *Women's Studies: An Inter-Disciplinary Journal* 6, no. 3 (1979): 237–257.

Sarton, May. *Journal of a Solitude.* New York: Norton, 1973.

Settle, Gary. "We Tend to Do the Right Thing When We Get Scared." Interview with Octavia Butler in *The New York Times* (Jan. 1, 2000).

Shriver, Maria. "Maria Shriver Interviews the Famously Private Poet Mary Oliver." *Oprah* (March 09, 2011).

Sparks, Muriel. *The Prime of Miss Jean Brodie*. New York: Lippincott, 1962.

Tepper, Sheri. *Raising the Stones*. New York: Bantam, 1991.

Tolkien, J. R. R. *The Lord of the Rings*. 1954–55. New York: Houghton Mifflin, 1991.

Trembley, Elizabeth. *Mysteries of Gender: The Development of Individuality in the Harriet Vane Novels of Dorothy L. Sayers*. Chicago: University of Chicago Press, 1991.

Uhlmann, E. L., et al. "Implicit Puritanism in American Moral Cognition." *Journal of Experimental Social Psychology* 47 (2011): 312–320.

von Franz, Marie-Louise. *The Feminine in Fairy Tales*. Rev. ed. Boston: Shambhala, 1993.

Walker, Alice. *The Color Purple*. Orlando, FL: Harvest, 1982.

Weisberger, Lauren. *The Devil Wears Prada*. New York: Random House, 2003.

Wiseman, Rosalind. *Queen Bees and Wannabes: Helping Your Daughter Survive Cliques, Gossip, Boyfriends, and Other Realities of Adolescence*. New York: Three Rivers, 2009.

Woodman, Marion. *Addiction to Perfection: The Still Unravished Bride*. Toronto: Inner City, 1982.

_____. *Leaving My Father's House: The Journey to Conscious Femininity*. Boston: Shambhala, 1992.

Yousafzai, Ziauddin. "My Daughter, Malala." Presentation, TED2014, March 2014. http://www.ted.com/talks/ziauddin_yousafzai_my_daughter_malala.

Additional Bibliography

Archetypal and Depth Psychology

Amatruda, Kate, and Lauren Cunningham. *The Witch and the Queen: Psychotherapy with Women at Midlife and Beyond*. www.psychceu.com. Downloaded May 10, 2012.

Christ, Carol P. "Spiritual Quest and Women's Experience." *WomanSpirit Rising*. Edited by Carol P. Christ and Judith Plaskow. New York: HarperCollins, 1979: 228–245.

Cowan, Lyn. "Dismantling the Animus." *Reflections on Psychology, Culture, and Life: The Jung Page* (November 22, 2002). Accessed June 23, 2012.

de Castillejo, Irene Claremont. *Knowing Woman: A Feminine Psychology*. Boston: Shambhala, 1973.

Dinnerstein, Dorothy. *The Mermaid and the Minotaur*. 1976. New York: Other, 1999.

Downing, Christine. *Psyche's Sisters: Reimagining the Meaning of Sisterhood*. New Orleans: Spring, 2007.

Harding, Esther. *The Way of All Women*. Boston: Shambhala, 1970.

Hillman, James. *The Dream and the Underworld*. New York: HarperPerennial, 1979.

Hunt, Nan. "In the Laps of the Mothers." *To Be a Woman: The Birth of the Conscious Feminine*. Edited by Connie Zweig. Los Angeles: Jeremy P. Tarcher, 1990: 64–75.

Lauter, Estella, and Cynthia Rupprecht, eds. *Feminist Archetypal Theory: Interdisciplinary Re-Visions of Jungian Thought*. Knoxville: University of Tennessee Press, 1985.

LeBoeuf, Tawny. "Weeping for the Loss of Strength in Femininity: The Implications of the Historical Shift of the Cinderella Archetypes to the Psyche of the Feminine." Presentation, Popular Culture Association/American Culture Association Conference, San Antonio, TX, April 2011.

Luke, Helen M. *The Way of Woman: Awakening the Perennial Feminine*. New York: Doubleday, 1995.

Mattoon, Mary Anne, and Jenette Jones. "Is the Animus Obsolete?" *The Goddess Re-Awakening: The Feminine Principle Today.* Edited by Shirley J. Nicholson. Wheaton: Quest Books, 1989: 142–65.

Murdock, Maureen. *Fathers' Daughters: Breaking the Ties that Bind.* 1994. Revised edition, New Orleans: Spring, 2005.

Rowland, Susan. *Jung: A Feminist Revision.* Malden, MA: Blackwell, 2002.

Ulanov, Ann Belford. *Receiving Woman: Studies in the Psychology and Theology of the Feminine.* 1981. Einsiedeln: Daimon, 2001.

Wehr, Demaris S. *Jung and Feminism: Liberating Archetypes.* Boston: Beacon, 1987.

_____. "Religious and Social Dimensions of the Archetype." *Feminist Archetypal Theory: Interdisciplinary Re-Visions of Jungian Thought.* Edited by Estella Lauter and Cynthia Rupprecht. Knoxville: University of Tennessee Press, 1985: 32–45.

Wolff, Toni. "Structural Forms of the Feminine Psyche." 1932. Translated by Gela Jacobson. *Psychological Perspectives* 31, no.1 (Spring 1995): 77–90.

Literary Analysis

Amiran, Minda Rae. "What Women's Literature?" *College English* 39, no. 6 (February 1978): 653–662.

Armstrong, Nancy. *How Novels Think: The Limits of Individualism from 1719–1900.* New York: Columbia University Press, 2005.

Baym, Nina. *Woman's Fiction: A Guide to Novels by and about Women in America, 1820–1870.* Ithaca, NY: Cornell University Press, 1978.

Beher, Valerie. "'You Can't Imagine How that Feels': Stephenie Meyer's *Twilight* and the Problem of the Literal Figural." Presentation, Popular Culture Association/American Culture Association Conference, San Antonio, April 2011.

Doniger, Wendy. "Mother Goose and the Voices of Women." *The Implied Spider: Politics and Theology in Myth.* New York: Columbia University Press, 1998: 109–136.

Donovan, Josephine. "Toward a Women's Poetics." *Studies in Women's Literature* 3, nos. 1–2 (Spring–Autumn 1984): 98–110.

Fleckenstein, Kristie S. "Images, Words, and Narrative Epistemology." *College English* 58, no. 8 (December 1996): 914–944.

Gilbert, Sandra M., and Susan Gubar. *The Madwoman in the Attic: The Woman Writer and the Nineteenth-Century Literary Imagination.* Second edition. New Haven: Yale University Press, 2000.

Graham, Elspeth, Hilary Hinds, Elaine Hobby, and Helen Wilcox, eds. *Her Own Life: Autobiographical Writings by Seventeenth-Century Englishwomen.* New York: Routledge, 1989.

Hardy, Barbara. "Towards a Poetics of Fiction: 3) An Approach through Narrative." *Novel: A Forum on Fiction* 2, no. 1 (Autumn 1968): 5–14.

Kaplan, Carla. "'Jane Eyre' and the Romance of Women's Narration." *Novel: A Forum on Fiction* 30, no. 1 (Autumn 1996): 5–31.

Rosenblatt, Louise M. *The Reader, the Text, the Poem: The Transactional Theory of the Literary Work*. Carbondale: Southern Illinois University Press, 1978.

Schleiner, Louise. *Tudor and Stuart Women Writers*. Bloomington: Indiana University Press, 1994.

Showalter, Elaine, ed. *New Feminist Criticism: Essays on Women, Literature, and Theory*. New York: Pantheon, 1985.

Sturges, Robert S. *Medieval Interpretation: Models of Reading in Literary Narrative, 1100–1500*. Carbondale: University of Southern Illinois Press, 1991.

Wilson, Katharina M., ed. *Women Writers of the Renaissance and Reformation*. Athens, GA: University of Georgia Press, 1987.

Mythology and Folk and Fairy Tales

Aisenberg, Nadya. *Ordinary Heroines: Transforming the Male Myth*. New York: Continuum, 1994.

Bolen, Jean Shinoda. *Goddesses in Every Woman*. New York: HarperCollins, 1984.

Campbell, Joseph. "Joseph Campbell on the Great Goddess." *Parabola: The Magazine of Myth and Tradition* 5, no. 4 (Fall 1980): 74–85.

Chinen, Allan. *In the Ever After: Fairy Tales and the Second Half of Life*. Wilmette, IL: Chiron, 1989.

_____. *Once upon a Midlife: Tales for the Midlife Traveler*. Bloomington, IN: Xlibris, 2003.

Downing, Christine. *Gods in Our Midst: Mythological Images of the Masculine; A Woman's View*. New Orleans: Spring Publications, 1993.

Frankel, Valerie E. *From Girl to Goddess: The Heroine's Journey through Myth and Legend*. Jefferson, NC: McFarland, 2010.

Grimm, Wilhelm and Jacob. *The Complete Grimm's Fairy Tales*. New York: Pantheon, 1944.

Harries, Elizabeth Wanning. *Twice upon a Time: Women Writers and the History of the Fairy Tale*. Princeton, NJ: Princeton University Press, 2001.

Hubbs, Joanna. *Mother Russia: The Feminine Myth in Russian Culture*. Bloomington: Indiana University Press, 1988.

Knapp, Bettina. *Women in Myth*. Albany, NY: SUNY, 1997.

Kolbenschlag, Madonna. *Kiss Sleeping Beauty Good-Bye: Breaking the Spell of Feminine Myths and Models*. New York: Bantam, 1979.

Lyons, Deborah. *Gender and Immortality: Heroines in Ancient Greek Myth and Cult.* Princeton, NJ: Princeton University Press, 1996.

Matthews, John. *Gawain, Knight of the Goddess: Restoring an Archetype.* Wellingborough, UK: Aquarian, 1990.

Phelps, Ethel Johnson, ed. *Tatterhood and Other Tales.* New York: Feminist Press, 1978.

Sparks, Elisa Kay. "The Female Hero." Clemson University online essay page, 2000. Accessed February 10, 2010.

Tatar, Maria. *The Annotated Classic Fairy Tales.* London: Norton, 2002.

_____. *The Hard Facts of the Grimms' Fairy Tales.* 1987. Princeton, NJ: Princeton University Press, 2003.

Walker, Barbara. *Feminist Fairy Tales.* New York: HarperCollins, 1976.

Yolen, Jane. *Not One Damsel in Distress: World Folktales for Strong Girls.* Boston: HMH Books for Young Readers, 2000.

Zipes, Jack David. *Breaking the Magic Spell: Radical Theories of Folk and Fairy Tales.* 1979. Lexington: University of Kentucky Press, 2002.

_____. *Don't Bet on the Prince: Contemporary Feminist Fairy Tales in North America and England.* New York: Methuen, 1986.

Neuroscience and Mainstream Psychology

Betsch, Tilmann. "The Nature of Intuition and Its Neglect in Research on Judgment and Decision-Making." *Intuition in Judgment and Decision-Making.* Edited by Henning Plessner. New York: Taylor and Francis, 2008.

Phan, Michel Tuam, Joel B. Cohen, John W. Pracejus, and G. David Hughes. "Affect Monitoring and the Primacy of Feelings in Judgment." *Journal of Consumer Research* (September 28, 2001): 167–188.

Solms, Mark, and Oliver Turnbull. *The Brain and the Inner World: An Introduction to the Neuroscience of Objective Experience.* New York: Other, 2000.

Weisstein, Naomi. "Psychology Constructs the Female." 1986. Chicago Women's Liberation Website, http://www.uic.edu/orgs/cwluherstory/CWLUArchive/psych.html. Accessed June 30, 2012.

Philosophy, Culture, and Social Studies

Alémán, Ana J. Martínez. "Understanding and Evaluating Female Friendship's Educative Value." *Journal of Higher Education* 68, no. 2 (March–April 1997): 119–159.

Bachofen, Johann Jakob. *Mother Right: An Investigation of the Religious and Juridical Character of Matriarchy in the Ancient World.* 1861.

Blanton, DeAnne. "Women Soldiers of the Civil War." *Prologue* 25, no.1 (Spring 1993): 27–33.

Bordo, Susan R. *The Flight to Objectivity: Essays on Cartesianism and Culture.* Albany: SUNY, 1987.

Cowan, Lyn. *Tracking the White Rabbit: A Subversive View of Modern Culture.* New York: Taylor and Francis, 2002.

Dezso, Cristian L. and David Gaddis Ross. "Does Female Representation in Top Management Improve Firm Performance? A Panel Data Investigation" (March 9, 2011). Robert H. Smith School. Research paper no. RHS 06–104, http://ssrn.com/abstract=1088182.

Eisler, Riane. *The Chalice and the Blade: Our History, Our Future.* New York: HarperCollins, 1987.

Gilligan, Carol. *In a Different Voice: Psychological Theory and Women's Development.* Cambridge: Harvard University Press, 1982.

Gilligan, Carol, and Lyn Mikel Brown. *Meeting at the Crossroads: Women's Psychology and Girls' Development.* New York: Random House, 1992.

Gimbutas, Marija. *The Civilization of the Goddess.* New York, HarperCollins, 1992.

Kitzinger, Celia. "Therapy and How It Undermines the Practice of Radical Feminism." *Radically Speaking: Feminism Reclaimed.* Edited by Renate Klein and Diane Bell. North Melbourne: Spinifex, 1996: 92–101.

Smith-Rosenberg, Carroll. "The Female World of Love and Ritual: Relations between Women in Nineteenth-Century America." *Signs: The Journal of Women Culture Society* 1, no. 1 (1975): 1–23.

Stone, Merlin. *When God Was a Woman.* Orlando, FL: Harcourt Brace, 1976.

Twist, Lynne, and Teresa Barker. *The Soul of Money: Reclaiming the Wealth of Our Inner Resources.* New York: Norton, 2003.

Yalom, Marilyn. *A History of the Wife.* New York: HarperCollins, 2002.

Works of Fiction, Autobiography, and Biography

Alcott, Louisa May. *Little Women.* 1868.

Apuleis, Lucius. *Metamorphoses.* Mid-second century CE.

Atwood, Margaret. *Cat's Eye.* Toronto: W. A. Toad, 1988.

Baker, Harriette Newell. *Juliette.* 1869.

Behn, Aphra. *Love-Letters between a Nobleman and His Sister.* 1684–87.

Bradley, Marion Zimmer. *The Mists of Avalon.* New York: Ballantine, 1982.

Brittain, Vera. *Testament of Friendship*. 1940. London: Virago, 1985.

Brontë, Emily. *Wuthering Heights*. 1847.

Bujold, Lois McMaster. *Curse of Chalion*. New York: HarperCollins, 2001.

———. *Paladin of Souls*. New York: HarperCollins, 2003.

Burnett, Frances Hodgson. *A Little Princess*. 1904.

Burney, Fanny. *Evelina*. 1778.

Butler, Octavia. *The Parable of the Sower*. New York: Time Warner, 1993.

Byatt, A. S. *Possession: A Romance*. New York: Random House, 1990.

Chopin, Kate. *The Awakening*. 1899.

Clayton, Jo. *Diadem from the Stars*. New York: DAW, 1986.

Collins, Suzanne. *The Hunger Games*. New York: Scholastic, 2008.

D'Aulnoy, Madame. *Fairy Tales*. 1697.

DeFoe, Daniel. *Moll Flanders*. 1722.

De Pizan, Christine. *The Book of the City of Ladies*. 1405.

Dickens, Charles. *Our Mutual Friend*. 1864–65.

Drabble, Margaret. *The Radiant Way*. New York: Knopf, 1987.

Eliot, George. *Adam Bede*. 1859.

———. *Daniel Deronda*. 1876.

Godwin, Gail. *The Odd Woman*. New York: Ballantine, 1974.

Kidd, Sue Monk. *The Secret Life of Bees*. New York: Penguin, 2003.

Le Guin, Ursula. *The Left Hand of Darkness*. New York: Bantam, 1969.

———. *A Wizard of Earthsea*. 1968. New York: Bantam, 2004.

Lessing, Doris. *The Summer before the Dark*. New York: Vintage, 1973.

Martin, George R. R. *Game of Thrones (A Song of Ice and Fire, Book I)*. New York: Bantam, 1996.

McCarthy, Mary. *The Group*. Orlando, FL: Harcourt, 1954.

Montgomery, Lucy Maud. *Anne of Green Gables*. 1908.

Morrison, Toni. *Beloved*. New York: Knopf, 1987.

———. *Sula*. New York: Penguin, 1973.

Perrault, Charles. *Tales of Mother Goose*. 1697.

Piercy, Marge. *Small Changes*. New York: Ballantine, 1972.

Pratchett, Terry. *A Hat Full of Sky: The Continuing Adventures of Tiffany Aching and the Wee Free Men*. New York: HarperCollins, 2004.

———. *The Wee Free Men*. New York: HarperCollins, 2003.

———. *Wyrd Sisters*. New York: HarperCollins, 1980.

Pullman, Phillip. *The Golden Compass: His Dark Materials*. New York: Knopf, 1996.

Richardson, Dorothy. *Pilgrimage*. Chicago: University of Illinois Press, 1989.

Roth, Veronica. *Divergent*. New York: HarperCollins, 2011.

Rowling, J. K. *Harry Potter and the Sorcerer's Stone*. New York: Scholastic, 1997.

Sayers, Dorothy. *Gaudy Night*. 1936. New York, HarperCollins, 1993.

———. *Have His Carcase*. 1932. New York: HarperCollins, 1993.

———. *Strong Poison*. 1930. New York, HarperCollins, 1995.

Schwartz, Lynne Sharon. *Disturbances in the Field*. 1983. Berkeley, CA: Counterpoint, 2005.

Shakespeare, William. *Twelfth Night*. Circa 1601.

Steinem, Gloria. *Revolution from Within: A Book of Self-Esteem*. New York: Little, Brown, 1991.

Stewart, Mary. *Madam Will You Talk?* 1955. New York: HarperTorch, 2003.

———. *Nine Coaches Waiting*. 1958. Chicago: Chicago Review, 2006.

———. *Wildfire at Midnight*. Greenwich, CT: Fawcett, 1956.

Stowe, Harriet Beecher. *Uncle Tom's Cabin,* 1852.

Strayed, Cheryl. *Wild: From Lost to Found on the Pacific Crest Trail*. New York: Vintage, 2013.

Warner, Susan. *The Wide Wide World*. 1850.

Weisberger, Lauren. *The Devil Wears Prada*. New York: Random House, 2003.

Wharton, Edith. *The House of Mirth*. 1905.

Wiggins, Kate Douglas. *Rebecca of Sunnybrook Farm*. 1903.

Woolf, Virginia. *Mrs. Dalloway*. 1925. Orlando, FL: Harcourt, 1995.

———. *To the Lighthouse*. 1927. Orlando, FL: Harcourt, 1989.

Wroth, Lady Mary. *The Countesse of Mountgomeries Urania*. 1621.

Index

H

X

Y

Z

Quest Books
encourages open-minded inquiry into
world religions, philosophy, science, and the arts
in order to understand the wisdom of the ages,
respect the unity of all life, and help people explore
individual spiritual self-transformation.

Its publications are generously supported by
The Kern Foundation,
a trust committed to Theosophical education.

Quest Books is the imprint of
the Theosophical Publishing House,
a division of the Theosophical Society in America.
For information about programs, literature,
on-line study, membership benefits, and international centers,
see www.theosophical.org
or call 800-669-1571 or (outside the U.S.) 630-668-1571.

To order books or a complete Quest catalog,
call 800-669-9425 or (outside the U.S.) 630-665-0130.